Math Workout for the New

GMAT®

The Princeton Review

Math Workout for the New

GMAT®

Fourth Edition

Jack Schieffer

PrincetonReview.com

Random House, Inc. New York

The Princeton Review, Inc.
111 Speen Street, Suite 550
Framingham, MA 01701
E-mail: editorialsupport@review.com

ISBN: 978-0-375-42749-7
ISSN: 2163-6036

Editor: Selena Coppock
Production Editor: Kathy G. Carter
Production Coordinator: Deborah A. Silvestrini

Printed in the United States of America on partially recycled paper.

10   9   8   7   6   5   4   3   2   1

Fourth Edition

Editorial

Robert Franek, VP, Test Prep Books, Publisher
Laura Braswell, Senior Editor
Calvin Cato, Editor
Selena Coppock, Editor
Meave Shelton, Editor

Random House Publishing Group

Tom Russell, Publisher
Nicole Benhabib, Publishing Manager
Ellen L. Reed, Production Manager
Alison Stoltzfus, Managing Editor

Acknowledgments

I'd like to thank all of the people at The Princeton Review, both those I've known personally and those I've never met. You have made the "big red arrow" a fun and interesting place to work, and I have learned a tremendous amount from you over the years. Special thanks go to Jerry Pederson, for hiring me and introducing me to the wacky world of test preparation; to Mike Gamerl, for the long-lasting appellation "GMAT Jack"; and to John Katzman, for creating The Princeton Review and making this all possible. Thanks also to David Ragsdale, Suzanne Markert, Patricia Dublin, and Marc Williams.

I'd also like to thank my family and friends for their love and support. I've immortalized some of you in story problems in this book, which I hope brings you fame and respect, rather than infamy and embarrassment.

Finally and most importantly, I want to thank my lovely wife, Christina. Your patience with my weird job and general test-geekiness is amazing. You have my love and gratitude forever.

Special thanks to Adam Robinson, who conceived of and perfected the Joe Bloggs approach to standardized tests and many of the other successful techniques used by The Princeton Review.

The Princeton Review would like to thank Oliver Pope for his hard work updating the fourth edition of this book, and John Fulmer for his guidance and expertise on the changing GMAT.

Contents

Introduction

WELCOME

You want to get an MBA and you know that you need a good GMAT score to get into your top-choice business school. It may be that your math skills are a bit rusty. For example, you may not have taken many (or even any) math classes in college. These days, you probably use a calculator or computer to balance your checkbook, to crunch numbers at work, and to handle any other calculations that come your way. The result is that you haven't really used your math muscles for several years or more. On the other hand, you may be rather comfortable with your math skills. Maybe you were the kid everyone cheated off in math class. However, you lack that edge necessary to push you over the top. You need a strong system you can use to reach that elite score. That's the bad news.

However, there is good news. In either case, at least at some point, you did learn the math that's tested on the GMAT. None of the concepts is more advanced than high school algebra and geometry. No trigonometry, no calculus, and no multi-variable regression analysis (whatever that is). Even the most challenging problems don't require you to learn a lot of new stuff; you just need to refresh your memory.

Another piece of good news is that you bought this book. (If you're reading this in the bookstore, go over to the register and pay up.) In the following chapters, you'll cover the math you need to know for the GMAT—and only that. If it's not on the test, it's not in this book. You'll also learn some test-taking strategies specific to the GMAT. This stuff probably won't help you in your first-year statistics course, but it will help you to get there in the first place. In addition, this book includes an introduction to the new Integrated Reasoning section of the GMAT. This new GMAT is referred to as the Next Generation GMAT.

THE GMAT AND BUSINESS SCHOOL ADMISSIONS

You already know that you have to take the GMAT to get into business school, but there may be a number of other things you're not so sure about. How important is the GMAT? What's a good score? What other things do schools consider?

The importance of the GMAT depends on several factors. One is how long you've been out of school. If you graduated a long time ago, say more than five years, then MBA programs will place more weight on your GMAT score than they would if you graduated a year or two ago. That's because they will de-emphasize your college GPA in considering your application, thereby making your GMAT score more important in the mix.

Another factor in the importance of your GMAT score is the particular GMAT score in question. In addition to the overall score (200–800 range), you will receive a separate Math score, Verbal score, Integrated Reasoning score, and AWA (Analytical Writing Assessment) essay score. With the introduction of the new Integrated Reasoning section (as part of the Next Generation GMAT), the scoring breakdown has changed. At the time of this printing, GMAC (Graduate Management Admissions Council)—the people who write the GMAT—had not yet released specific scoring information about the Next Generation GMAT. Check out www.PrincetonReview.com and www.mba.com for further information. As far as scoring goes, most schools concentrate on the overall score and the Math score in their admissions decisions. They look at the overall score because it's a broad measure of your ability. They look at the Math score because many MBA courses require significant use of quantitative skills, and the schools want to ensure that entering students have the necessary mathematical ability.

A good GMAT score is one that will make you competitive with other applicants to the programs of your choice. Check with the programs you're considering to find out the average GMAT score and GPA for the latest entering class. That GMAT score gives you a good target. If your GPA is below the average, you should shoot for a higher GMAT score to compensate.

Business schools consider many factors in the application process, with GMAT scores, undergraduate GPA, and work experience making up the "big three." GPA is fairly self-explanatory, and GMAT scores are discussed above. The work experience factor includes both the length of your full-time experience and its nature. Several years of experience are virtually mandatory for the top programs. Schools like to see leadership roles and increasing responsibility in your career to date.

MBA programs will also look at several other factors, including letters of recommendation and your application essays. Although these elements are not counted as heavily as the three factors discussed above, they are still important. If your "big three" qualifications are average for a given program, strong essays and recommendations can help you stand out from the pack.

A full discussion of the various criteria in MBA admissions is beyond the scope of this book; it is, after all, a GMAT math review. However, it is important to give due consideration to all of the elements in your application, not just your GMAT scores.

STRUCTURE OF THE GMAT

The GMAT lasts approximately four hours. The test is administered by computer.

Section	Questions	Time
AWA—Argument	1 essay	30 minutes
Integrated Reasoning	12 questions	30 minutes
Quantitative	37 multiple-choice	75 minutes
Verbal	41 multiple-choice	75 minutes

The test starts with the AWA essay. You will have 30 minutes to write one essay that's an Analysis of an Argument. The section after the essay is the new Integrated Reasoning section. You will have 30 minutes to answer 12 questions, which sounds like a piece of cake, right? Most of those questions have multiple parts, though. So you'll need all of that time to tackle these multi-part questions.

Then you'll come to the Quantitative section (what we call the Math section), which is the first computer-adaptive section of the GMAT. We'll explain computer-adaptive tests more in a moment. For now, know that all of the math questions are multiple-choice and you may not use a calculator on this section.

In the Math section, you will have 75 minutes to answer 37 questions, which come in two formats: problem solving and data sufficiency. The problem solving questions are the more familiar format. For these questions, you work the problem, come up with an answer, and choose the answer choice that matches. The data sufficiency format, which is totally unfamiliar to most test takers, is discussed in detail in Chapter 3.

After the Math section, you will have an optional break before the Verbal section, in which you will have 75 minutes to answer 41 questions. The questions come in three formats: sentence correction, critical reasoning, and reading comprehension. Sentence correction questions involve grammar and other issues of sentence construction. Critical reasoning questions require you to analyze the logic of short arguments. Reading comprehension questions require you to find information in long passages.

Approximately one fourth of the questions will be experimental questions. These questions are not labeled in any way, so you will not know whether a question is experimental. Unlike the others, experimental questions do not affect your score in any way. These questions are being tested for future use, and you are essentially serving as a guinea pig, providing statistical information on the difficulty of the questions through your performance on them relative to the scored questions. Additionally, the difficulty of these questions does not track your performance, as does the difficulty of the scored questions. Therefore, some questions that seem much easier or more difficult than those in the rest of the section may be experimental.

HOW A CAT WORKS

CAT is an acronym for "computer adaptive test." The test is adaptive because it tries to match the difficulty of the questions to your performance. The better you do, the harder the questions get. The Math and Verbal sections of the GMAT are computer-adaptive tests. The Integrated Reasoning and Essay sections are not.

In the Verbal and Math sections, each section starts with a question of medium difficulty and initially assigns you a medium score. When you answer a question correctly, the computer raises your score and gives you a harder question. When you choose a wrong answer, the computer lowers your score and gives you an easier question.

At the beginning of a section, the computer knows very little about you, so each answer, right or wrong, can change your score a lot. By the end of the section, in contrast, the computer already has a very strong idea of your performance, so your answers to the last few questions won't change its mind much at all.

Do you really need to know all this? Well, you don't need to be an expert in computer adaptive testing, but it's good for you to know a little so that you don't freak out when the test gets harder and harder and harder. In Chapter 2, you'll examine some of the implications for pacing and the best way to attack the Math section.

For now, you should realize that you cannot skip questions, because the computer can't determine which question to give you next until it sees your performance on the current one. You also cannot go back to change an answer to a previous question. Therefore, you will sometimes have to move ahead without knowing how to work a particular question, and strong guessing skills will be an important factor in doing your best on the GMAT.

HOW TO USE THIS BOOK

Each chapter in this book reviews one particular area of math or one type of problem. The chapters are arranged sequentially so that later chapters assume familiarity with the material covered in earlier chapters. Spaced throughout each chapter are quizzes that will test your knowledge of the material in each subsection. At the end of each chapter is a set of problems that covers all of the material in that chapter. Explanations are provided for all the problems in the quizzes and practice sets.

Ideally, you'll work through the book from front to back, taking the time to review each subject area thoroughly, work all of the practice sets, and check all of the explanations. You should give yourself several weeks (at least!) for this plan, so that you have plenty of time to review the practice sets and learn from your mistakes.

Of course, we don't live in an ideal world, and you may not have the time to review each subject, work every problem, and read every explanation. If this is your situation, you should skip over the topics with which you're familiar. Try a few of the problems. If you are comfortable with them, move on to something else that gives you more trouble. If you're not comfortable with them, review that topic more thoroughly and do most or all of the problems. You should definitely spend some time with Chapters 2, 3, 8, and 10. Those chapters contain a lot of test-taking strategies specific to the GMAT that you are unlikely to have seen previously. You still need at least a couple of weeks for this approach.

In general, the more time you spend preparing for the test, the better you'll do. Give yourself plenty of time and set up a disciplined practice schedule.

As you use this book, you should do all of your calculations and other work on separate scratch paper, instead of writing on the problems in the book. This practice simulates the situation during the test, when you can't write on the computer screen. (The testing sites get a bit touchy about that.) Get used to copying key information and diagrams from the problem to your scratch paper. Watch out for mistakes in your copying. Also, writing A, B, C, D, E will help you keep track of answers as you eliminate them. Physically crossing off answer choices not only provides enjoyment but also prevents careless mistakes.

In addition to working problems from this book, you should take some practice tests on the computer to help you get comfortable with the format and also work on pacing strategies. You can take an online practice test on The Princeton Review's website. Go to **PrincetonReview.com/mba** and click on the link to take a free practice test, complete with adaptive question selection and a full range of question types. In addition to the practice GMAT, you'll also find lots of useful information on the site about preparing for the test and applying to business school.

Another source for practice tests is GMAC. Their GMATPrep software is available for free download at their website, **www.mba.com**. Another helpful GMAT tool is GMAC's GMAT preparation book, *The Official Guide for GMAT Review.*

CALCULATION PRACTICE

Although the GMAT tests knowledge of concepts and problem analysis more than calculation skills, you're going to do a significant amount of number-crunching during the test. You want to make sure that your number manipulation skills are sharp so that you won't make careless mistakes or waste precious time struggling with the calculations.

Chances are good that you do most of your calculations with the aid of a calculator or a computer spreadsheet. When was the last time you did long division by hand? Hmm, that's what we thought.

Starting today, do all your day-to-day math by hand: Balance your checkbook, figure out a 15-percent tip, calculate your softball batting average, and so forth. You can check your results with a calculator, but force yourself to exercise those math muscles.

ANSWER CHOICES

On the real GMAT, the answer choices are not labeled by the letters A, B, C, D, and E. In all of the examples in this book, the answer choices are marked by bubbles similar to those you'll see on the test. In the explanations for the questions and in the quizzes and practice sets, however, this book uses the letters to identify the answer choices. We refer to the first answer choice as A, the second as B, and so forth. This notation is simply less cumbersome than referring to "the first answer," "the second answer," and so on.

WHAT IS THE PRINCETON REVIEW?

The Princeton Review is one of the leaders in helping people prepare for standardized tests such as the GMAT. We started by offering courses and tutoring for the SAT in 1981. Now we offer courses, books, and software to an audience of more than two million people each year.

The Princeton Review's central philosophy is that the tests are beatable. Standardized tests measure test-taking skills more than they do fundamental knowledge or intelligence. We are dedicated to teaching people the test-taking skills they need to perform their best and beat the standardized tests.

Glad to meet you!

General Test-Taking Tips

The GMAT, like all other standardized tests, follows certain predictable patterns. That's why it's "standardized." The test writers must follow these patterns so that everybody who takes a GMAT gets tested on the same criteria. Otherwise, their scores wouldn't be comparable and schools couldn't use those scores to evaluate applicants.

By learning the methods and patterns that the test writers follow, you can use some general test-taking strategies that will help you beat the test. These guidelines apply no matter what specific topic the question covers, so they are useful throughout the test. Don't underestimate how much these tips can help your score.

PACING

Time is your most precious resource on the GMAT. In the Math section, you have only 75 minutes to answer the 37 questions; be sure you use your time wisely. You should keep three pacing goals in mind as you take the test:

1. **Answer every question.** You'll receive a significant penalty to your score if you don't answer all of the questions in each section. Therefore, you should answer every question, even if you have to guess on the last few. However, the test is smart enough to figure out you're guessing if you answer more than three or four questions in only a couple of minutes, and it penalizes you for that. So, it's very important to use your time wisely and pace yourself to at least come close to finishing each section and then guess on the remaining few questions.

2. **Start slowly.** On a CAT, the computer first gives you a medium question. If you answer it correctly, the computer gives you a slightly harder question. If you answer it incorrectly, the computer gives you a slightly easier question, and so on. The idea is that the computer will zero in on your exact level of ability very quickly and make a finely honed assessment of your abilities. Because of this system, the earlier questions are more important than the later questions, in that you are attempting to prove to GMAC that you are a high-caliber student and can breeze through hard questions. Go slower and be more careful on the earlier, more important questions. Don't spend five minutes on a question; just try to minimize your chances of making a careless mistake. As you progress through the section and get to less and less important questions, you should gradually pick up some speed. If you make a careless mistake on a question near the end, it will have a very small effect on your final score.

3. **Don't waste time on "impossible" questions.** Almost everyone comes across a handful of questions that are too difficult to do. No matter how much time you spend staring at them, you're not improving your chances of answering them correctly. Cut your losses on these questions. Once you realize that it's an impossible question, take an educated guess (more on this later) and move on. Spend your time on the questions that will get you points.

Let's integrate these ideas into an overall strategy. The following chart shows how your pacing and accuracy goals should change as you progress through the Math section.

	Questions			
	1–10	**11–20**	**21–30**	**31–37**
Time allowed	30 min.	20 min.	15 min.	10 min.
Accuracy goal	90%+	75%+	60%+	60%+

On questions 1 to 10 of the Math section, accuracy is your primary goal. Your performance on these questions sets the tone for the whole section. Think of it as making a good first impression on someone you just met. You should aim for 90 to 100 percent accuracy, and allow yourself plenty of time to work each question thoroughly so that you avoid careless mistakes. If you do encounter an "impossible" question, spend a reasonable amount of time using good elimination methods to make the best possible guess.

In questions 11 to 20, you need to significantly pick up speed so that you will be on pace to answer every question. You can allow yourself an average of two minutes per question. Therefore, you must become more selective. If a question seems likely to take an excessive amount of time, you should quickly eliminate some answers and take a guess. You cannot afford to spend several minutes working a problem and then end up guesing after all. If you hit your accuracy goal of 75 percent or higher, your score will still be increasing.

With questions 21 to 30, your objective shifts from rapidly raising your score to damage control. If you hit your accuracy targets in the earlier questions, your score should be pretty high, and the remaining questions will correspondingly be more difficult. If you can keep improving your score, that's great, but first you must "do no harm." Time is running short, so you will need to be more selective. You can afford to aggressively eliminate and guess on tougher problems so that you will have time to thoroughly work the others. For example, you could spend two minutes on each of six to seven questions, and make educated guesses on the others.

In the end game, questions 31 to 37, the top priority is answering every question, one way or another. Ideally, you will have time to read each one and either solve the problem or make a quick guess. However, you should make absolutely certain that you answer all 37 questions, even if that means blindly choosing answers in the last minute.

GUESSING

No matter how prepared you are, there's always the possibility that you could run into a problem that you just don't know how to solve. If this happens, stay calm, eliminate any answers you can, and make the best guess possible. As a general rule, 3 minutes is as much time as you should spend on any given problem. If you get to 3 minutes and you're not on the verge of solving the problem, then it's time to cut your losses, eliminate any answers you can, and take a guess. Remember that the test is adaptive, so the material gets harder the better you're doing. Therefore, you're probably going to run into a few problems that you don't know how to solve. In that case, it's better to make the best guess you can and move on, rather than to stubbornly waste time on a question. Don't forget that it could be experimental!

USING NOTEBOARDS

Because the questions are presented on a computer screen, you do not have a test booklet on which you can scribble notes. You can't write directly on the problem to label diagrams, cross off answers, and so forth. In an effort to be environmentally conscious, the GMAT is no longer administered with scrap paper. Instead of paper, you will be given noteboards, which are reusable dry-erase sheets for your scratch work. If you manage to fill up all of the space on your noteboards, you can raise your hand and have the test administrator clean them for you. So, use them! Don't try to do calculations in your head in order to save time. Chances are the time you'll spend thinking about the numbers is at least as much time as it would take you to write them down, and the accuracy of mental math is never as good.

When you first sit down at your computer—before the timer starts—take a few minutes to divide your noteboards into eight boxes per board, leaving one column of boxes empty for any formulas you might want to write down or outlines you may want to make for the AWA. In each box, write A, B, C, D, E so that you can physically cross off answers as you eliminate them. This will help you keep track of where you are as you work the problem.

When you practice questions from this book, you should do your work on separate sheets of scratch paper, just as you do with the noteboards on test day. Doing so will help you get used to copying stuff to your noteboards.

READ CAREFULLY

For most people, a substantial number of their wrong answers in the Math section are caused by nothing more than reading errors. You may know exactly how to do the math, but that won't help you if you answer the wrong question. Be sure to read each question carefully. Take a look at some examples of traps for unwary readers.

1. If $3x + 12 = 21$, then $x + 4 =$

   ◯ 3
   ◯ 4
   ◯ 5
   ◯ 7
   ◯ 9

Most people will start solving the equation. Subtract 12 from each side to get $3x = 9$. Then divide by 3 to get $x = 3$. Aha, the answer is A! Um…no, actually. Although $x = 3$, that's not what the question asked. If $x = 3$, then $x + 4 = 7$, so the answer is D. It is usually a good idea to reread the problem, especially the question stem (at the end), before choosing an answer choice.

Here is another example.

2. In a classroom containing only fifth- and sixth-graders, fifth-graders are seated in $\frac{1}{2}$ of the desks and sixth-graders are seated in $\frac{2}{3}$ of the remainder. In what fraction of the desks in use are sixth-graders seated?

- ◯ $\frac{5}{6}$
- ◯ $\frac{2}{3}$
- ◯ $\frac{3}{5}$
- ◯ $\frac{2}{5}$
- ◯ $\frac{1}{3}$

A good way to start with such a problem is to choose a number for the desks in the room. (This handy strategy, called Plugging In, is covered in Chapter 8.) Suppose there are 60 desks in the room. That means there are fifth-graders in $\frac{1}{2} \times 60 = 30$ of the desks, with $60 - 30 = 30$ desks remaining. So there are $\frac{2}{3} \times 30 = 20$ desks with sixth-graders. Therefore, sixth-graders take up $\frac{20}{60} = \frac{1}{3}$ of the desks, and E must be the answer. Right? Again, sloppy reading has led to a wrong answer designed to trap you. The question asked for the fraction of the desks in use containing sixth-graders, so the answer should be $\frac{20}{50} = \frac{2}{5}$, or answer choice D.

If you avoid reading mistakes, these questions may seem relatively easy, but that's exactly the point. You don't want to choose wrong answers when you know how to do the math. Careless mistakes can wreak havoc on your GMAT score.

There are several ways to decrease the number of reading mistakes you make in the Math section. As suggested, reread the question, particularly the stem, before selecting your answer. Also, when you copy numbers and diagrams to your scratch paper, double-check your notes before working the problem. Finally, pay extra attention to key phrases such as "of the…" in word problems.

JOE BLOGGS

Choose a number and write it down here: _____
Don't read any further until you've chosen your number. You'll need to refer to this number in a few minutes.

When the test writers write questions for the GMAT, they need to generate questions that cover the range of difficulty from pretty easy to really tough. However, they're restricted by the topics they're allowed to test. They can't write questions about calculus or other difficult topics in order to get hard questions. Instead, they have to use the same topics, yet somehow they have to make the questions hard. One way the test writers make a question hard is to include things that will trick you into choosing the wrong answer.

People tend to think in predictable patterns. For example, look at the number you wrote down earlier. You could have chosen any number, including 0.08, –7.5, $\frac{2}{3}$, $\sqrt{7}$, and similar numbers. However, no one chooses those numbers; almost everyone chooses a whole number such as 1, 2, or 3. In addition, most people choose a whole number from 1 to 10.

People choose these numbers because they are "programmed" to think that way.

This type of thinking is called the Joe Bloggs response. Joe Bloggs is the completely predictable person who lives inside each of us. When you look at a math problem, watch your initial reaction to the question—your "five seconds or less" solution. That's the Joe Bloggs answer.

The test writers use those predictable thinking patterns against you. They write questions in such a way that being Joe Bloggs will lead you to the wrong answer. You should be suspicious of a solution that you come up with too quickly. If you don't use at least 30 seconds to solve the question, you should double-check your answer. That doesn't mean that the easy answers are *never* correct, just that they are *usually* traps. Look at this next example.

1. Cathy's Boutique is a store that sells silk scarves at an everyday 20% discount from the normal list price. During a Mother's Day sale, all the scarves are sold at an additional 10% discount from the everyday price. The sale price is what percent of the normal list price?

   ◯ 28%
   ◯ 30%
   ◯ 70%
   ◯ 72%
   ◯ 80%

The Joe Bloggs instinct says, "Simple. A 20% discount plus a 10% discount is a 30% discount." Joe would choose C or, if he misread the question, B. So you want to be suspicious of those answers. If you come up with one of those answers, double-check your work and see if there's a different approach you could take. Take a look at another example.

2. If $w + 2x = 150$, $2w + 3y = 100$, and $x + 3z = 50$, what is the value of $w + x + y + z$?

- ◯ 12.5
- ◯ 20
- ◯ 50
- ◯ 100
- ◯ It cannot be determined from the information provided.

Your first instinct is probably something like, "Wow. There's no way I can solve for all those variables. With four variables, I'm going to need four equations!" If so, you're absolutely right. However, the Joe Bloggs answer, E, is not the correct answer.

EXPLANATIONS FOR THE JOE BLOGGS EXAMPLES

1. **D** Suppose a scarf has a retail price of $100. Cathy's Boutique sells that scarf at an everyday 20% discount, or $80. During the Mother's Day sale, the store reduces the everyday price another 10%, or $8 (10% of $80). So the sale price is $72, which is 72% of the retail price.

2. **D** Combine all the equations into one and you get $(w + 2x) + (2w + 3y) + (x + 3z) = 150 + 100 + 50$. If you simplify each side, you get $3w + 3x + 3y + 3z = 300$. Divide everything by 3 and you find that $w + x + y + z = 100$. Even though you can't solve for each individual variable, you can answer the question.

QUIZ 1

Identify the Joe Bloggs answer for each of the following questions:

1. Alex drives to and from work each day along the same route. If she drives at a speed of 80 miles per hour on the way to work, and she drives at a speed of 100 miles per hour on the way home from work, which of the following most closely approximates her average speed, in miles per hour, for the round trip?

- ◯ 80.0
- ◯ 88.9
- ◯ 90.0
- ◯ 91.1
- ◯ 100.0

2. For which of the following values of n is $(-0.5)^n$ the greatest?

- ◯ 5
- ◯ 4
- ◯ 3
- ◯ 2
- ◯ 1

Got Answers?
The answers to the quizzes can be found at the end of this chapter.

3. $\left(\sqrt{3} + \sqrt{3} + \sqrt{3}\right)^2 =$

○ 27
○ 18
○ 9
○ $3\sqrt{3}$
○ 3

BALLPARKING

On the GMAT, you will need to do some calculations. However, the primary purpose of the GMAT is not to test your calculation abilities. In fact, you can often shortcut a problem to save some time or eliminate answers when you're unsure of how to solve a problem.

Even when you get stuck and can't completely solve a problem, you can often eliminate some answers that are "out of the ballpark." This won't necessarily lead you to the one and only right answer (although it might), but it will help you narrow down the possible answers before you guess. Approach the question on very simple terms and try to get a rough idea of what the answer is. Then eliminate answers that aren't very close. Try this approach to eliminate some answers on this example from Quiz 1.

1. Alex drives to and from work each day along the same route. If she drives at a speed of 80 miles per hour on the way to work, and she drives at a speed of 100 miles per hour on the way from work, which of the following most closely approximates her average speed in miles per hour for the round trip?

○ 80.0
○ 88.9
○ 90.0
○ 91.1
○ 100.0

You know that Alex's average speed should be pretty close to 90 mph. That narrows down the possible answers to B, C, and D. You also know that A is wrong because the average of 80 and a higher speed must be more than 80. The same reasoning lets you eliminate E. Factor in the Joe Bloggs technique to eliminate C and you're down to a 50-50 guess, even if you don't know the real solution to the problem. As you will see in the answers at the end of the chapter, the correct answer is B.

With some additional thought, you can turn this 50-50 guess into a sure thing, still without "really" solving the problem. Of the remaining two answers, one is a little more than 90 mph and the other is a little less. The trip to work takes longer than the trip home, because Alex drives the "to" trip at a slower speed. Since she spends more time at the slow speed (80 mph), the average must be closer to 80 than to 100. Imagine driving at a steady, slow speed for a long trip and then driving as fast as possible for the last block. Despite your high speed at the end, your average speed for the whole trip would be very close to the steady, slow speed, because virtually the whole trip was made at that speed. The final burst of speed has little effect on the average because it is so short in duration. Alex's situation is similar: More time at the slow speed than the fast means her average is closer to 80 than to 100. Thus, B is the correct answer. To see the real way to solve this problem, check out the explanation for question 1 in the practice set in Chapter 11.

The second aspect of Ballparking is saving time by approximating. Because time is precious, you don't want to waste it when you don't need to. On the GMAT, you can use approximations to make the calculations easier and faster. Whenever you see a calculation that looks difficult, try to round off the numbers to something you can handle easily. Then see which answers are in the ballpark. If there's only one reasonably close answer, you don't need to calculate the precise answer. If there's more than one reasonably close answer, go back and do the calculation to find the closest one. Wait a minute, isn't that a waste of time? Not really. The time you spend Ballparking is really short and it will save you from choosing the wrong answer by mistake. For example, you may misplace the decimal point, or accidentally multiply a fraction instead of dividing. However, you won't pick that trap answer if you already eliminated it through Ballparking. Try the Ballparking approach to simplify the calculation on this next example.

2. Maggie has four quart-sized bottles of water, each of which is partially empty. The first bottle currently contains $\frac{1}{8}$ of a quart. The second bottle currently contains $\frac{1}{6}$ of a quart. The third bottle currently contains $\frac{1}{2}$ of a quart. The fourth bottle currently contains $\frac{3}{4}$ of a quart. How many additional quarts of water does Maggie need to fill each of these bottles?

○ $\frac{7}{8}$

○ $\frac{37}{24}$

○ $\frac{23}{12}$

○ $\frac{59}{24}$

○ $\frac{51}{12}$

You could solve this problem by adding up the missing fractions. However, you can avoid some of the messy math by taking a Ballpark approach. Say that Maggie needs a full quart for each of the first two bottles (rounding up a bit). She needs one half of a quart for the third bottle. Then round down the fourth bottle (to offset the earlier rounding up) and say she doesn't need any water for it. All together, she needs approximately $2\frac{1}{2}$ quarts of water to fill the four bottles. A is too small—less than 1 quart. B is also too small—between 1 (or $\frac{24}{24}$) and 2 (or $\frac{48}{24}$) quarts. C is also too small—less than 2 (or $\frac{24}{12}$) quarts. D seems about right—between 2 (or $\frac{48}{24}$) and 3 (or $\frac{72}{24}$) quarts. E is too big—more than 4 (or $\frac{48}{12}$) quarts. The correct answer must be D. Note that B is a trap answer. It is the amount of water currently in the bottles, not the missing amount.

Ballparking is particularly effective for questions with a drawn figure, including many geometry problems. Even if you don't know the formulas or how to set up the solution, you can make a rough estimate of the answer. Compare the thing the question wants (e.g., area or length of a line) to some known value in the diagram. Try this method on the following example:

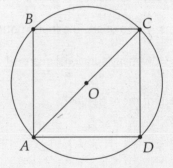

3. In the figure above, square *ABCD* has an area of 25. What is the area of the circle with center *O*?

○ $\dfrac{5\sqrt{2}}{2}\pi$

○ $\dfrac{25}{4}\pi$

○ $\dfrac{25}{2}\pi$

○ 25π

○ $25\sqrt{2}\pi$

Imagine that you have forgotten every geometry formula you've ever known. Just from "eyeballing" the diagram, you can see that the circle is bigger than the square, but less than twice as big. Since the square has an area of 25, the area of the circle is probably in the neighborhood of 35 or 40. The next step is to determine which answers are reasonably close to this estimate and which aren't, eliminating the latter.

Geometry answers often contain $\sqrt{2}$, $\sqrt{3}$, and π, so it's helpful to know some approximations for them: $\sqrt{2}$ is about 1.4, $\sqrt{3}$ is about 1.7, and π is about 3.

Using these approximations, you can find a value for each answer choice. Feel free to round off the numbers to make the calculation easier; after all, you're working with approximations anyway. Answer A is between 10 and 11, and B is close to 19. Both are smaller than the square's area of 25, so you can eliminate them as possibilities for the circle's area. Answer C is between 37 and 38, which is in line with your estimate. Answer D is about 75, which is way too big, and E is even worse, at more than 100. Given your rough estimate of 35 to 40, only C seems at all reasonable, and it is actually the correct answer. For a non-Ballparking solution to this problem, see the explanation for question 9 in the practice set in Chapter 9.

Caution: Ballparking on geometry problems depends on having an accurate diagram. If a diagram is labeled with something like "Note: Figure not drawn to scale," you should not use a Ballparking approach. Likewise, the diagrams for data sufficiency questions cannot be trusted, whether or not they carry a warning label. So do not try Ballparking with data sufficiency questions. *Note:* While Ballparking is effective in many cases, don't use it as your primary technique for solving most questions. Don't worry; you will learn all of the techniques necessary for the GMAT in later chapters.

Quiz 2

Use the Ballparking approach to narrow down your choices.

1. Jeff opens a savings account with a $3,000 deposit and makes no other deposits or withdrawals. The account pays interest at the rate of 6 percent, compounded monthly. How much money, rounded to the nearest dollar, is in the account at the end of 1 year?

   ○ $2,160
   ○ $3,180
   ○ $3,185
   ○ $5,160
   ○ $6,037

2. After a performance review, Steve's salary is increased by 5 percent. After a second performance review, Steve's new salary is increased by 20 percent. This series of raises is equivalent to a single raise of

   ○ 25%
   ○ 26%
   ○ 27%
   ○ 30%
   ○ 32%

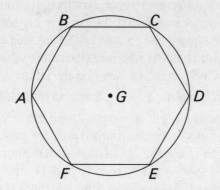

3. In the figure above, equilateral hexagon *ABCDEF* is inscribed in the circle with center *G*, which has a diameter of 16. What is the length of *AB*?

   ○ 16

   ○ $8\sqrt{3}$

   ○ $6\sqrt{3}$

   ○ 8

   ○ $4\sqrt{3}$

ANSWERS AND EXPLANATIONS

Quiz 1

1. **B** C is the Joe Bloggs trap answer. Your first instinct is simply to average 80 and 100 to get 90. If only it were that easy! The correct answer is B. For a more complete explanation, see the explanation for question 1 in the practice set in Chapter 11.

2. **D** A is the Joe Bloggs trap answer. When the question asks for the greatest value, your initial reaction is probably to look for the largest number. So you should be suspicious of that answer. The correct answer is D.

3. **A** C is the Joe Bloggs trap answer. The simplest-looking thing to do is square each of the $\sqrt{3}$s to get $3 + 3 + 3 = 9$. Unfortunately, you can't do that. Joe Bloggs might also pick D because it contains a square root, and that reminds him of the numbers in the problem. The correct answer is A.

Quiz 2

1. **C** The account doesn't lose money, so you can eliminate choice A. If the account pays simple interest (compounded annually) of 6%, the interest earned would be $6\% \times \$3,000 = \$180$, for a total of $\$3,000 + \$180 = \$3,180$. However, the monthly compounding means that the account earns interest slightly faster because it pays interest on the interest. So you would choose an answer that is more than $3,180 but still in that ballpark. The only possible answer is C. Answers D and E are much bigger than the simple interest amount. For more on compound interest, see Chapter 6.

2. **B** Choices B and C are in the ballpark. Using the Joe Bloggs concept, you know that simply adding 5% and 20% to get 25% would be too easy. So the answer is unlikely to be A. However, it's got to be pretty close to 25%, so you can narrow it down to B and C. The correct answer is B. For a more complete explanation, see the explanation for question 2 in the practice set in Chapter 5.

3. **D** Compare segment AB to the distance from A to D, the diameter of the circle. It appears to be about half as long, approximately 8. Using 1.7 as an approximation for $\sqrt{3}$, you can check each of the answer choices. A is 16, which is too long. B is about 13.6, which is also too long. C is closer, at 10.2. D is a good fit at 8. E is close, at 6.8. You should definitely eliminate A and B. The others are all close, but D is the closest to your estimate and is actually the correct answer. For the real solution, see the explanation for question 19 in the practice set in Chapter 9.

Data Sufficiency 1

Data sufficiency questions give many test takers headaches. Merely figuring out what you're asked to do can be awkward. You may know the concept a question is testing but still miss it because you are confused by the data sufficiency format.

In this chapter, you'll decipher what it all means and learn a simple but extremely effective approach for those data sufficiency questions.

WHAT DOES IT ALL MEAN?

The first time you get a data sufficiency question, you will see a screen describing the directions for that type of question. It will say something like this:

> This data sufficiency problem consists of a question and two statements, labeled (1) and (2), in which certain data are given. You have to decide whether the data given in the statements are *sufficient* for answering the question. Using the data given in the statements *plus* your knowledge of mathematics and everyday facts (such as the number of days in July or the meaning of *counterclockwise*), you must indicate whether
>
> - statement (1) ALONE is sufficient, but statement (2) alone is not sufficient to answer the question asked;
>
> - statement (2) ALONE is sufficient, but statement (1) alone is not sufficient to answer the question asked;
>
> - BOTH statements (1) and (2) TOGETHER are sufficient to answer the question asked, but NEITHER statement ALONE is sufficient;
>
> - EACH statement ALONE is sufficient to answer the question asked;
>
> - statements (1) and (2) TOGETHER are NOT sufficient to answer the question asked, and additional data specific to the problem are needed.

You could easily spend a large amount of time trying to understand that confusing morass of instructions. If you do that during the test, you're throwing away precious minutes that you need to answer the questions. Instead, you should understand the data sufficiency format forward and backward before you ever set foot inside a testing center. So let's break it apart and see what those directions really mean.

Your mission on a data sufficiency problem is to determine which statement or combination of statements gives you enough information to answer the question. Then you choose the answer choice that matches that combination. The following chart shows you what the answers mean:

Answer Choice	Statement (1) Alone	Statement (2) Alone	(1) and (2) Together
A	enough	not enough	—
B	not enough	enough	—
C	not enough	not enough	enough
D	enough	enough	—
E	not enough	not enough	not enough

Here's another way to think about what each answer choice means.

A   ①   ✗   (1) only

B   ✗   ②   (2) only

C   ⟨ 1   2 ⟩   Teamwork

D   ①   ②   Either/or

E   ⟨ 1   2 ⟩   Cannot answer

These answer choices are the same for every data sufficiency problem. Memorize the "definition" of each answer choice so that you never need to read the directions or the text of the answer choices.

> *Note:* Since the answers are always the same for each data sufficiency problem, the questions presented later in this book do not supply the answer choices. Practice answering the questions without looking back at the choices.

AD OR BCE

Don't try to look at both statements at the same time to sort out which answer fits. That way leads to madness. Instead, you should look at one statement at a time, determine whether you can answer the question using the statement, and eliminate the appropriate answer choices. Follow this flowchart:

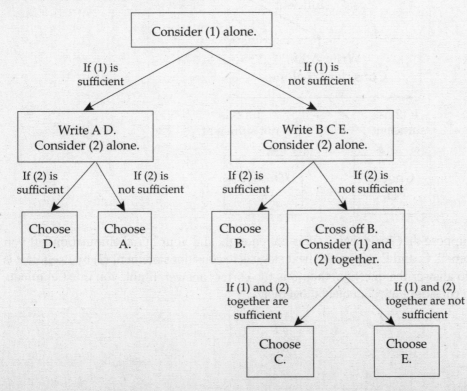

Your first step on any data sufficiency question is to consider statement (1) alone and narrow your choice to AD or BCE. Do *not* read statement (2) yet. If statement (1) provides enough information to answer the question, then A and D are the only possible answer choices. If statement (1) is insufficient, then only B, C, and E are possible. Based on statement (1) alone, you will eliminate half of the answer choices.

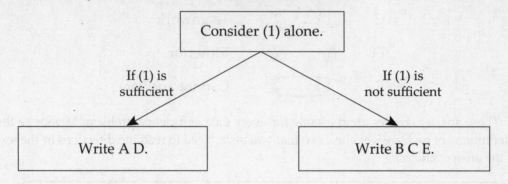

Next, you will consider statement (2) alone. It is extremely important that you forget what you saw in statement (1). Avoid the common mistake of rushing immediately into considering both statements together. Suppose that statement (1) was sufficient to answer the question, and you are left with A and D as possible answers. If statement (2) is not enough (by itself) to answer the question, then A must be the answer. If statement (2) is enough, then D is the correct answer.

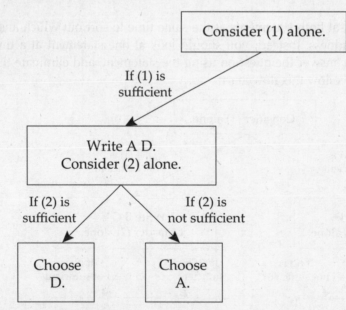

Now, suppose that statement (1) was not enough, and your initial elimination left you with answers B, C, and E. Again, the next stage is to consider statement (2) by itself. If it is sufficient to answer the question, then B is the correct answer. If not, you must eliminate B and then consider both statements together.

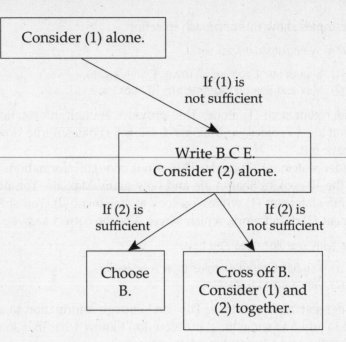

If you are down to C and E as the remaining answers, then, and only then, will you consider both statements together. At that point, if statements (1) and (2) combined provide enough information to answer the question, C is the correct answer. Otherwise, the question cannot be answered, and you should choose E.

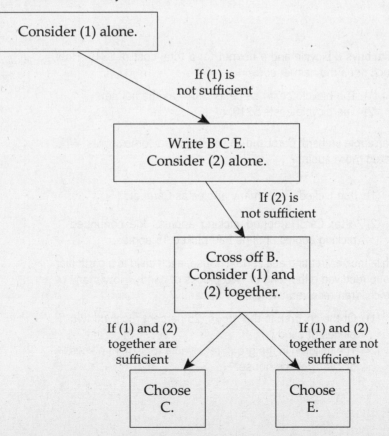

The next examples show this approach in action.

1. How many cookies did Max eat?

   (1) Sharon ate 4 cookies, 2 fewer than Max ate.
   (2) Max and Sharon together ate 10 cookies.

First, consider statement (1) alone. This provides enough information to answer the question. Sharon ate 4 cookies, so Max ate 4 + 2 = 6 cookies. Write down "A D" as the answers you have left.

Next, consider statement (2) alone. This is not enough information. You don't know how many of the 10 cookies Sharon ate and how many Max ate. You need to forget the information from statement (1) while you look at statement (2). You should eliminate D because statement (2) didn't work, which leaves A as the correct answer.

2. How many marbles does Karl have?

   (1) Karl has 6 more marbles than Jennifer has.
   (2) Jennifer has 8 marbles.

First, consider statement (1) alone. This isn't enough information to answer the question. You need to add 6 to something, but you don't know what that something is. Write down "B C E" as the answers you have left.

Next, consider statement (2) alone. This isn't enough either. Forget statement (1) during this step. Cross off B because statement (2) isn't enough, and go on to the next step.

Consider statements (1) and (2) together. Now you can find that Karl has 8 + 6 = 14 marbles. Choose C.

QUIZ 1

Remember!
For Data Sufficiency problems in this book, we do not supply the answer choices. The five possible answer choices are the same every time.

1. Mike buys a bicycle and a helmet for a total cost of $315. How much does the helmet cost?

   (1) The bicycle costs twice as much as the helmet.
   (2) The bicycle costs $210.

2. In an apple orchard, Carol and Joe each picked some apples. Who picked more apples?

   (1) Joe picked $\frac{3}{4}$ as many apples as Carol did.
   (2) After Carol stopped picking apples, Joe continued picking apples until he had picked 15 apples.

3. While trick-or-treating at a certain house, each child in a particular group received either one or two pieces of candy. How many of the children received two pieces of candy?

   (1) Of the children in the group, 25 percent received two pieces of candy.
   (2) The children in the group received a total of 15 pieces of candy at the house.

4. The rents on both Doug's apartment and Magda's apartment were increased. Which tenant paid the larger dollar increase in rent?

    (1) Doug's rent increased 2 percent.
    (2) Magda's rent increased 8 percent.

5. How many guitars does Rick own?

    (1) Rick owns three times as many electric guitars as acoustic guitars.
    (2) If Rick owned 6 fewer guitars, he would own only two-thirds as many guitars as he actually owns.

ELIMINATE CONFUSION

The data sufficiency format is very confusing. The key to consistent success is following the step-by-step method of eliminating answer choices. Go slowly and carefully as you start practicing this approach; taking the time to master it will pay off with high accuracy, even on the toughest data sufficiency questions.

DON'T FIND THE ANSWER

You usually don't need to find the actual value asked for in a data sufficiency question. You just need to know whether you could figure it out with the information in the statements. So don't waste your time solving the problem to come up with the numbers; just setting up the problem will usually be enough.

There is one situation in which you might want to find the number: when you're not sure whether the problem is actually solvable with the information in the statement. In that case, you should set up the problem and work through it until you are sure, even if you find yourself calculating the solution.

AVOID COMMON MISTAKES

Here are ways to avoid some common mistakes on data sufficiency questions:

- When you consider statement (2) alone, you must forget what statement (1) said. Physically covering up the statement with your finger can help. (But be careful about fingerprints on the computer screen!) Otherwise, you may think that statement (2) provides more information than it really does.

- Don't rush to consider both statements combined. A common tendency is to read the question and both statements, and then try to juggle all of the information at once. This mistake will lead to choosing C too frequently, even though it is wrong. It's important to consider each of the statements on its own, eliminating answers as you go, before considering them in combination.

- Don't try to do everything in your head. It is a common error for people to answer data sufficiency questions without writing anything on their scratch paper. That's a big no-no. Even though you don't need to calculate an answer, you should write down AD or BCE to help you eliminate. Also, writing down the given pieces of information, setting up equations, and the like often help you determine when you have enough pieces of the puzzle to answer the question.

- As always, read carefully. Data sufficiency questions are notorious for deliberate trickery. Be on the lookout for misleading phrases, and give yourself enough time to read the question slowly and completely.

PRACTICE SET

1. If $q = 7$, what was the total cost to place q long distance telephone calls?

   (1) Each call lasted at least 2 minutes.
   (2) The rate for long distance calls is $0.32 per minute.

Remember!
For Data Sufficiency problems in this book, we do not supply the answer choices. The five possible answer choices are the same every time.

2. If s and t are positive, what is the value of s ?

   (1) $t = 2.7$
   (2) $s = 3.1t$

3. What is the value of x ?

   (1) $3x + y = 12$
   (2) $y = 9$

4. Tom spent the day baking cookies. Of the first three dozen cookies, one third contained chocolate chips. Of the remaining cookies baked that day, one half contained chocolate chips. How many cookies containing chocolate chips did Tom bake that day?

   (1) Tom baked five dozen cookies.
   (2) Of all the cookies Tom baked, two fifths contained chocolate chips.

5. The usual price for a bagel was reduced during a sale. How much money could be saved by purchasing 10 bagels at the sale price rather than at the usual price?

   (1) The usual price for the bagels was $0.50 per bagel.
   (2) The sale price for the bagels was $0.40 per bagel.

6. How many sandwiches were sold at a certain delicatessen yesterday?

   (1) A total of 64 sandwiches were sold at the delicatessen today, 12 more than half the number sold yesterday.
   (2) The number of sandwiches sold at the delicatessen today was 40 fewer than the number sold yesterday.

7. If a total of 30 puppies is displayed in the two windows of a pet store, how many of the 30 puppies are female?

   (1) $\dfrac{3}{4}$ of the puppies in the left window are male.

   (2) $\dfrac{1}{3}$ of the puppies in the right window are female.

8. By what percent did the price of a particular stock increase?

   (1) The price of the stock increased by $10.
   (2) The price of the stock doubled to $20.

9. What is the value of $a + b$?

   (1) $a = 7$
   (2) $a + b - 9 = 0$

10. How much did a certain taxi ride cost?

    (1) The taxi ride covered 3.75 miles.
    (2) The cost for the taxi ride was $2.00 plus $0.30 for every 0.25 miles.

11. If a certain parking lot contains 40 motor vehicles, how many of the vehicles are red trucks?

    (1) Of the motor vehicles in the parking lot, 20 percent are painted red.
    (2) Of the motor vehicles in the parking lot, 15 are trucks.

12. Bruce, John, Linda, and Mark stand, in that order, in a straight line. If Linda stands 7 feet away from Mark, what is the distance from Bruce to John?

    (1) Bruce stands 7 feet away from Linda.
    (2) John stands 11 feet away from Mark.

13. What is the value of x ?

    (1) $x + y + z = 17$
    (2) $x + y = 11$

14. The regular price for a box of Crunch-O cereal is $3.50. How much money will be saved on the purchase of five boxes of Crunch-O cereal if the regular price is specially reduced?

    (1) The reduced price is more than 50% of the regular price.
    (2) The reduced price is $0.75 less per box than the regular price.

15. Mike bought a computer system for $4,000 and later sold it. For what price did Mike sell the computer system?

    (1) Mike sold the computer system for 60% of the price he paid for it.
    (2) Mike advertised the computer system in a newspaper at a price of $3,000, which was 25% more than the price for which he actually sold it.

16. How old, rounded to the nearest year, was Jim in May 1989?

    (1) Jim's friend Steve, who is exactly 2 years older than Jim, turned 25 years old in 1972.
    (2) In March 1982, Jim turned 33 years old.

17. Of the 3,000 cars manufactured in Factory Q last year, how many were still in operation at the end of the year?

    (1) Of all of the cars manufactured in Factory Q, 60% were still in operation at the end of last year.
    (2) A total of 48,000 cars manufactured in Factory Q were still in operation at the end of last year.

18. Norman is practicing shooting free throws, alternating right-handed shots with left-handed shots. He shoots 50 free throws in this manner, takes a break, and then shoots another 50 free throws in the same manner. How many successful free throws did Norman shoot?

    (1) Norman successfully shot 90% of his free throws before the break and 60% of his free throws after the break.
    (2) Norman shot 10 more successful left-handed free throws than he did successful right-handed free throws.

19. Of the 40 guests at a party, 20 eat exactly one bowl of ice cream. How many of the guests at the party eat exactly one bowl of chocolate ice cream?

    (1) Of the guests, 10 eat exactly one bowl of vanilla ice cream.
    (2) Of the guests, 5 eat exactly one bowl of strawberry ice cream.

20. How many apples can Roger hold at maximum in his basket?

(1) Roger's basket currently carries 12 apples.
(2) If Roger were to remove 4 apples from his basket when it's one quarter filled with apples, the number of apples contained within the basket would decrease by 20%.

Challenge!
Take a crack at this high-level GMAT question.

ANSWERS AND EXPLANATIONS

Quiz 1

1. **D** Start with statement (1). You know that the bicycle costs twice as much as the helmet and that the two together cost $315. The only possible prices are $105 for the helmet and $210 for the bicycle. You can answer the question, so narrow it down to A and D. Next, look at statement (2). You can simply subtract $210 from $315 to get $105 for the cost of the helmet. Statement (2) also answers the question, so choose D.

2. **A** Start with statement (1). You don't know how many apples either person picked, but you do know that Joe picked fewer than Carol. Statement (1) answers the question, so narrow the choices to A and D. Next look at statement (2). You know that Joe took longer to pick his apples, but you don't know whether he picked more or fewer than Carol did. Statement (2) doesn't answer the question, so choose A.

3. **C** Start with statement (1). Although you know the percentage of the group that received two pieces, you don't know how many children that is. You can't answer the question, so narrow it down to B, C, and E. Next, look at statement (2). You can't tell how many of the 15 pieces went to "two-piece" children and how many went to "one-piece" children. Maybe 1 child received 2 pieces and 13 children received 1 piece each. Maybe 7 children received 2 pieces each and 1 child received 1 piece. You can't answer the question, so eliminate B. Now, try both statements together. If there are x children, then 75% of x receive 1 piece and 25% of x receive 2 pieces. Given that the total number of pieces is 15, you can set up this equation: $(0.75 \times 1 \times x) + (0.25 \times 2 \times x) = 15$. You could solve this equation and find the total number of children. Then you'd be able to answer the question by finding 25% of that number. Choose C.

4. **E** Start with statement (1). This mentions only Doug's increase, so you can't compare that to Magda's increase because you don't know their starting rents. You can't answer the question, so narrow it down to B, C, and E. Next, look at statement (2). This tells you only about Magda's increase. Again, you can't answer the question because you don't know their starting rents, so eliminate B. Next, look at both statements together. Even though Magda's percent increase is larger, you don't know anything about the actual dollar increases because you don't know their starting rents. This eliminates C. You can't answer the question, so choose E.

5. **B** Start with statement (1). This doesn't tell you anything about the total number of guitars, just about the ratio of electric to acoustic. You can't answer the question, so narrow it down to B, C, and E. Next, look at statement (2). If Rick owns y guitars, you can set up the equation $y - 6 = \frac{2}{3}y$. You could solve this equation to find how many guitars Rick owns. Don't waste time actually solving for y! You know that you can answer the question using statement (2), so choose B.

Practice Set

1. **E** Start with statement (1). This tells you nothing about the cost of the calls. You can't answer the question, so narrow down the possible answers to B, C, and E. Look at statement (2). Now you know the cost per minute, but you don't know how many minutes the calls lasted. You can't answer the question, so eliminate B. Look at (1) and (2) together. You know more, but you still don't know the exact number of minutes—only that the total was at least 14 minutes. This eliminates C. You can't answer the question, so choose E.

2. **C** Start with statement (1). This doesn't tell you anything about s. You can't answer the question, so narrow down the choices to B, C, and E. Look at statement (2). Alone, this statement doesn't help. You don't know t, so you can't solve for s. You can't answer the question, so eliminate B. Look at statements (1) and (2) combined. You can plug $t = 2.7$ into the second equation to get $s = (3.1)(2.7)$. Now you can solve for s and answer the question. Choose C.

3. **C** Start with statement (1). You can't solve for x because you don't have a number to plug in for y. Narrow the answers to B, C, and E. Look at statement (2). This tells you only about y, not about x. You can't answer the question, so eliminate B. Look at (1) and (2) together. Now you can plug $y = 9$ into the first equation and solve for x. You can answer the question, so choose C.

4. **D** Start with statement (1). You know that one third of the first 36 cookies, or 12 cookies, contain chocolate chips. Since there are 5 dozen cookies total, that leaves 24 cookies of which one half, or 12 cookies, are also chocolate chip. That's $12 + 12 = 24$ cookies containing chocolate chips. You can answer the question, so narrow your choices to A and D. Look at statement (2). You can set up the equation $\frac{1}{3}x + \frac{1}{2}y = \frac{2}{5}(x+y)$, in which x is the first set of cookies (3 dozen), and y is the number of remaining cookies. Since you know that $x = 36$, you can plug that into the equation and solve for y. The total number of chocolate chip cookies would then be $\frac{2}{5}(x+y)$. You could answer the question, so choose D.

5. **C** Start with statement (1). You don't know anything about the sale price, so you can't determine how much money is saved. You can't answer the question; narrow it down to B, C, and E. Look at statement (2). Now you know the sale price, but not the regular price. You can't find the difference to answer the question, so eliminate B. Look at statements (1) and (2) together. You know that you save $0.50 – $0.40 = $0.10 per bagel. If you buy 10 bagels, that's $1.00 saved. You can answer the question; choose C.

6. **A** Start with statement (1). If x is the number of sandwiches sold yesterday, you can set up the equation $64 = \frac{1}{2}x + 12$. You don't actually need to solve the equation; just know that you could find x. You can answer the question, so narrow down the choices to A and D. Look at statement (2). You could set up an equation, $y = x - 40$, but you can't solve it because you don't know y, the number of sandwiches sold today. You can't answer the question with only B, so choose A.

7. **E** Start with statement (1). You can turn the statement around to say that $\frac{1}{4}$ of the puppies in the left window are female, but you don't know anything about the proportion of females in the right window. You can't answer the question so far, so you've got answers B, C, and E left. Look at statement (2). Same problem, just with the other window. Again you can't answer the question, so eliminate B. Look at (1) and (2) together. Although you know the male-to-female proportion in each window, you don't know how many puppies are in each window. If there are 24 puppies in the left window and 6 in the right, then there are $6 + 2 = 8$ female puppies. If there are 12 puppies in the left window and 18 puppies in the right, then there are $3 + 6 = 9$ female puppies. Don't assume the puppies are split evenly. You can't answer the question, so choose E.

8. **B** Start with statement (1). You know the dollar amount of the increase, but you don't know the original price, so you can't find the percentage increase. You can't answer the question, so narrow it down to B, C, and E. Look at statement (2). This tells you that the old price was $10 and the new price is $20. That's a 100% increase. You can answer the question, so choose B.

9. **B** Start with statement (1). This gives you information only about a. You can't answer the question, so narrow your choices to B, C, and E. Look at statement (2). You can use statement (2) to determine that $a + b = 9$, which answers the question. You don't know what a and b are individually, but you don't need to in order to answer the question. Choose B.

10. **C** Start with statement (1). This tells you the length of the trip, but not how to determine the cost from that. You can't answer the question, so your choices are now B, C, and E. Look at statement (2). This tells you the formula for determining the cost, but you don't know how many miles long the trip was. *Remember:* You need to forget statement (1) at this point. Now look at statements (1) and (2) together. You can take the miles from (1) and plug them into the formula from (2) to find the cost. You don't need to actually find the answer, just to be certain that you could. Choose C.

11. **E** Start with statement (1). You know that overall 20% of the motor vehicles are painted red, but you don't know how many trucks there are or if the trucks are different from the rest of the motor vehicles. They may be more or less likely to be painted red. You can't answer the question, so narrow the choices to B, C, and E. Look at statement (2). You now know that there are 15 trucks, but you don't know anything about the percentage that are painted red. You can't answer the question; eliminate B. Look at (1) and (2) together. There are 15 trucks and 20% of all motor vehicles are painted red, but you can't assume that the 20% statement applies to trucks specifically. Perhaps none of the trucks are red and all the red motor vehicles are non-trucks. You can't answer the question, so choose E.

12. **C** Start by drawing a picture. It should look something like this.

Now, look at statement (1). From the question, you know that LM is 7 feet. This statement tells you that BJ plus JL is also 7 feet. But you don't know how much of the 7 feet is BJ. You can't answer the question, so narrow your potential answers to B, C, and E. Look at statement (2). This tells you that JM is 11 feet, which means that JL is 4 feet because, from the question, LM is 7 feet. However, you don't know anything about B or how far away he is from the others. You can't answer the question, so eliminate B. Look at statements (1) and (2) together. From the question, you know that LM = 7. From (1) you know that BJ + JL = 7. From (2) you know that JL = 4. Substitute that into BJ + JL = 7 and you find that BJ = 3. That answers the question, so choose C.

13. **E** Start with statement (1). You can't solve for x because you don't know the values of y and z. You can't answer the question, so narrow your choices to B, C, and E. Look at statement (2). You can't solve for x because you don't know the value of y. Eliminate B. Try statements (1) and (2) together. You can solve for z by substituting $x + y = 11$ into the first equation, but you can't solve for x. You can't answer the question, so choose E.

14. **B** Start with statement (1). Because the statement says "more than 50%," you can't tell whether it's 51%, 99%, or somewhere in between. You can't answer the question, so narrow it down to B, C, and E. Look at statement (2). This tells you that you save $0.75 per box, or $3.75 for five boxes. That answers the question, so choose B.

15. **D** Start with statement (1). You just need to find 60% of $4,000 (it's $2,400) and that's the price for which Mike sold the computer system. You can answer the question, so narrow your choices to A and D. Look at statement (2). You know that 25% of the sale price is $3,000, so you could solve for the sale price and answer the question. Choose D.

16. **B** Start with statement (1). Because Steve turned 25 in 1972, you can determine that Jim turned 23 in 1972. So Jim must have turned 40 in 1989, but you don't know whether he was 39 or 40 in May. His birthday may have been later in the year. You can't answer the question, so narrow the choices to B, C, and E. Look at statement (2). If Jim turned 33 in March 1982, then he turned 40 in March 1989 and he would still be 40 in May. You can answer the question, so choose B.

17. **E** Start with statement (1). The 60% refers to all cars *ever* manufactured in Factory Q, not just those made last year. You can't answer the question, so your potential answers narrow to B, C, and E. Look at statement (2). Again, the 48,000 refers to all cars ever manufactured in Factory Q. You don't know how many of those are from last year's batch. You can't answer the question, so eliminate B. Look at (1) and (2) together. You still don't have any information about last year's batch, and you can't assume the 60% rate applies to them as well. You can't answer the question. Choose E.

18. **A** Start with statement (1). Before the break, Norman made 90% of 50, or 45 free throws. After the break, he made 60% of 50, or 30 free throws. The total is 45 + 30 = 75 successful free throws. You can answer the question, so narrow your choices to A and D. Look at statement (2). This statement doesn't help you because you don't know how many successful left-handed free throws or successful right-handed free throws he made. You can't find the total, so you can't answer the question. This eliminates D, so choose A.

19. **E** Start with statement (1). You can determine that there are 10 other ice cream eaters, but you don't know how many of them eat chocolate ice cream. You can't answer the question. Narrow your choices to B, C, and E. Look at statement (2). This leaves 15 other ice cream eaters, but you still don't know how many eat chocolate ice cream. You can't answer the question, so eliminate B. Look at statements (1) and (2) together. You may be tempted to think that 10 guests eat vanilla ice cream and 5 eat strawberry ice cream, leaving 5 to eat chocolate ice cream. However, you don't know whether any other flavors of ice cream (such as my favorite—mint chocolate chip) are available. You can't answer the question, so choose E.

20. **B** Start with statement (1). Knowing the number of apples currently in Roger's basket is irrelevant to the number of apples the basket could hold at maximum. This is not sufficient, so your remaining choices narrow to B, C, and E. Look at statement (2). At first glance, this may not look sufficient. However, it is possible to translate this statement into an equation. If a represents the maximum apples in the basket, the equation from statement (2) would read as follows: $0.25a - 4 = (0.8)0.25a$. This equation could then be solved to yield the answer. Choose B.

Terms of Endearment

Many of the questions in the GMAT Math section use a lot of math vocabulary. You probably learned most of these terms in junior high and high school. However, if you're like most GMAT takers, you haven't used them in years, so your memory of them is pretty hazy.

This chapter reviews the terms that are most common on the GMAT. We'll look at the definitions and, more importantly, the way those words are used in GMAT questions. Even if you feel comfortable with the definitions, you should work some or all of the examples to be certain you know how to apply those definitions.

NUMBERS

It's often helpful to use a number line to describe different types of numbers and their properties. Here's an example of a number line.

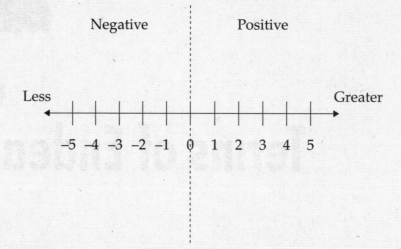

Greater means "to the right" on the number line, while less means "to the left." So 7 is greater than 5 and 2 is less than 3. Most people find that pretty intuitive. However, it's easy to get mixed up when you deal with negative numbers. For example, –5 is actually less than –3 even though 5 looks bigger than 3. You can avoid this mistake if you think in terms of "right" and "left" rather than "bigger" and "smaller."

Positive numbers are greater than zero. Negative numbers are less than zero.

Zero itself is neither positive nor negative. It is usually referred to as neutral.

There are some rules for multiplying (and dividing) positive and negative numbers.

Positive × or ÷ Positive = Positive	$2 \times 3 = 6$ and $10 \div 5 = 2$
Positive × or ÷ Negative = Negative	$2 \times (-3) = -6$ and $10 \div (-5) = -2$
Negative × or ÷ Negative = Positive	$(-2) \times (-3) = 6$ and $(-10) \div (-5) = 2$

The absolute value of a number refers to that number's distance from zero. The symbol for absolute value is a pair of vertical lines; e.g., the absolute value of 7 is written as $|7|$. The easiest way to deal with it is simply to omit the negative sign if the number is negative. For example, $|-4| = 4$. For positive numbers, the absolute value is the same as the number itself. For example, $|3| = 3$.

Distinct numbers are numbers that are not equal. For example, 2 and 3 are distinct numbers, but 4 and 2^2 are not distinct.

QUIZ 1

1. Which of the following numbers has the greatest value?

   ○ -8.3

   ○ $|-7.7|$

   ○ 2

   ○ $|4.5|$

   ○ 6.8

2. What is the value of x?

   (1) $|x| = 7$

   (2) When x is divided by a negative number, the result is negative.

INTEGERS

An integer is what you commonly think of as a positive or negative "counting number." All of the numbers marked on the number line are integers. The numbers between the marks are not integers. More formally, integers include all positive whole numbers, all negative whole numbers, and 0. For example, numbers such as 1, 2, 3, 0, –1, and –2 are all integers. Numbers such as $\frac{1}{2}$, 0.072, $-\frac{2}{3}$, and $\sqrt{3}$ are not integers.

Even integers are divisible by 2 with no remainder. Odd integers are not divisible by 2. It's important to realize that the terms "even" and "odd" apply only to integers. Note that zero is an even integer. There are some rules for multiplying (but not dividing) even and odd integers. If you forget these rules, you can recreate them by trying out some simple numbers.

Even × Even = Even	$2 \times 4 = 8$
Even × Odd = Even	$2 \times 3 = 6$
Odd × Odd = Odd	$3 \times 5 = 15$

There are also some rules for adding and subtracting odd and even integers.

Even + or − Even = Even	$2 + 4 = 6$	$8 − 2 = 6$
Even + or − Odd = Odd	$2 + 3 = 5$	$8 − 3 = 5$
Odd + or − Odd = Even	$3 + 5 = 8$	$7 − 5 = 2$

Consecutive integers are integers listed in order of increasing value without any integers in between. For example, 1, 2, 3,… is a series of consecutive integers. The GMAT may also ask questions about consecutive even integers, such as 2, 4, 6, 8,…, or consecutive multiples of 7, such as 7, 14, 21, 28,….

The test writers sometimes set traps based upon the terms in the question, hoping that you're not paying close attention to these important words. Suppose a problem states that "x is a number greater than 0." If you consider only integers, such as 1 or 5, as possible values for x, you may miss something important. Non-integers have unusual properties in some circumstances. For example, squaring typical integers, such as 2 or 3, results in a larger number. However, squaring the non-integer $\frac{2}{3}$ results in a smaller number. These subtle terminology traps are especially prevalent in data sufficiency questions.

Quiz 2

1. If m and n are negative integers, which of the following must be true?

    I. $m + n < 0$
    II. $mn > 0$
    III. $mn > n$

    ○ I only
    ○ II only
    ○ I and II
    ○ I and III
    ○ I, II, and III

2. If both v and w are odd integers, which of the following could be an even integer?

    ○ vw

    ○ $v + w + 1$

    ○ $\dfrac{v}{w}$

    ○ $2(v + w)$

    ○ $2v + w$

3. If a, b, and c are consecutive integers, which of the following must be an odd integer?

○ $a + b + c$
○ abc
○ $a + b + c + 1$
○ $ab(c - 1)$
○ $abc - 1$

MANIPULATING NUMBERS

A sum is the result obtained from addition, and a difference is the result from subtraction. A product is the result of multiplication, and a quotient is the result of division.

Whenever you see one of these terms in a problem, you know to perform that operation (add, subtract, multiply, divide).

A remainder is the integer left over from division. This is the way you did division in third grade—no decimals or fractions allowed. Just keep dividing until you get down to something smaller than the number you're dividing by. That something is the remainder.

For example, let's divide 7 by 2. Set up the long division like this: $2\overline{)7}$. You know that 2 goes into 7 three times (because $2 \times 3 = 6$).

However, there's still 1 left over. 1 is smaller than 2, so you can't continue without getting into decimals. That means 1 is the remainder.

The reciprocal of a number is the number you multiply it by to get 1. In other words, if the product of two numbers, m and n, is 1, then the numbers are reciprocal. If you're not quite sure what that means, consider some actual numbers. What is the reciprocal of 2? Well, what number can 2 be multiplied by in order to yield a product of 1? $2 \times \frac{1}{2} = 1$. So, the reciprocal of 2 is $\frac{1}{2}$. If the number you're starting with is a fraction, the reciprocal can be determined by simply swapping the numerator and denominator in the original fraction. For example, the reciprocal of $\frac{3}{4}$ is $\frac{4}{3}$.

QUIZ 3

1. When 12 is divided by the positive integer k, the remainder is $k - 3$. Which of the following could be the value of k ?

○ 3
○ 4
○ 6
○ 9
○ 10

2. If the product xy is negative, which of the following must be true?

    ◯ $x < 0$

    ◯ $y < 0$

    ◯ $\dfrac{x}{y} > 0$

    ◯ $\dfrac{x}{y} < 0$

    ◯ $x + y < 0$

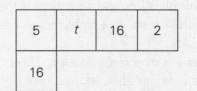

3. In the figure above, the product of the two numbers in the vertical column equals the sum of the four numbers in the horizontal row. What is the value of t ?

    ◯   0.5
    ◯   3
    ◯   21
    ◯   57
    ◯   80

ZERO

Zero is a special number because it is unique in a lot of ways. Some of the trickier questions require that you be aware of some of these special characteristics. Zero is an integer, but it is neither positive nor negative. It's usually referred to as neutral. However, zero does qualify as even.

You can't divide anything by zero. Division by zero is said to be undefined. Multiplying anything by zero is always zero. Also, zero divided by anything else equals zero.

FACTORS, MULTIPLES, AND DIVISIBILITY

An integer, x, is a factor of another integer, y, if y is divisible by x. In other words, $y = nx$, where y, n, and x are all integers. For example, $3 \times 6 = 18$, so 3 and 6 are factors of 18. It's best to identify factors in pairs. Also, when you're trying to find all the factors of a number, start with 1 and work your way up. That way you're less likely to forget a pair.

List all the factors of 24.

$$1 \times 24$$

$$2 \times 12$$

$$3 \times 8$$

$$4 \times 6$$

When the numbers get close together, like 4 and 6, you know you've got them all.

For the quantities x and y, we say that y is a multiple of x if $y = nx$ for some integer n. In other words, to find the multiple of a number, just multiply that number by any integer, for example 1 or 2. The GMAT is generally concerned with only the positive multiples of a number. For example, the multiples of 4 are 4, 8, 12, 16, 20, 24, and so on. Don't worry about negative numbers or zero, even though they technically can be multiples of a given number. There are an infinite number of multiples for any given number.

If there is no remainder when integer x is divided by integer y, then x is said to be divisible by y. In other words, *divisible* means you can evenly divide the bigger number by the smaller number. For example, $8 \div 2 = 4$, so 8 is divisible by 2. However, $10 \div 4 = 2.5$, so 10 is not divisible by 4.

Here are some shortcuts to help you determine divisibility:

- A number is divisible by 2 if it is an even integer.

- A number is divisible by 3 if the sum of its digits is a number divisible by 3. For example, see whether 108 is divisible by 3. The sum of the digits is $1 + 0 + 8 = 9$. Since 9 is divisible by 3, the number 108 is also divisible by 3.

- A number is divisible by 4 if the number formed by its last two digits is divisible by 4. For example, see whether 624 is divisible by 4. The number formed by the last two digits is 24 (just ignore all of the digits except the last two). Since 24 is divisible by 4, the number 624 is also divisible by 4.

- A number is divisible by 5 if it ends in 0 or 5.

- A number is divisible by 6 if it is divisible by both 2 and 3, using the rules above.

- A number is divisible by 9 if the sum of its digits is a number divisible by 9. This is very similar to the "divisible by 3" rule. For example, see whether 902,178 is divisible by 9. The sum of the digits is $9 + 0 + 2 + 1 + 7 + 8 = 27$. Since 27 is divisible by 9 (use the rule again if you're not sure), the number 902,178 is also divisible by 9.

- A number is divisible by 10 if it ends in 0.

Some tougher problems may require you to break a number into its prime factors, which can be thought of as the building blocks of the number. These prime factors play a big role in determining the divisibility of a number and in finding its multiples. You'll learn more about these concepts later in this chapter.

Quiz 4

1. How many multiples of 3 are there between 10 and 90, inclusive?

   ○ 26
   ○ 27
   ○ 28
   ○ 29
   ○ 30

2. Which of the following is the least positive integer that is divisible by each of the integers from 2 through 5, inclusive?

   ○ 30
   ○ 60
   ○ 120
   ○ 180
   ○ 240

3. How many of the factors of 42 are divisible by 3 ?

   ○ 2
   ○ 3
   ○ 4
   ○ 6
   ○ 8

PRIME NUMBERS

A prime number is a number that has exactly two distinct factors, 1 and itself. This means that the number isn't divisible by anything besides itself and the number 1. The first ten prime numbers are 2, 3, 5, 7, 11, 13, 17, 19, 23, and 29.

Another thing to note is that 2 is the only even prime number. That's because all other even numbers are divisible by 2.

If an integer x is a factor of integer y, then x is called a prime factor of y. For example, the prime factors of 6 are 2 and 3 because $2 \times 3 = 6$. The prime factors of 24 are 2, 2, 2, and 3 because $2 \times 2 \times 2 \times 3 = 24$. You could also write this as $2^3 \times 3 = 24$, which is sometimes called the prime factorization of 24. However, if the question asked for the *distinct* prime factors of 24, they are 2 and 3. You wouldn't count the extra 2s, because distinct means "not the same."

An easy way to find the prime factors of a number is a factor tree: Find two factors of the number. Then, find two factors for each factor that isn't a prime number. Stop when all you have are prime numbers. The following diagram is of a factor tree for 100:

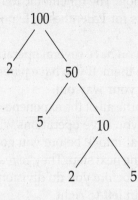

Prime factorization of 100 = 2 × 2 × 5 × 5

Distinct prime factors of 100 are 2 and 5

Quiz 5

1. If a and b are distinct prime numbers, which of the following could be the product of a and b ?

   ○   4
   ○   5
   ○   10
   ○   11
   ○   25

2. What is the greatest integer that is a sum of four different prime numbers, each less than 30 ?

   ○   67
   ○   88
   ○   98
   ○   104
   ○   126

3. If x is a prime number greater than 3, what is the remainder when x^2 is divided by 8 ?

   ○   0
   ○   1
   ○   3
   ○   4
   ○   5

ORDER OF OPERATIONS

There is an order you want to follow when you're solving a mathematical expression that contains more than one operation. The mnemonic to help you remember the order of operations is **P E M D A S**. It stands for **P**arentheses, **E**xponents, **M**ultiplication, **D**ivision, **A**ddition, and **S**ubtraction.

Parentheses are the first step. If you have several operations within a set of parentheses, just apply the order of operations to them. If you have parentheses inside parentheses, start with the innermost ones and work your way out.

Exponents are the next step. Handle all of the exponents before you move on to the other operations. The one exception is if you have operations within an exponent. For example, if you see 3^{2+3}, you need to turn that into 3^5 before you go any further.

Multiplication and division are the next step. They're really the same thing, so you won't necessarily do all the multiplication before you do division. Treat them as though they are at the same level and just work from left to right.

Addition and subtraction are the last step. Just as multiplication and division are at the same level, so are addition and subtraction. Just work from left to right.

Quiz 6

1. $24 - 12 + \dfrac{36}{6} - 3 =$

   - ○ 3
   - ○ 5
   - ○ 12
   - ○ 15
   - ○ 24

2. $(1 + 5) - 3^2 + 8 \div 2 \times 2 =$

   - ○ −5
   - ○ −1
   - ○ 1
   - ○ 5
   - ○ 15

MORE FACTORING

Earlier in this chapter, you learned about the factors of a number and how to break down a number into its prime factorization. It is often useful to think of a number in terms of its factors, which are the building blocks of a number. You will usually be concerned with the prime factors of a number.

For example, take a look at the number 20. Its factors are 1, 2, 4, 5, 10, and 20. Its prime factorization is $2 \times 2 \times 5$, or $2^2 \times 5$. Each factor of 20 (except 1), is formed from a subset of the prime factors of 20. The factor 2 uses one of the prime factors 2. The factor 10 incorporates one of the prime factors 2 and the prime factor 5, because $2 \times 5 = 10$. Once you know the prime factorization of a number, its factors are formed by grouping the prime factors in different ways. Try these concepts in the next problem.

1. Which of the following is NOT divisible by the product of 5, 6, and 8 ?

   ○ $2^4 \times 3 \times 5$
   ○ $2^3 \times 3^2 \times 5$
   ○ $2^5 \times 3 \times 5$
   ○ $2^4 \times 3^3 \times 5 \times 7$
   ○ $2^5 \times 3^2 \times 5 \times 11$

First, look at the prime factorizations of 5, 6, and 8. 5 is already prime. You can break 6 into 2×3 and 8 into $2 \times 2 \times 2$ or 2^3. Thus, the product $5 \times 6 \times 8$ can be expressed in prime factorization form: $(5)(2 \times 3)(2^3) = 2^4 \times 3 \times 5$. Whatever that product is, it includes four factors of 2, one factor of 3, and one factor of 5.

Four of the answers will be divisible by the product. Another way of saying that is the product is a factor of those four answer choices. Each of these four answers must include four factors of 2, one factor of 3, and one factor of 5 (or $2^4 \times 3 \times 5$). The only answer that doesn't include at least those factors is B. It has only three factors of 2, not four. Choose B.

2. If m and n are integers, and m is a multiple of 5, is mn a multiple of 135 ?

   (1) m is a multiple of 3.
   (2) n is a multiple of 9.

A multiple of 135 must be a multiple of all of the factors of 135. If you break 135 into its prime factors, you get $135 = 3 \times 5$. Thus, mn must include three factors of 3 and one factor of 5 if it is a multiple of 135. You already know that m includes a factor of 5, so you need to look for the factors of 3.

With statement (1), you learn that m is also a multiple of 3, so it includes at least one factor of 3. However, you need three factors of 3. Without more information, statement (1) is insufficient. Narrow the possible answers to B, C, and E.

In statement (2), you learn that n is a multiple of 9, so it must include at least two factors of 3 (because $9 = 3$). Again, you need three factors of 3, so (2) alone is not enough. Eliminate B.

Remember!
For Data Sufficiency problems in this book, we do not supply the answer choices. The five possible answer choices are the same every time.

With both statements together, you have at least one factor of 3 in m and at least two more in n. Combined with the knowledge that m is a multiple of 5, you can determine that mn contains at least the factors 3×5, which makes it a multiple of 135. That answers the question, so C is the correct answer.

FACTORIALS

A factorial is closely related to the idea of factors. An exclamation mark after a number, such as 5!, indicates a factorial. The factorial is the product of the indicated numbers and all positive integers less than that number. For example, $5! = 5 \times 4 \times 3 \times 2 \times 1$. Although you could calculate the value of the factorial (e.g., $5! = 120$), most factorial problems will be easier if you leave it in factored form. That allows you to cancel like terms and otherwise simplify the numbers. Look at the following example:

3. What is the value of $\dfrac{6!}{8!}$?

○ $\dfrac{1}{56}$

○ $\dfrac{1}{48}$

○ $\dfrac{1}{8}$

○ $\dfrac{1}{4}$

○ $\dfrac{3}{4}$

First, write out each factorial in factored form: $\dfrac{6!}{8!} = \dfrac{6 \times 5 \times 4 \times 3 \times 2 \times 1}{8 \times 7 \times 6 \times 5 \times 4 \times 3 \times 2 \times 1}$. You can cancel the 6, 5, 4, 3, 2, and 1 in the top and the bottom to reduce the fraction to $\dfrac{1}{8 \times 7} = \dfrac{1}{56}$. The correct answer is A.

4. If $\dfrac{9!}{3^k}$ is an integer, what is the greatest possible value of k?

○ 9
○ 6
○ 4
○ 3
○ 2

First, write out the factorial in factored form: $\dfrac{9!}{3^k} = \dfrac{9 \times 8 \times 7 \times 6 \times 5 \times 4 \times 3 \times 2 \times 1}{3 \times \ldots \times 3}$. To make the fraction an integer, each of the factors of 3 on the bottom must cancel with a factor of 3 on the top. The 9 on the top has two factors of 3, the 6 has one factor of 3, and the 3 has one factor of 3. That's four factors of 3 on the top, so the largest that k could be is 4. Four factors of 3 on the bottom would exactly cancel with the four on the top, leaving an integer. The correct answer is C.

PRACTICE SET

1. If x is a positive integer, then $x(x - 1)$ is

    ○ divisible by 5 whenever x is even.
    ○ divisible by 9 whenever x is odd.
    ○ odd only when x is odd.
    ○ always odd.
    ⊗ always even.

2. Which of the following CANNOT result in an integer?

    ○ The product of two integers divided by the reciprocal of a different integer
    ○ An even integer divided by 7
    ○ The quotient of two distinct prime numbers
    ○ A multiple of 11 divided by 3
    ○ The sum of two odd integers divided by 2

3. If $a + b + c = 36$, what is the value of abc ?

    (1) a, b, and c are consecutive even integers.
    (2) a, b, and c are distinct positive integers.

4. How many positive integers less than 28 are prime numbers, odd multiples of 5, or the sum of a positive multiple of 2 and a positive multiple of 4 ?

    ○ 27
    ○ 25
    ○ 24
    ○ 22
    ○ 20

Remember!
For Data Sufficiency problems in this book, we do not supply the answer choices. The five possible answer choices are the same every time.

5. If a positive integer q is divisible by both 3 and 11, then q must also be divisible by which of the following?

 I.   14
 II.   33
 III. 66

- ○ I only
- ○ II only
- ○ III only
- ○ I and II
- ○ II and III

6. If positive integers q and r are both even, which of the following must be odd?

- ○ $q - r$

- ○ $\dfrac{q}{r}$

- ○ $\dfrac{q}{r} + 1$

- ○ $qr - 1$

- ○ $q(r - 1)$

7. What is the value of the two-digit integer n ?

 (1) n is divisible by 9.
 (2) The tens digit of n is 4.

8. In a decreasing sequence of seven consecutive even integers, the sum of the first four integers is 68. What is the product of the last three integers in the sequence?

- ○ 1,000
- ○   960
- ○   925
- ○   30
- ○   25

9. What is the value of the integer p ?

 (1) p is a prime factor of 33.
 (2) $3 \leq p \leq 15$

10. If m is an odd integer and $n = 5m + 4$, which of the following could be a divisor of n ?

   ○ 2
   ○ 3
   ○ 4
   ○ 5
   ○ 6

11. $(3 + 1)^2 + (5 - 4 \times 2) =$

   ○ 7
   ○ 12
   ○ 13
   ○ 18
   ○ 19

12. If positive integer n is less than or equal to 20, what is the value of n ?

   (1) n is divisible by 2 and 5.
   (2) n has 2 distinct prime factors.

13. If x is a member of the set {12, 15, 18, 24, 36, 45}, what is the value of x ?

   (1) x is divisible by 6.
   (2) x is a multiple of 9.

14. What is the value of the sum of a sequence of x consecutive even integers?

   (1) $x = 5$
   (2) The least integer in the sequence is 6.

15. If x and z are integers, how many even integers y are there such that $x < y < z$?

   (1) $z - x = 4$
   (2) x is odd.

16. What is the value of q ?
   (1) $q = \sqrt{9}$
   (2) $|q| = 3$

17. What is the value of the three-digit integer t if t is divisible by 9 ?

   (1) The tens digit and the hundreds digit of t are both 7.
   (2) The units digit of t is less than both the tens digit and the hundreds digit.

18. If x is a factor of positive integer y, then which of the following must be positive?

○ $x - y$
○ $y - x$
○ $2x - y$
○ $x - 2y$
○ $y - x + 1$

19. What is the remainder when n is divided by 3 ?

(1) n is divisible by 5.
(2) n is divisible by 6.

Challenge!
Take a crack at this high-level GMAT question.

20. In a certain game, scoring plays result in 2, 7, or 11 points only. How many times did a team playing this game score 2 points on a play?

(1) The team scored 7 points on a scoring play exactly 3 times.
(2) The product of the point values from all of the team's scoring plays is 6,860.

ANSWERS AND EXPLANATIONS

Quiz 1

1. **B** The question asks for the greatest value, so you want the number farthest to the right on a number line. The two absolute values convert to 7.7 and 4.5. Of all five numbers, 7.7 is the greatest, so B is the best answer.

2. **C** Start with statement (1). You know that $x = 7$ or -7, but that's not enough. You can't answer the question, so narrow down the answers to B, C, and E. Look at statement (2). From the rules for multiplying and dividing positive and negative numbers, this statement tells you that x is positive, but you don't have a single value. You can't answer the question, so eliminate B. Look at (1) and (2) together. You know that x is positive so the only possible value is 7. Choose C.

Quiz 2

1. **E** Adding two negative numbers will just result in an even smaller (farther to the left) negative number. So $m + n < 0$ and I is true. You know that a negative multiplied by a negative results in a positive number. So $mn > 0$ and II is true. This also means that mn is greater than any negative number, including n. Therefore $mn > n$ and III is true. So the answer is E.

2. **D** You know that an odd integer multiplied by an odd integer results in an odd integer. So vw is odd and you can eliminate A. An odd integer plus an odd integer results in an even integer. So $v + w$ is even, but $v + w + 1$ is odd and you eliminate B. Dividing an odd integer by an odd integer gives you either an odd integer, such as $\frac{15}{5} = 3$, or a non-integer, such as $\frac{17}{5} = 3\frac{2}{5}$. So eliminate C. An even times an odd is even, so $2v$ is even. Adding an even to an odd is odd, so $2v + w$ is odd and you should cross off E. As we saw earlier, $v + w$ is even, and multiplying by 2 keeps it even. (Even if $v + w$ were odd, multiplying by 2 would make it even.) So D is the best answer.

3. **E** This is a great problem to approach by Plugging In. Start by setting the values of a, b, and, c equal to 1, 2, and 3, respectively, and then test the answer choices using these numbers. That will eliminate A, B, and D. Next, test C and E by replacing the values of a, b, and c with 2, 3, and 4, respectively. (The first round of plugging in used two odd numbers, and this round will use two even numbers.) When you test C and E with these new numbers, E is the only one that works: $2 \times 3 \times 4 - 1 = 23$. (*Note:* You'll study Plugging In in Chapter 7.)

Quiz 3

1. **A** For this question, just try out each answer choice and see what the remainder is. If $k = 3$ then $12 \div 3 = 4$ with a remainder of 0. Because $k - 3 = 0$, answer A is correct. In answer B, the remainder is 0 and $k - 3 = 1$; eliminate it. In answer C, the remainder is 0 and $k - 3 = 3$; cross it off. In answer D, the remainder is 3 and $k - 3 = 6$; get rid of it. In answer E, the remainder is 2 and $k - 3 = 7$, so that's not right either.

2. **D** Because xy is negative, you know that either x is negative and y is positive or vice versa. However, you don't know which way it is, so eliminate A and B. The rule tells you that division with a positive and a negative results in a negative. Eliminate C and choose D. You can cross off E because $x + y$ could be either positive or negative. For example, $3 + (-5) = -2$ but $(-3) + 5 = 2$. It just depends on the particular numbers you use for x and y.

3. **D** Product means multiply, so the product of the numbers in the vertical column is $5 \times 16 = 80$. The sum of the horizontal numbers needs to equal 80 as well. Sum means add, so the sum is $5 + t + 16 + 2 = 23 + t$. If $23 + t = 80$, then $t = 57$. Choose D.

Quiz 4

1. **B** The simplest way to solve this problem is to list every multiple of 3 from 10 to 90 and then count them. It sounds tedious but it doesn't really take as long as you think it will. The multiples of 3 are 12, 15, 18, 21, 24, 27, 30, 33, 36, 39, 42, 45, 48, 51, 54, 57, 60, 63, 66, 69, 72, 75, 78, 81, 84, 87, and 90. You include 90 because the question said *inclusive*. That's a total of 27 numbers.

2. **B** The correct answer must be divisible by 2, 3, 4, and 5. You may think the easiest way is simply to multiply those numbers together, but that's a trap. Instead, start with the smallest answer choice and see whether it's divisible by all of those numbers. If not, try the next smallest answer choice. Use the divisibility shortcuts. 30 is divisible by 2, 3, and 5, but not by 4. Eliminate A. 60 is divisible by 2, 3, 4, and 5. Choose B. The trap is answer C. If you multiply $2 \times 3 \times 4 \times 5$ you'll get 120, which is divisible by all of those numbers, but it's not the *least* number divisible by them.

3. **C** First, list all of the factors of 42: 1×42, 2×21, 3×14, and 6×7. Of these factors, 42, 21, 3, and 6 are all divisible by 3. That's 4 numbers, so choose C.

Quiz 5

1. **C** For each answer, list all the factor pairs and see if any contain two distinct prime numbers. The factors of 4 are 1×4 and 2×2. Although 2 is a prime number, you need two distinct prime numbers. Eliminate A. The factors of 5 are 1×5. *Remember:* 1 is not a prime number. Eliminate B. The factors of 10 are 1×10 and 2×5. Since 2 and 5 are both prime numbers, choose C.

2. **B** The question asks for the greatest integer, so add up the four largest prime numbers that are less than 30. The numbers are 29, 23, 19, and 17. Remember that not all odd integers are prime. The sum is $29 + 23 + 19 + 17 = 88$. Choose B.

3. **B** Just pick a prime number greater than 3, such as 5. Square it and you get $5^2 =$ 25. Divide 25 by 8 and you get 3 with a remainder of 1. You can try other prime numbers, but you'll always get a remainder of 1. Choose B.

QUIZ 6

1. **D** There are no parentheses or exponents, so start with the division.
$36 \div 6 = 6$. Then, do the addition and subtraction from left to right. $24 - 12 = 12$.
$12 + 6 = 18$. $18 - 3 = 15$. Choose D.

2. **D** First, do the parentheses to get $(6) - 3^2 + 8 \div 2 \times 2$. Then do the exponent to get
$6 - 9 + 8 \div 2 \times 2$. Next, do the multiplication and division, left to right, to get
$6 - 9 + 8$. Last do the addition and subtraction, left to right, to get 5. Choose D.

PRACTICE SET

1. **E** You can eliminate A because some, but not all, even numbers for x will result in a number divisible by 5. Same with B. When x is even, $x - 1$ is odd. When x is odd, $x - 1$ is even. From the odd/even rules, you know that the product of an even integer and an odd integer will always be even. So $x(x - 1)$ will always be even. Choose E.

2. **C** For this question, you need to check each answer to see if there is some combination of numbers that would result in an integer. In A, try the product of 4 and 5 divided by the reciprocal of 2. $4 \times 5 \div \frac{1}{2} = 40$, which is an integer. Eliminate A. In B, try 14 divided by 7, which is 2; 2 is an integer, so eliminate B. In D, try 66 divided by 3. The result is 22, which is an integer. Eliminate D. In E, try 3 + 5 divided by 2, which is 4, an integer. Eliminate E. In C, one prime number divided by a different prime number will never result in an integer because a prime number is only divisible by 1 and itself. Choose C.

3. **A** Start with statement (1). The three numbers must be 10, 12, and 14, so you could multiply them to find the product. You can answer the question, so the answer must be A or D. Look at statement (2). This doesn't help because a, b, and c could be any three integers that add up to 36. They could be 10, 12, and 14, but they could also be 1, 2, and 33 or many other combinations. You can't answer the question, so choose A.

4. **D** Just list all the numbers and circle the ones that meet one or more of the criteria. The prime numbers are 2, 3, 5, 7, 11, 13, 17, 19, and 23. The odd multiples of 5 are 5, 15, and 25. The numbers that can be expressed as the sum of a positive multiple of 2 and a positive multiple of 4 are all the even numbers over 4. That gives you 22 numbers. Be sure you don't double count any of them. Choose D.

5. **B** Numbers that are divisible by 3 and 11 include 33, 66, 99, 132, and so forth. You can eliminate I and III because not all these numbers are divisible by 14 or 66. All these numbers are divisible by 33, so choose B.

6. **D** An even integer minus another even integer will always give an even result. Eliminate A. An even integer divided by another even integer could be even, odd, or not an integer. Eliminate B. You can also eliminate C because adding 1 changes odd to even and vice versa. E is wrong because this is even times odd, which will give an even result. qr will always be even because even times even is even. So $qr - 1$ will always be odd. Choose D.

7. **C** Start with statement (1). If n is divisible by 9, then the sum of its digits is a multiple of 9. However, n could be 18, 27, 36, 45, and so forth. You can't answer the question, so narrow the choices to B, C, and E. Look at statement (2). By itself, this statement tells you that n is in the 40s, but it could be 40, 41, 42, and so forth. You can't answer the question, so eliminate B. Try statements (1) and (2) together. The only number in the 40s that is divisible by 9 is 45. You can answer the question, so choose C.

8. **B** The first four integers must be 20, 18, 16, and 14. You can find them by dividing 68 by 4 to get 17. Then, try out different groups of consecutive even integers near 17 until you find the ones that fit. The remaining three numbers are 12, 10, and 8. The product is $12 \times 10 \times 8 = 960$. Choose B.

9. **E** Start with statement (1). 33 has two prime factors: 3 and 11, so you can't answer the question. Narrow the possible answers to B, C, and E. Look at statement (2). p could be any integer from 3 to 15. You can't answer the question, so eliminate B. Look at (1) and (2) together. p could still be either 3 or 11. You can't answer the question, so choose E.

10. **B** As you'll see in more detail in Chapter 8, problems like this can also be solved by Plugging In. Since the problem specifies that m is an odd integer, start by plugging in a value for m in order to solve for n; then determine which of the answer choices divides evenly into your value for n. If you chose 1 for your value for m, the equation could be rewritten as $n = 5(1) + 4$. So, if $m = 1$, $n = 9$. The only answer choice that divides evenly into 9 is 3.

11. **C** Use the order of operations. Start with the parentheses. Within the second parentheses, do the multiplication before you do the subtraction. This all becomes $(4)^2 + (5 - 8) = 16 + (-3) = 13$. Choose C.

12. **E** Look at statement (1). n could be 10 or 20. You can't answer the question, so narrow the choices to B, C, and E. Look at statement (2). n could be several numbers, including 6 (prime factors 2 and 3), 10 (prime factors 2 and 5), 12 (prime factors 2 and 3), 14 (prime factors 2 and 7), 15 (prime factors 3 and 5), 18 (prime factors 2 and 3), and 20 (prime factors 2 and 5). You can't answer the question, so eliminate B. Look at statements (1) and (2) together. n could be 10 or 20. You can't answer the question, so choose E.

13. **E** Look at statement (1). There are 4 numbers in the set that are divisible by 6: 12, 18, 24, and 36. You can't answer the question, so narrow the choices to B, C, and E. Look at statement (2). There are 3 numbers in the set that are divisible by 9: 18, 36, and 45. You can't answer the question, so eliminate B. Look at (1) and (2) together. There are still 2 numbers that are divisible by 6 and 9: 18 and 36. You can't answer the question, so choose E.

14. **C** Look at statement (1). This tells you how many numbers to add up, but you don't know which numbers they are. You can't answer the question, so narrow the choices to B, C, and E. Look at statement (2). You know that the sequence starts with 6, but you don't know how many numbers are in the sequence. You can't answer the question, so eliminate B. Look at (1) and (2) together. The sequence is 6, 8, 10, 12, and 14. You could easily find the sum, so choose C.

15. **C** Look at statement (1). It tells you that there are 3 integers between x and z. If x is odd, then there are 2 even integers between x and z. If x is even, there is 1 even integer between x and z. You can't answer the question, so narrow the choices to B, C, and E. Look at statement (2). This doesn't help by itself because you don't know how much greater z is. You can't answer the question, so eliminate B. Look at (1) and (2) together. Since x is odd, there are 2 even integers between x and z. You can answer the question, so choose C.

16. **A** Start with statement (1). Since $\sqrt{9} = 3$, you can find the value of q and answer the question. Narrow your choices to A and D. Look at statement (2). This only tells you that $q = 3$ or -3. Don't let the information you learned in statement (1) affect your interpretation of statement (2). You can't answer the question with the information from (2), so choose A.

17. **A** Start with statement (1). You know from the question that the sum of the digits of t is a multiple of 9. The sum of the tens and hundreds digits is 14. The only possible value for the units digit is 4, which makes $t = 774$. You can answer the question, so narrow the choices to A and D. Look at statement (2). This leaves many possibilities for t, including 990, 972, 540, and so forth. You can't answer the question with statement (2), so choose A.

18. **E** This problem becomes far more approachable if you use Plugging In. Remember that the largest factor of any integer is the number itself. So, in order to solve this problem, you can start by simply substituting in the same number for x and y. That will immediately eliminate A, B, and D. Next, choose a larger number for y, such as 10, and make x a smaller factor, like 2. Use those values to test C and E; the only answer that works is E. (*Note:* You'll learn more about Plugging In in Chapter 7.)

19. **B** Start with statement (1). n could be many different numbers, such as 5, 10, 15, and so forth. $\frac{5}{3}$ leaves a remainder of 2. $\frac{10}{3}$ leaves a remainder of 1. $\frac{15}{5}$ leaves a remainder of 0. You can't pin it down to one value, so you can't answer the question. Narrow the choices to B, C, and E. Look at statement (2). Any number that's divisible by 6 is also going to be divisible by 3. So the remainder will always be 0. You can answer the question, so choose B.

20. **B** First take a look at statement (1). Knowing that the team scored 7 points exactly three times does not help you to determine how many times the team scored any of the other point increments. Statement (1) is not sufficient. Your remaining choices are B, C, and E. Now, look at statement (2). This statement may initially look insufficient, but since the point increments are prime factors, you should first factor 6,860 to get $2 \times 2 \times 5 \times 7 \times 7 \times 7$. Therefore, knowing the product of the points is 6,860, you can determine the number of times 2 points were scored. Choose B.

Fractions, Decimals, and Percents

FRACTIONS

Fractions are used to express division. The top number (the numerator) is divided by the bottom number (the denominator). Just think of the fraction bar as a division symbol. For example, $\frac{12}{3}$ means the same thing as $12 \div 3$, or 4.

Fractions also represent part of a whole. Simply put the part over the whole and you have the fraction. This approach is very useful for word problems that involve fractions. For example, suppose Oscar has a marble collection containing 2 blue marbles, 5 green marbles, and 8 red marbles. His total collection is $2 + 5 + 8 = 15$ marbles. To find the fraction of his collection that is blue, put the part (2 blue marbles) over the whole (15 marbles total) and you find that $\frac{2}{15}$ of Oscar's marbles are blue.

REDUCING FRACTIONS

A common mistake in solving fraction problems is failing to reduce the answer. If you solve the problem but don't see your answer among the choices, check to see whether you need to reduce the fraction.

To reduce a fraction, divide the numerator and the denominator by the same number. Continue until there are no other numbers that will divide into both parts of the fraction.

Look at Oscar's marble collection again. Suppose you need to know what fraction of his marbles are green. Putting part over whole, you find that $\frac{5}{15}$ of the marbles are green. You look at the answers, but you don't see $\frac{5}{15}$ anywhere. Did you miss something? No. You just need to reduce the answer. Both 5 and 15 are divisible by 5. Divide each of them by 5 and $\frac{5}{15}$ becomes $\frac{1}{3}$. You can't divide any further, so you're done.

ADDING AND SUBTRACTING FRACTIONS

A simple way to add or subtract fractions with different denominators is by using "the Bowtie." First, multiply the denominator of the second fraction by the numerator of the first fraction and place the result above the left numerator. Then, multiply the denominator of the first fraction by the numerator of the second fraction and place the result above the right numerator. Next, multiply the denominators of the fractions to get the denominator of the answer. Last, add (or subtract) the numerators to get the numerator of the answer. It's easier than it sounds; look at this example:

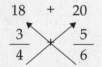

Multiply 6 by 3 to get 18 and put that above the left numerator. Multiply 4 by 5 to get 20 and put that above the right numerator. Next, multiply 4 by 6 to get 24, the denominator. The criss-cross shape gives the Bowtie its name. Putting it all together, you have $18 + 20$ in the numerator and 24 in the denominator. That's $\dfrac{38}{24}$, which reduces to $\dfrac{19}{12}$.

Subtraction undergoes exactly the same treatment; you just subtract the numerators instead of adding them. For example, try $\dfrac{2}{3} - \dfrac{1}{5}$. For the numerators, you get $5 \times 2 = 10$ and $3 \times 1 = 3$. For the denominators, you get $3 \times 5 = 15$. Put it all together and you get $\dfrac{10-3}{15} = \dfrac{7}{15}$.

COMPARING FRACTIONS

You can also use the Bowtie to compare fractions. Suppose you need to compare $\dfrac{3}{5}$ and $\dfrac{7}{11}$ so that you can determine which is greater. Write down the fractions and use the Bowtie as if you were going to add them. However, you should stop before you reach the third step (multiplying the denominators). You should have something like this.

The 35, which is over $\dfrac{7}{11}$, is bigger than 33, which is over $\dfrac{3}{5}$, so $\dfrac{7}{11}$ is the greater of the two fractions.

MULTIPLYING FRACTIONS

Multiplying fractions is rather straightforward. Multiply the numerators to get the numerator of the answer, and multiply the denominators to get the denominator of the answer. For example, $\dfrac{2}{3} \times \dfrac{1}{5} = \dfrac{2 \times 1}{3 \times 5} = \dfrac{2}{15}$. Then reduce if necessary.

What if you're multiplying a fraction and a whole number? Just turn the whole number into a fraction by putting a 1 in the denominator. Then multiply normally. For example, $3 \times \dfrac{1}{5}$ becomes $\dfrac{3}{1} \times \dfrac{1}{5} = \dfrac{3}{5}$.

Sometimes it's helpful if you cancel the numbers before you multiply. This will make the calculation simpler. Canceling is virtually the same thing as reducing, but you do it before the calculation, not after. You can cancel any number in the numerator with any number in the denominator. Just divide them both by the same number. For example, $\frac{4}{5} \times \frac{3}{8}$ becomes $\frac{1}{5} \times \frac{3}{2}$ because you can divide both the 4 and the 8 by 4. Note that the answer is exactly the same regardless of whether you cancel before you multiply or reduce after you multiply. Just use whichever is more comfortable for you.

DIVIDING FRACTIONS

To divide fractions, multiply the first fraction by the reciprocal of the second fraction (the one you're dividing by). Just flip over the second fraction and multiply. For example, $\frac{1}{3} \div \frac{3}{4}$ becomes $\frac{1}{3} \times \frac{4}{3}$. Multiply it to get $\frac{4}{9}$.

Sometimes you'll see a fraction composed of two fractions, such as $\frac{\frac{3}{6}}{\frac{3}{5}}$. Just remember that you're dividing the numerator by the denominator. Rewritten, this becomes $\frac{3}{6} \div \frac{3}{5}$ or $\frac{3}{6} \times \frac{5}{3}$. Once you've written it as a multiplication problem you can cancel. It's easier to do this after, rather than before, converting it to a multiplication problem. Canceling, you get $\frac{1}{6} \times \frac{5}{1} = \frac{5}{6}$.

What if the division contains a fraction and a whole number? Turn the whole number into a fraction by putting a 1 in the denominator, just as you did in multiplication. For example, $\frac{4}{15} \div 2$ becomes $\frac{4}{15} \div \frac{2}{1}$. When you flip the second fraction and multiply, you get $\frac{4}{15} \times \frac{1}{2} = \frac{2}{15}$. Don't to forget either cancel or reduce the fractions.

MIXED FRACTIONS

A mixed fraction consists of a whole number and a fraction, such as $5\frac{1}{4}$. If a problem contains mixed fractions, the first thing you should do is convert them to improper fractions (improper fractions are fractions in which the numerators are larger than or equal to the denominators). Multiply the whole number (the 5 in $5\frac{1}{4}$) by the denominator. Then add it to the numerator. So $5\frac{1}{4}$ becomes $\frac{20+1}{4} = \frac{21}{4}$.

THE REST

Word problems involving fractions can sometimes complicate things. Look at this example.

1. Oscar has 15 marbles. If he gives $\frac{1}{3}$ of his marbles to Sally and $\frac{1}{5}$ of the rest to Mike, how many marbles does Oscar have left?

    ○ 1
    ○ 3
    ○ 5
    ○ 7
    ○ 8

Looks simple enough. One third of his marbles is 5 marbles and one fifth of his marbles is 3 marbles. So he gives away 5 to Sally and 3 to Mike, leaving 15 – 5 – 3 = 7 marbles for Oscar. A little too simple, perhaps. Remember our friend Joe Bloggs? That's the kind of calculation he would make, and the test writers know it. D is the trap answer.

Look at the problem again carefully. Oscar gives $\frac{1}{3}$ of his marbles, or 5 marbles, to Sally. He gives $\frac{1}{5}$ *of the rest* to Mike. So that's $\frac{1}{5}$ of the remaining 10, not $\frac{1}{5}$ of the original 15. Oscar gives only 2 marbles to Mike, leaving himself with 15 – 5 – 2 = 8 marbles. So the correct answer is E. This is a very common pattern on the GMAT. Always be on the lookout for phrases such as "the rest" or "the remainder." They're there to trap the unwary.

QUIZ 1

1. $\left(\dfrac{1}{2}-\dfrac{1}{3}\right)\times\left(\dfrac{2}{3}+\dfrac{1}{6}\right)=$

   ○ $\dfrac{1}{18}$

   ○ $\dfrac{1}{9}$

   ○ $\dfrac{5}{36}$

   ○ $\dfrac{5}{18}$

   ○ 1

2. Which of the following is greater than $\dfrac{3}{5}$?

   ○ $\dfrac{1}{2}$

   ○ $\dfrac{2}{7}$

   ○ $\dfrac{6}{11}$

   ○ $\dfrac{5}{9}$

   ○ $\dfrac{2}{3}$

3. Ian owns a collection of 60 baseball cards. If he gives $\dfrac{1}{5}$ of his collection to Kevin and $\dfrac{1}{4}$ of the remainder to Paul, how many baseball cards does Ian have left?

   ○ 54
   ○ 36
   ○ 33
   ○ 24
   ○ 3

DECIMALS

Decimals are a way to express numbers that are not integers. The digits to the left and right of the decimal point are referred to as decimal places. Starting at the decimal point and moving left, the places are ones (or units), tens, hundreds, thousands, and so forth. To the right of the decimal point, the places are tenths, hundredths, thousandths, and so forth. This diagram shows how it all fits together for the number 10,325.0218.

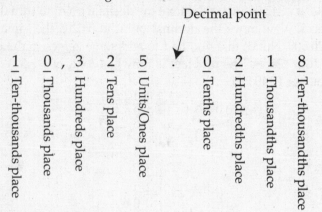

ADDING AND SUBTRACTING DECIMALS

Adding and subtracting decimals is fairly simple. Just line up the decimal points and put a decimal point in the same spot in your answer. You may need to add some zeroes to one of the numbers. For example, 0.0732 + 1.56 would look like this:

$$
\begin{array}{r}
0.\overset{1}{\cancel{0}}732 \\
+\ 1.\ 5600 \\
\hline
1.\ 6332
\end{array}
$$

And 7.23 – 3.105 would look like this:

$$
\begin{array}{r}
7.2\overset{2}{3}\overset{1}{0} \\
-\ 3.105 \\
\hline
4.125
\end{array}
$$

MULTIPLYING DECIMALS

To multiply decimals, just ignore the decimal points and multiply the numbers. Then count the number of decimal places in the original numbers. In other words, how many digits are to the right of the decimal place in the original numbers? That's the total number of decimal places you want in your answer.

For example, look at 1.05 × 2.2. First, ignore the decimal points and just multiply: 105 × 22 = 2310. Then, count the number of decimal places. There are two digits to the right of the decimal point in 1.05 and one digit to the right of the decimal place in 2.2. So you need three decimal places in your answer. 2310 becomes 2.310 or just 2.31. You should leave off any ending zeroes.

DIVIDING DECIMALS

To divide decimals, you must move the decimal points in both numbers. Move the decimal point all the way to the right in the second number (the one you're dividing by) and count the number of places you moved it. Then move the decimal point in the first number (the one that's being divided) the same number of places to the right. Add zeroes if you run out of digits. Then simply do the long division.

As an example, try 342.06 ÷ 0.0003. Move the decimal point to turn 0.0003 into 3. That's four decimal places. Now move the decimal point in 342.06 the same number of places (four) to get 3,420,600. Notice that you had to add some zeroes to the end of the number so that you had four places. The problem is now just 3,420,600 ÷ 3. When you work the long division, you get 1,140,200.

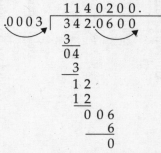

Here's another example: 1.175 ÷ 0.05. Move the decimal point two places to the right in each number. That changes the problem to 117.5 ÷ 5. Again, work the long division to find the answer, 23.5.

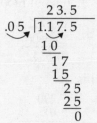

QUIZ 2

1. $\dfrac{30.3}{4.04} =$

   ○ 0.75
   ○ 1.01
   ○ 7.5
   ○ 10.1
   ○ 75

2. $\dfrac{(0.15)-(0.03)}{(0.2)(0.3)} =$

- ◯ 0.02
- ◯ 0.12
- ◯ 0.2
- ◯ 2
- ◯ 1.2

PERCENTS AND CONVERSION

Percents are just like fractions and decimals; they are just another way to express non-integer numbers. The word percent means "for each 100." So 50% translates to "50 for each 100" or the fraction $\dfrac{50}{100}$, which reduces to $\dfrac{1}{2}$. You can also turn percents into decimals by moving the decimal point two places to the left. So 50% would become 0.5. After converting the percent, make the calculation using the methods you just learned for fractions and percents.

You've learned how to convert percents into fractions and decimals. You should also know how to convert the other way—fractions and decimals into percents. Last but not least, you should understand how to turn fractions into decimals and vice versa.

To convert decimals into percents, simply move the decimal point two places to the right. So 0.4 becomes 40% and 0.654 becomes 65.4%.

To convert fractions into percents, multiply the numerator and denominator of the fraction by the same number. Decide what multiplier is necessary to turn the denominator into 100. Then use that multiplier for both the numerator and denominator. For example, suppose you want to convert $\dfrac{3}{4}$ into a percent. You must first multiply the 4 by 25 to get 100, so that's the multiplier for both the numerator and the denominator. So you get $\dfrac{3}{4} = \dfrac{3 \times 25}{4 \times 25} = \dfrac{75}{100}$, which you know is the same as 75%. If you can't easily find the multiplier for the fraction (if you have a fraction such as $\dfrac{2}{9}$), just convert the fraction to a decimal (as described below) and then change the decimal to a percent by moving the decimal point two places to the right.

Converting fractions to decimals is relatively straightforward: Just divide the numerator by the denominator. So $\frac{1}{8}$ becomes 0.125.

$$\frac{1}{8} \longrightarrow 8 \overline{\smash{\big)}\,1.000}$$

$$\begin{array}{r} 0.125 \\ 8\,\overline{\smash{\big)}\,1.000} \\ \underline{8} \\ 20 \\ \underline{16} \\ 40 \\ \underline{40} \\ 0 \end{array}$$

To convert a decimal to a fraction, first determine the place of the rightmost digit of the fraction. For example, in 0.125, the 5 is in the thousandths place. Therefore, the denominator should be 1,000. The numerator of the fraction is just the number without the decimal point. So 0.125 is the same as $\frac{125}{1,000}$. Of course, you should reduce the fraction if you can, so the result is $\frac{1}{8}$.

The following chart shows the conversions for the most common fractions, decimals, and percents. You should know these by heart so that you won't spend precious time calculating the converted values.

Fraction	Decimal	Percent
$\frac{1}{2}$	0.5	50%
$\frac{1}{3}$	$0.\overline{33}$	$33\frac{1}{3}\%$
$\frac{2}{3}$	$0.\overline{66}$	$66\frac{2}{3}\%$
$\frac{1}{4}$	0.25	25%
$\frac{3}{4}$	0.75	75%
$\frac{1}{5}$	0.2	20%
$\frac{2}{5}$	0.4	40%
$\frac{3}{5}$	0.6	60%
$\frac{4}{5}$	0.8	80%

TRANSLATION

In fraction and percent problems, especially word problems, you can get confused about which numbers to multiply, divide, add, or subtract. Translating the words into an equation is often helpful in starting a problem. Take the "stem" of the question (the part that contains the question word such as "what") and translate each word using this chart.

Word	Translation
is, are, does (verbs)	=
of	× (multiply)
what	n (variable)
n percent	$\dfrac{n}{100}$

So the question "What percent of 50 is 10?" becomes $\dfrac{n}{100} \times 50 = 10$. Then you would solve for n to get the answer, which is 20%. Refer to the beginning of Chapter 7 if you need a quick refresher on solving these types of equations.

You can often use translation to help you solve long word problems. Translate the question stem, usually the last sentence, to set up the equation. Replace the items described with numbers from the problem.

1. Paul owns 10 television sets, of which 2 do not work. Of the working television sets, 2 have black-and-white screens and the rest have color screens. What percent of Paul's working television sets have color screens?

   ○ 20%
   ○ 25%
   ○ 40%
   ○ 60%
   ○ 75%

When you translate the question stem, you should get something like $\dfrac{n}{100} \times \text{working} = \text{color}$. From the problem, you know that there are 10 – 2 = 8 working television sets and 8 – 2 = 6 with color screens. Plugging these numbers into the equation, you get $\dfrac{n}{100} \times 8 = 6$. Solving the equation, you get $n = 75$, so E is the correct answer.

Translation is not always the fastest way to solve a problem. For example, you could answer the question about Paul's television sets by dividing the color televisions by the number of working televisions: $\frac{6}{8} = \frac{3}{4} = 75\%$. (Remember your common fraction-to-percent conversions.) However, translating is a reliable way to set up a problem when you don't immediately see the solution.

Translation can also be useful for data sufficiency word problems. Although you don't need to calculate a numerical answer, setting up the equation can help you determine whether you have enough pieces of information to answer the question. Just set up the equation, but don't solve it.

2. Brady, Charlie, and Daryl play on the same baseball team. The number of home runs hit by Brady in a particular season is what fraction of the total home runs hit by the three players in that season?

    (1) Brady hit 12 home runs in that season.
    (2) In that season, the number of home runs hit by Brady was twice the number hit by Charlie and Daryl combined.

When you translate the question stem, you get $b = n \times (b + c + d)$ or $n = \frac{b}{b+c+d}$. Consider statement (1). If you plug in $b = 12$, you get $n = \frac{12}{12+c+d}$. You can't solve that equation for n, so narrow your choices to B, C, and E. Now consider statement (2). You can translate that statement into $b = 2(c + d)$. If you insert that into your equation from the question stem, you get $n = \frac{2(c+d)}{2(c+d)+c+d}$ or $n = \frac{2(c+d)}{3(c+d)}$. You can solve that by canceling the $(c + d)$ in both the top and bottom of the fraction. (You get $n = \frac{2}{3}$.) So statement (2) is sufficient and the correct answer is B.

PERCENT CHANGE

You will probably see at least one problem in which the value of some number increases or decreases, and you need to find the percent change. A question might also compare two numbers and ask you to state the difference in percentage terms. For both of these cases, use this formula:

$$\text{Percent change} = \frac{\text{difference}}{\text{original number}} \times 100$$

Finding the actual difference is usually pretty simple; just subtract the two numbers. The key is determining which number is the original number. Sometimes the test writers will try to trick you. Just remember the following guidelines:

- If the question mentions "increase" or "greater," you're going from a smaller number to a larger number. So the original number is the smaller one.

- If the question says "decrease" or "less," you're going from a larger number to a smaller number. So the original number is the larger one.

Quiz 3

1. In a group of 20 tourists, 12 brought cameras. If one half of the tourists with cameras brought disposable cameras, what percent of all the tourists brought disposable cameras?

   ○ 12%
   ○ 20%
   ○ 30%
   ○ 40%
   ○ 60%

2. Lenny can bench press 320 pounds. Ollie can bench press 400 pounds. The weight Ollie can bench press is what percent greater than the weight Lenny can bench press?

   ○ 20%
   ○ 25%
   ○ 32%
   ○ 40%
   ○ 80%

3. The original price of a model X200 laptop computer is reduced by $1,000 to the new price of $2,000. What is the percentage change in the price of the X200 laptop computer?

   ○ $12\frac{1}{2}\%$

   ○ 20%

   ○ $33\frac{1}{3}\%$

   ○ 40%

   ○ 50%

PRACTICE SET

1. In an engineering class that contained 50 students, the final exam consisted of two questions. Three fifths of the students answered the first question correctly. If four fifths of the remainder answered the second question correctly, how many students answered both questions incorrectly?

   - ○ 4
   - ○ 6
   - ○ 10
   - ○ 12
   - ○ 24

2. Forty percent of $\frac{1}{8}$ of what is 20 ?

   - ○ 400
   - ○ 320
   - ○ 100
   - ○ 4
   - ○ 1

3. After a performance review, Steve's salary is increased by 5%. After a second performance review, Steve's new salary is increased by 20%. This series of raises is equivalent to a single raise of

   - ○ 25%
   - ○ 26%
   - ○ 27%
   - ○ 30%
   - ○ 32%

4. Of the 2,400 animals at the zoo, $\frac{1}{4}$ are primates. If the number of primates were to be reduced by $\frac{1}{4}$, what percent of the remaining animals would then be primates?

   - ○ 50%
   - ○ $33\frac{1}{3}$%
   - ○ 25%
   - ○ 20%
   - ○ 6.25%

5. If each of the following fractions were written as a decimal, which would have the fewest number of digits to the right of the decimal point?

○ $\dfrac{1}{8}$

○ $\dfrac{1}{5}$

○ $\dfrac{1}{3}$

○ $\dfrac{2}{3}$

○ $\dfrac{3}{4}$

6. Poetry books make up what percent of the books on Beth's bookshelf?

    (1) Of the 60 books on Beth's bookshelf, 15 are novels.
    (2) There are 12 poetry books on Beth's bookshelf.

7. $\dfrac{3\frac{1}{2}-2\frac{1}{3}}{\frac{2}{3}-\frac{3}{4}} =$

○ −14

○ $-\dfrac{1}{14}$

○ $\dfrac{1}{14}$

○ $1\dfrac{1}{3}$

○ 14

8. During one day, a door-to-door brick salesman sold three fourths of his bricks for $0.25 each. If he had 150 bricks left at the end of the day, how much money did he collect for brick sales that day?

○ $12.50
○ $37.50
○ $50.00
○ $112.50
○ $150.00

Remember!
For Data Sufficiency problems in this book, we do not supply the answer choices. The five possible answer choices are the same every time.

9. In a group of 24 musicians, some are pianists and the rest are violinists. Exactly $\frac{1}{2}$ of the pianists and exactly $\frac{2}{3}$ of the violinists belong to a union. What is the least possible number of union members in the group?

- ◯ 12
- ◯ 13
- ◯ 14
- ◯ 15
- ◯ 16

10. Which of the following fractions is equal to the decimal 0.375 ?

- ◯ $\frac{1}{6}$
- ◯ $\frac{2}{7}$
- ◯ $\frac{3}{8}$
- ◯ $\frac{4}{9}$
- ◯ $\frac{5}{11}$

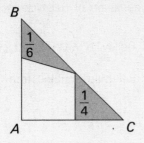

Note: Figure not drawn to scale.

11. In the triangle *ABC* shown above, the two shaded regions make up $\frac{1}{4}$ and $\frac{1}{6}$ of the area of the triangle. The unshaded region makes up what fractional part of the area of the triangle?

○ $\frac{1}{24}$

○ $\frac{5}{12}$

○ $\frac{7}{12}$

○ $\frac{9}{10}$

○ $\frac{23}{24}$

12. Justin, Max, and Paul each have a collection of marbles. Justin has 50% fewer marbles than Max has. Max has 30% more marbles than Paul has. If Paul's collection contains 80 marbles, how many marbles does Justin's collection contain?

○ 32
○ 48
○ 52
○ 56
○ 64

13. By what percent did the population of Belleville increase from 2001 to 2003 ?

    (1) The population of Belleville was 72,000 people in 2003.

    (2) The population of Belleville doubled from 2001 to 2003.

14. $$\frac{1}{2+\dfrac{2}{1+\dfrac{1}{4}}} =$$

○ $\dfrac{5}{18}$

○ $\dfrac{5}{9}$

○ $\dfrac{13}{18}$

○ $\dfrac{18}{13}$

○ $\dfrac{18}{5}$

15. If 12 is 20% of 40% of a certain number, what is the number?

○   20
○   24
○   72
○   96
○   150

16. The fuel efficiency of a certain make of car was increased from 30 miles per gallon for last year's model to 45 miles per gallon for this year's model. By what percent was the fuel efficiency of the car increased?

○   15%

○ $33\dfrac{1}{2}\%$

○   50%

○ $66\dfrac{2}{3}\%$

○   75%

17. In 2002, 30% of the students at Maxwell State University were engineering majors. The number of engineering majors at the university increased by what percent between 2002 and 2003 ?

    (1) In 2003, 45% of the students at the university were engineering majors.

    (2) The number of engineering majors at the university increased by 750 between 2002 and 2003.

18. $\dfrac{(4)(0.06)}{(0.12)} =$

    ◯   0.18
    ◯   0.2
    ◯   1.8
    ◯   2.0
    ◯   20

19. If Kim makes a $30,000 down payment on a house, which represents 20% of the sale price of the house, how much money does Kim still owe on the house?

    ◯ $90,000
    ◯ $120,000
    ◯ $140,000
    ◯ $150,000
    ◯ $170,000

20. If the fractions $\dfrac{1}{2}, \dfrac{2}{5}, \dfrac{3}{8}, \dfrac{4}{11}$, and $\dfrac{5}{7}$ were ordered from least to greatest, the second smallest fraction in the resulting sequence would be

    ◯ $\dfrac{1}{2}$

    ◯ $\dfrac{2}{5}$

    ◯ $\dfrac{3}{8}$

    ◯ $\dfrac{4}{11}$

    ◯ $\dfrac{5}{7}$

21. In 1991, the price of a house was 80% of its original price. In 1992, the price of the house was 60% of its original price. By what percent did the price of the house decrease from 1991 to 1992 ?

  ○ 20%

  ○ 25%

  ○ $33\frac{1}{3}$%

  ○ 40%

  ○ 60%

22. $1 + \dfrac{5}{10} + \dfrac{3}{1,000} + \dfrac{9}{10,000} =$

  ○ 1.539
  ○ 1.5309
  ○ 1.5039
  ○ 1.50309
  ○ 1.05039

23. Of the 400 people in an auditorium, $\dfrac{1}{4}$ are wearing hats. Of those, $\dfrac{1}{5}$ are wearing fedoras. How many people in the auditorium are not wearing fedoras?

  ○　20
  ○　80
  ○　180
  ○　220
  ○　380

24. What fraction of the cookies in a certain bakery's window display contains nuts?

  (1) Of the cookies in the display, 22 contain nuts.
  (2) Of the cookies in the display, 90% do not contain nuts.

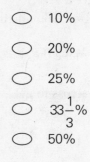

25. A process manager in a plant wishes to decrease the hours logged by his workforce by 20%, while still retaining the exact same production. If all of the workers in the workforce produce at the same constant rate, by what percent would the workforce need to increase its production?

- ○ 10%
- ○ 20%
- ○ 25%
- ○ $33\frac{1}{3}$%
- ○ 50%

Challenge!
Take a crack at this high-level GMAT question.

ANSWERS AND EXPLANATIONS

Quiz 1

1. **C** Use the Bowtie on the first parentheses to get $\frac{1}{2} - \frac{1}{3} = \frac{3-2}{6} = \frac{1}{6}$. Bowtie the second parentheses to get $\frac{2}{3} + \frac{1}{6} = \frac{12+3}{18} = \frac{15}{18} = \frac{5}{6}$. You'll make the calculations easier if you reduce as you go. Now just multiply straight across to get $\frac{1}{6} \times \frac{5}{6} = \frac{5}{36}$. Choose C.

2. **E** You could use the Bowtie to compare all five answer choices to $\frac{3}{5}$. However, you'll save yourself some time if you first eliminate a few answers by Ballparking. You can eliminate A and B because $\frac{3}{5}$ is greater than $\frac{1}{2}$. You can tell because 3 is more than half of 5. Similarly, $\frac{2}{7}$ is less than $\frac{1}{2}$ so it's also less than $\frac{3}{5}$. When you Bowtie $\frac{2}{3}$ and $\frac{3}{5}$, you get 10 versus. 9. The 10 goes with $\frac{2}{3}$, so choose E.

3. **B** Ian gives $\frac{1}{5} \times 60 = 12$ baseball cards to Kevin, so he has 60 − 12 = 48 left. Then he gives $\frac{1}{4} \times 48 = 12$ baseball cards to Paul, so he has 48 − 12 = 36 left. Choose B.

Quiz 2

1. **C** Move the decimal point two places to the right in both the numerator and the denominator. This gives you $\frac{3,030}{404}$. Do the long division and you get 7.5. Choose C.

2. **D** In the numerator, subtract the decimals by lining up the decimal points. The numerator becomes 0.12. In the denominator, multiply 2 × 3 = 6. There is one decimal place in each for a total of two. Put two decimal places in the denominator and it becomes 0.06. When you divide, you need to move the decimal point two places to the right in each number. That gives you $\frac{12}{6} = 2$. Choose D.

Quiz 3

1. **C** One half of the 12 tourists with cameras have disposable cameras, so that's $\frac{1}{2} \times 12 = 6$ disposable cameras. There are 20 tourists, so $\frac{6}{20} = \frac{3}{10}$ of the tourists have disposable cameras. To change this fraction to a percent, multiply the top and the bottom by 10. That becomes $\frac{3 \times 10}{10 \times 10} = \frac{30}{100}$, or 30%. Choose C.

2. **B** Divide the difference by the original amount. The difference is $400 - 320 = 80$.

   To find the original amount, remember that "greater" means starting small and getting big, so the original is the smaller number, 320. The percent difference is $\frac{80}{320}$, or 25%. Notice that the trap answer of 20% is there to fool you if you mistakenly divide by 400. Choose B.

3. **C** Use the percent change formula. The difference is $1,000. The original price is $2,000 + $1,000 = $3,000. So the percent change is $\frac{1,000}{3,000} = \frac{1}{3}$, or $33\frac{1}{3}$%. Choose C.

Practice Set

1. **A** The number of students that answered the first question correctly is $\frac{3}{5} \times \frac{50}{1} = 30$ students. That leaves $50 - 30 = 20$ students who answered the first question incorrectly. Of these 20, $\frac{4}{5} \times \frac{20}{1} = 16$ answered the second question correctly. That leaves $20 - 16 = 4$ students who missed both questions. Choose A.

2. **A** Use the translation technique to help you set up this problem. You get the equation $\frac{40}{100} \times \frac{1}{8} \times n = 20$. Simplifying, you get $\frac{1}{20}n = 20$. Multiply both sides by 20 to get $n = 400$. Choose A.

3. **B** The Joe Bloggs answer is A, so you should be suspicious of that. It may help for you to make up a number for Steve's initial salary, say $100 (sorry, Steve). The 5% raise takes him to $105. The 20% raise is 20% of the new, $105 salary, not 20% of the old, $100 salary. 20% × $105 = $21. So his new salary is $105 + $21 = $126. That's the same as if he had gotten a raise of 26% of his original $100 salary. Choose B. You'll see this "making up numbers" method more in Chapter 7. It's called Plugging In.

4. **D** The number of primates is $\frac{1}{4} \times 2,400 = 600$. The reduction in primates is $\frac{1}{4} \times 600 = 150$ primates, leaving $600 - 150 = 450$ primates. Don't forget, however, that this also reduces the total number of animals at the zoo to $2,400 - 150 = 2,250$. The fraction of animals at the zoo that are primates is $\frac{450}{2,250}$ (part over whole), which reduces to $\frac{1}{5}$. From the conversion chart, you know that's the same as 20%. Choose D.

5. **B** Just write each of these fractions as a decimal. You probably know some of them from the conversion chart, but you can always use the division method if you forget. The conversions are: $\frac{1}{8} = 0.125$, $\frac{1}{5} = 0.2$, $\frac{1}{3} = 0.\overline{33}$, $\frac{2}{3} = 0.\overline{66}$, and $\frac{3}{4} = 0.75$. 0.2 is the answer because it has only one digit to the right of the decimal point. Choose B.

6. **C** You want to find $\frac{\text{\# of poetry books}}{\text{\# of books total}} \times 100$. With statement (1), you know the total number of books, but not the number of poetry books. The number of novels is irrelevant because you don't know whether there are types of books other than poetry books and novels. Narrow the choices to B, C, and E. With statement (2), you know the number of poetry books, but not the total. Eliminate B. With both statements, you know both the total and the number of poetry books, allowing you to find the percentage. Choose C.

7. **A** Do two subtractions first, using the Bowtie, and then do the division. In the numerator, you'll need to convert the mixed fractions. $3\frac{1}{2}$ becomes $\frac{6+1}{2} = \frac{7}{2}$. $2\frac{1}{3}$ becomes $\frac{6+1}{3} = \frac{7}{3}$. Applying the Bowtie, you get $\frac{7}{2} - \frac{7}{3} = \frac{21-14}{6} = \frac{7}{6}$ for the numerator. Applying the Bowtie to the denominator, you get $\frac{2}{3} - \frac{3}{4} = \frac{8-9}{12} = -\frac{1}{12}$. To divide fractions, you flip the divisor (in this case, the denominator) and multiply. This gives you $\frac{7}{6} \times \frac{-12}{1} = -14$. Choose A.

8. **D** The 150 bricks left are $\dfrac{1}{4}$ of his initial inventory of bricks, so he had

$4 \times 150 = 600$ bricks. He sold $600 - 150 = 450$ bricks at $0.25 each. His sales

revenue was $0.25 \times 450 = \$112.50$. Choose D.

9. **B** To get the least possible number of union members, you want as many pianists

as possible and as few violinists as possible, because $\dfrac{1}{2}$ is less than $\dfrac{2}{3}$. However,

you have to have some violinists because the problem states that there are some

of each. It's impossible to have fractional violinists, so the number of violinists

is a multiple of 3. It can't be 3 violinists and 21 pianists because that would give

you $\dfrac{1}{2} \times 21 = 10\dfrac{1}{2}$ union pianists. Try 6 violinists and 18 pianists. That gives

you $\dfrac{1}{2} \times 18 = 9$ union pianists. Combined with the $\dfrac{2}{3} \times 6 = 4$ union violinists,

that means $9 + 4 = 13$ union members total. Note that Joe Bloggs will probably

pick the smallest answer when the question asks for the "least possible number."

Choose B.

10. **C** You need to convert the fractions to decimals, either with the conversion chart

or by doing the division. $\dfrac{1}{6} = 0.1\overline{66}$, $\dfrac{2}{7} = 0.2857\ldots$, $\dfrac{3}{8} = 0.375$. If you want to

check the other two answers (depending on where you are in the section), they

are: $\dfrac{4}{9} = 0.\overline{44}$ and $\dfrac{5}{11} = 0.\overline{45}$. Another way of solving is to turn the decimal into a

fraction and reduce: $0.375 = \dfrac{375}{1000} = \dfrac{3}{8}$. Choose C.

11. **C** Use the Bowtie to find the total area of the shaded regions:
$\dfrac{1}{4} + \dfrac{1}{6} = \dfrac{6+4}{24} = \dfrac{10}{24} = \dfrac{5}{12}$. That leaves $\dfrac{7}{12}$ of the area for the unshaded region.
Choose C.

12. **C** Paul has 80 marbles, so Max has $30\% \times 80 = 24$ marbles more for a total of
$80 + 24 = 104$ marbles. Justin has $50\% \times 104 = 52$ fewer marbles than Max for a
total of $104 - 52 = 52$ marbles. Choose C.

13. **B** Use the percent change formula: $\dfrac{\text{difference}}{\text{original}} \times 100$. With statement (1), you know the final population, but not the original population. Narrow the choices to B, C, and E. With statement (2), you know that the population doubled, which is the same as increasing by 100%. Choose B. You don't need to be able to find the actual numbers as long as you can answer the question, so C is a trap.

14. **A** You'll need to work this problem from the innermost fraction outward. It helps if you rewrite the problem as you work each part. $1 + \dfrac{1}{4} = \dfrac{4+1}{4} = \dfrac{5}{4}$ for the bottom. For the next step, $2 \div \dfrac{5}{4} = 2 \times \dfrac{4}{5} = \dfrac{8}{5}$. Next, $2 + \dfrac{8}{5} = \dfrac{10+8}{5} = \dfrac{18}{5}$. Last, $1 \div \dfrac{18}{5} = 1 \times \dfrac{5}{18} = \dfrac{5}{18}$. Choose A.

15. **E** Use translation to set up the equation: $12 = \dfrac{20}{100} \times \dfrac{40}{100} \times n$. That simplifies to $12 = \dfrac{2}{25} n$. Multiply both sides by $\dfrac{25}{2}$ to get $n = 150$. Choose E.

16. **C** Use the percent change formula. The difference in fuel efficiency is $45 - 30 = 15$. The original number was 30, so the percent change is $\dfrac{15}{30} = \dfrac{1}{2} = 50\%$. The key is dividing by the right number. Choose C.

17. **E** The percent change formula is $\dfrac{\text{difference}}{\text{original}} \times 100$. Statement (1) initially looks like it might be sufficient. However, unless you also know how the overall student populations in the two years compare to each other, you can't determine whether 45% of the later group is more or less than 30% of the earlier group or by how much. Narrow the choices to B, C, and E. With statement (2) alone, you know the amount of the change (+750), but not the original number of engineering majors. Eliminate B. Even with both statements together, you can't find the original number of engineering majors. You could set up the equation $0.45y - 0.3x = 750$, but you can't solve it because there are two variables. Choose E.

18. **D** To get the numerator of the fraction, just multiply $4 \times 6 = 24$; then add in the two decimal places to get 0.24. To divide by 0.12, move the decimal point two places to the right in each decimal to make it $24 \div 12 = 2$. Choose D.

19. **B** Restate the information as "\$30,000 is 20% of the sale price." Then you can translate that sentence to the equation $30,000 = \frac{20}{100} \times n$. Solving the equation, you find that $n = \$150,000$. However, you need to know how much she owes. That's $\$150,000 - \$30,000 = \$120,000$. Choose B.

20. **C** First, put the fractions in order. You can quickly compare fractions to $\frac{1}{2}$ by seeing if the numerator is greater or less than one half the denominator. So $\frac{5}{7}$ is more than $\frac{1}{2}$, and the other fractions are less. You need the Bowtie to put the other three fractions in order. Comparing $\frac{2}{5}$ to $\frac{3}{8}$, you get $2 \times 8 = 16$ versus $5 \times 3 = 15$, so $\frac{2}{5}$ is greater. Comparing $\frac{3}{8}$ to $\frac{4}{11}$, you get $3 \times 11 = 33$ versus $8 \times 4 = 32$, so $\frac{3}{8}$ is greater. So the final order is $\frac{4}{11}$, $\frac{3}{8}$, $\frac{2}{5}$, $\frac{1}{2}$, and $\frac{5}{7}$. The second smallest fraction is $\frac{3}{8}$. Choose C.

21. **B** It's helpful to make up a number for the original sale price, say \$100,000. That means the price in 1991 was \$80,000 and the price in 1992 was \$60,000. Use the percent change formula. The difference is $\$80,000 - \$60,000 = \$20,000$. The original number is \$80,000 because you're measuring only the 1991 to 1992 time period. So the percent change is $\frac{20,000}{80,000} = \frac{1}{4} = 25\%$. Choose B.

22. **C** The easiest way to solve this problem is to convert each fraction to a decimal and then add them. $\frac{5}{10} = 0.5$, $\frac{3}{1,000} = 0.003$, and $\frac{9}{10,000} = 0.0009$. This is just like the way you convert decimals to fractions, except reversed. Adding the numbers, you get $1 + 0.5 + 0.003 + 0.0009 = 1.5039$. Choose C.

23. **E** The number of people wearing hats is $\frac{1}{4} \times 400 = 100$. The number of people wearing fedoras is $\frac{1}{5} \times 100 = 20$. So the number of people *not* wearing fedoras is $400 - 20 = 380$. Choose E.

24. **B** To find the fraction, you want $\frac{\text{\# with nuts}}{\text{total \#}}$. With statement (1), you know the number of cookies with nuts, but not the total. Narrow the choices to B, C, and E. With statement (2), you can find that 100% − 90% = 10% of the cookies contain nuts. A percent is just another way of showing a fraction, so you can answer the question even though you can't find the actual numbers. Choose B.

25. **C** Try Plugging In a number (pretty self-explanatory, but we have more information about this in our "Avoiding Algebra" chapter) to solve this problem. Say that the number of hours currently worked by the workforce is 50, and that each hour the work force is able to produce 2 units of production. This means the workforce is currently producing 100 total units in 50 hours. The manager wants to decrease the work hours by 20%. To determine this reduction, calculate 20% of 50, which is 10 hours. So, if the number of hours is reduced by 20%, the workforce will work only 40 hours. Since the manager wants the production to be the same, the work force must now produce 100 units in 40 hours. So, the work force must produce 2.5 units per hour, which is .5 more units an hour than before. Because .5 is one fourth of 2, the original production rate, the workforce must produce 25% more units. Choose C.

6
Assorted Topics 1

RATIOS

A ratio shows the relationship between two or more numbers, but it doesn't tell you the actual values of those numbers. Suppose you have a recipe for margaritas that calls for 1 ounce of tequila and 1 ounce of triple sec for every 2 ounces of lime juice. You would say that the ratio of tequila to triple sec to lime juice is 1 : 1 : 2. But the recipe alone doesn't tell you how much tequila you need for a particular batch of margaritas. For that, you also need to know some actual number, such as the total volume of the batch of margaritas.

The ratio box is an excellent tool to help you solve ratio problems. Make a grid with a row for each item in the ratio plus a row for the total. Use three columns: ratio value, multiplier, and actual value. The result will look like this.

	Item 1	Item 2	Item 3	Total
Ratio Value				
Multiplier				
Actual Value				

To use the ratio box, fill in all of the numbers from the problem. Then, find the multiplier by comparing the ratio value to the actual value for one item. This multiplier will be the same for all of the items. Just multiply the ratio value by the multiplier to find all of the other actual values. Look at this example.

1. The Kosmic Kickers is a coed soccer team with 24 players on its roster. If the ratio of male players to female players is 2 to 1, how many female players are on the Kosmic Kickers' roster?

   ○　1
   ○　2
   ○　8
   ○　12
   ○　16

First, draw a ratio box and fill in all the numbers from the problem. The ratio value for male players is 2. The ratio value for female players is 1. So the ratio total is 2 + 1 = 3. The roster contains 24 players, so that number goes in the box for actual total.

Here's what you've got so far.

	Male	Female	Total
Ratio	2	1	3
Multiplier			
Actual			24

The next step is to find the multiplier. The ratio total is 3 and the actual total is 24. So the multiplier must be 8. Write 8 in the multiplier box. If you're ever unsure of the multiplier, divide the total actual value by the total ratio value. The result is the multiplier.

To find the other actual values, multiply each ratio value by the multiplier, 8. Here's what the completed box will look like:

	Male	Female	Total
Ratio	2	1	3
Multiplier	8	8	8
Actual	16	8	24

So the actual number of male players is $2 \times 8 = 16$ and the actual number of female players is $1 \times 8 = 8$. The correct answer is C.

Quiz 1

1. If the ratio of male students to female students in a philosophy class is 3 : 5, and there is a total of 40 students in the class, how many female students are in the class?

   ○   8
   ○   15
   ○   16
   ○   24
   ○   25

2. The ratio of apples, bananas, cantaloupes, and oranges at a fruit stand is 5 : 3 : 2 : 6, respectively. The total number of these fruits is 64. If 4 cantaloupes are added to the fruit stand, what is the new ratio of bananas to cantaloupes?

   ○   1 : 2
   ○   2 : 3
   ○   1 : 1
   ○   3 : 2
   ○   2 : 1

3. Fred has a jarful of nickels, dimes, and quarters, in the ratio of 2 : 5 : 10, respectively. If the total value of these coins is $15.50, how many dimes are in Fred's jar?

   ○   17
   ○   25
   ○   50
   ○   85
   ○   155

PROPORTIONS

Proportions are very similar to ratios because they also show relationships between pairs of numbers. In fact, they're pretty much the same as ratios; they're just shown in a different way.

The way to solve a proportion question is to write two equal fractions, or ratios. Put the units in the same place in both fractions. For example, a question might ask, "If Carol can glaze 10 ceramic pots in 2 hours, how many pots can she glaze in 3 hours?" Set up the equal fractions as shown below.

$$\frac{10 \text{ pots}}{2 \text{ hours}} = \frac{x \text{ pots}}{3 \text{ hours}}$$

Notice that the number of pots is in the numerator of each fraction and the number of hours is in the denominator of each fraction. It's important to set up your fractions in the same way. It doesn't really matter which one (pots or hours) is in the numerator as long as it's the same in both fractions. Because you don't know the number of pots for the second fraction, use the variable x.

The next step is to cross-multiply the fractions. Multiply the denominator on the left by the numerator on the right and put the result on one side of the equals sign. Multiply the denominator on the right by the numerator on the left and put that on the other side of the equals sign. You end up with $10 \times 3 = 2x$. Solving the equation, you get $x = 15$, so Carol can glaze 15 pots in 3 hours.

QUIZ 2

1. Chris plays solitaire at the constant rate of 3 hands in 20 minutes. How many hands of solitaire can Chris play in 2 hours?

   ○ 6
   ○ 9
   ○ 12
   ○ 18
   ○ 20

2. A bottle-capping machine caps 12 bottles per minute. How many minutes does the machine take to cap 30 bottles?

   ○ 2.5
   ○ 5
   ○ 6
   ○ 12
   ○ 60

AVERAGES

An average tells you something about a group of people or things. The term arithmetic mean is also used to refer to averages. There are three numbers involved in any average question: the number of things in the group, the total amount, and the average amount. Given any two of these numbers, you can always find the third. The relationship of these three numbers is shown in the following formula:

$$\text{Average} = \frac{\text{total}}{\text{\# of things}}$$

With this many vague numbers flying around, things get confusing. A tool called the average circle will help you keep everything organized, and as soon as you try a couple of problems, you'll see that finding averages is pretty simple. Look at the diagram below. This gives you a place to put the three numbers for an average. Draw a separate circle for each average in the problem.

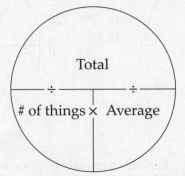

Fill in the two numbers the problem gives you and use that information to calculate the missing number. Notice that the line between the total and the other two numbers acts as the division line in a fraction. The total amount divided by the number of things gives you the average. The total amount divided by the average gives you the number of things. If you have the two bottom numbers, the number of things and the average, just multiply them to get the total amount. Try this problem.

1. Five friends play blackjack in Las Vegas and lose an average of $100 each. If the losses of two of the friends total $380, what is the average loss of the other friends?

   ○ $40
   ○ $60
   ○ $100
   ○ $120
   ○ $1,900

Draw two circles, one for the average of all five friends and one for the average of the other friends. In the first circle, fill in 5 for the number of things and $100 for the average. From this you can calculate the total loss, which is 5 × $100 = $500. For the second circle, fill in 5 − 2 = 3 for the number of things. The question asks for the average, so you first need to find the total loss of the other friends. You know the total lost by all five friends was $500 and that the two friends lost a total of $380, so the total loss of the other three friends must be $500 − $380 = $120. Fill that in for the total in the second circle. Now you can calculate the average loss of the three friends, which is $\frac{\$120}{3} = \$40$. The answer is A.

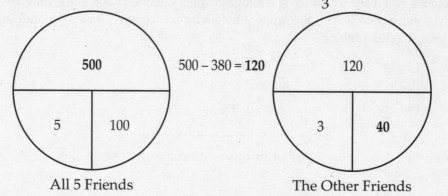

All 5 Friends   The Other Friends

Some questions require you to combine numbers from several circles. It's okay to add and subtract the numbers of things and the total amounts, but never, ever, combine the averages directly. Averages must either be taken from the questions or calculated from the other two numbers in the circle. You can see this trap in the next example.

2. A company composed of two divisions is reviewing managerial salaries. The two managers in Division A of the company earn an average annual salary of $75,000. The three managers in Division B of the company earn an average annual salary of $100,000. What is the average salary of all the managers in the company's two divisions?

    ○ $75,000
    ○ $85,000
    ○ $87,500
    ○ $90,000
    ○ $100,000

Under no circumstances should you average the averages. That answer, $87,500, is there, but it's a trap in this question. To correctly solve the problem, set up three circles: Division A, Division B, and the whole company. In Division A, the number of things is 2, the average is $75,000, and the total is 2 × $75,000 = $150,000. In Division B, the number of things is 3, the average is $100,000, and the total is 3 × $100,000 = $300,000. In the whole company, the number of things is 2 + 3 = 5, the total is $150,000 + $300,000 = $450,000. So the average is $\frac{\$450,000}{5} = \$90,000$. The correct answer is D.

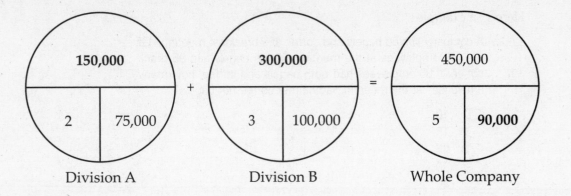

150,000		+	300,000		=	450,000	
2	75,000		3	100,000		5	90,000

Division A   Division B   Whole Company

QUIZ 3

1. The average (arithmetic mean) of four numbers is 5.5. When an additional number is included, the average of all five numbers is 6. What is the additional number?

    ◯   5.75
    ◯   6.5
    ◯   8.0
    ◯   22.0
    ◯   30.0

2. A set of 10 numbers has an average (arithmetic mean) of 12. When a subset of numbers, which has an average of 15, is removed from the original set, the sum of the remaining numbers is 60. How many numbers remain from the original set?

    ◯   3
    ◯   4
    ◯   5
    ◯   6
    ◯   8

GROUPS

Some GMAT problems deal with classifying a group of people or things into sub-groups. Many of these problems break the people into two classes, with some people in both classes and some people in neither class. Although these problems look complex, you can easily solve them by applying the following group formula:

$$\text{Total} = \text{Class 1} + \text{Class 2} - \text{Both} + \text{Neither}$$

Simply plug in the numbers the problem gives you and solve for the missing value. It's possible that the problem will stipulate that everyone belongs to one class or the other. In that case, just plug in 0 for the Neither category. If the problem states that no one belongs to both classes, just use 0 for the Both value.

Here's an example.

1. A company served bagels and coffee at a breakfast meeting. Of the 120 employees at the meeting, 50 ate bagels and 95 drank coffee. If 35 employees had both bagels and coffee, how many employees at the meeting had neither coffee nor bagels?

   ○ 10
   ○ 15
   ○ 25
   ○ 30
   ○ 45

Plug the numbers into the formula and you get 120 = 50 + 95 − 35 + Neither. When you solve the equation, you get Neither = 10. The answer is A. See, it's much easier than it seemed at first.

Sometimes group problems get tough and the formula doesn't help. These questions still feature two categories, but they will talk about the number of people that are and are not in each group. To solve these tough problems, you'll need to set up a grid like this one.

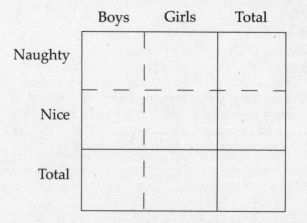

Each box in the grid shows the number of objects that match the labels above and to the left of the box. For example, the upper left box shows the number of naughty boys and the lower left box shows the total number of boys (naughty and nice). The middle box contains the number of nice girls. (Aha! So that's how Santa keeps track of them all.)

In each row, add the two leftmost boxes to get the total for the rightmost box. In each column, add the two upper boxes to get the total for the bottom box. Given any two of the three numbers in a row or column, you can determine the third number through addition or subtraction. Look at this next example.

2. Of the 200 employees at Company A, 70 work part-time and the rest work full-time. If 140 of the employees like their jobs and 10 of the part-time employees don't like their jobs, how many full-time employees like their jobs?

   ○ 50
   ○ 60
   ○ 80
   ○ 130
   ○ 140

Set up the grid as shown below. Plug in the numbers provided in the question. These are shown in bold type in the diagram. Now you can figure out the other numbers. There are 70 part-time employees out of 200 total, so there must be 130 full-time employees. Since 10 of the 70 part-time employees don't like their jobs, the other 60 must like their jobs. If 140 of the 200 employees like their jobs, the other 60 don't like their jobs. Of the 140 employees who like their jobs, 60 are part-time, so the other 80 must be full-time. Of the 130 full-time employees, 80 like their jobs, so the other 50 don't like their jobs. Every time you have two of the three numbers in a row or column, you can find the third number. The number of full-time employees who like their jobs is 80, so C is the correct answer.

	Part-time	Full-time	Total
Like job	60	80	**140**
Don't like job	**10**	50	60
Total	**70**	130	**200**

Quiz 4

1. The 2,000 students at College Q get one week for spring break. Each student takes the opportunity to travel to the beach, the mountains, or both. If 1,500 students take a trip to the beach and 700 take a trip to the mountains, how many students go to both the beach and the mountains?

    ○ 200
    ○ 500
    ○ 800
    ○ 1,300
    ○ 2,200

2. The 25 players on the Little Sluggers baseball team are supposed to take their caps and gloves to each game. At the first game of the season, 22 players took their caps and 18 took their gloves. If 6 players took their caps but not their gloves, how many players took neither cap nor glove to the first game?

    ○ 1
    ○ 2
    ○ 3
    ○ 4
    ○ 7

INTEREST

One of the few business-related topics that the GMAT tests is interest rates. To calculate the interest earned in a year, multiply the initial amount of money (also called the principal) by the percentage interest rate. For example, if $500 is deposited for one year in a savings account that earns 4% interest, then the account will earn $500 × 4% = $20 in interest for that year. So the total amount in the savings account after one year is $500 + $20 = $520. This type of interest calculation is sometimes called simple interest.

When the GMAT does test you on interest, the problem usually involves compound interest. Either the money will earn interest for a period longer than a year, or the interest will compound more frequently than once per year. For example, suppose that $500 is deposited for ten years in a savings account earning 4% interest. In the first year, the account earns $20 in interest, so during the second year, the account earns interest on $520, not $500. In the third year, the principal is even greater. Thus, the account earns interest on the interest. While this is great for your IRA account, it can make GMAT questions a little tougher.

Fortunately, you can usually avoid calculating the precise amount of compound interest. Instead, use Ballparking to find the answer. Start by finding the simple interest, which is, well, pretty simple. Then find an answer that's a little bit bigger. Look at the next example.

1. Allan deposits $1,000 into a bank account that pays 3% interest annually. If he makes no other deposits or withdrawals, approximately how much money is in the account after four years?

    ○ $120
    ○ $126
    ○ $1,120
    ○ $1,126
    ○ $1,200

Start by calculating the simple interest. The interest for one year is $1,000 × 3% = $30. For four years, that's $120 in simple interest, which makes the total amount in the account $1,000 + $120 = $1,120. Look for the answer that's a little bit bigger. The answer has to be D.

Every once in a while, you may need to know the formula for compound interest. You probably won't need to make the calculation, but you may need to set up the equation. The formula is

$$\text{Total amount} = \text{principal} \times (1 + r)^t,$$

in which r is the interest rate (expressed as a decimal) for the compounding period and t is the number of compounding periods. You'll need the formula for this next example.

2. Amy deposits $100 into an account that pays 8% interest, compounded semiannually. She makes no other deposits or withdrawals. Which of the following expresses the amount of money the account will contain in 2 years?

    ○ $100 × (1 + .04)^2$
    ○ $100 × (1 + .04)^4$
    ○ $100 × (1 + .04)^6$
    ○ $100 × (1 + .08)^2$
    ○ $100 × (1 + .08)^6$

You use 0.04 for r because the account earns 4% over six months; the 8% rate is for a full year. You use 4 for t because two years contains four six-month periods. So the correct answer is B. Notice that you're not going to complete the calculation. You'd need a calculator for that and it's not necessary; just setting up the equation is enough.

QUIZ 5

1. Mark deposits $1,000 into a bank account that pays annual interest of 7%. If he makes no other deposits or withdrawals, approximately how much interest has the account earned after four years?

   ○ $280
   ○ $311
   ○ $700
   ○ $1,280
   ○ $1,311

2. Gilbert deposits $200 into a bank account that earns interest at the rate of 8%. He makes no further transactions other than a $100 withdrawal after 3 years. Approximately how much money is in Gilbert's account after he makes the withdrawal?

   ○ $124
   ○ $127
   ○ $148
   ○ $152
   ○ $224

PRACTICE SET

1. Three hungry children, Sharon, Carol, and Elinor, agree to divide a batch of cookies in the ratio 3 : 5 : 7, respectively. If Sharon's share was 15 cookies, how many cookies were in that batch?

   ○   60
   ○   75
   ○   120
   ○   150
   ○   750

2. A company consists of two departments: sales and production. If 30 percent of the 150 employees in the sales department received a holiday bonus and 70 percent of the 250 employees in the production department received a holiday bonus, what percent of all employees did not receive a holiday bonus?

○ 40%
○ 45%
○ 50%
○ 55%
○ 60%

Remember!
For Data Sufficiency problems in this book, we do not supply the answer choices. The five possible answer choices are the same every time.

3. What is the ratio of a to b ?

(1) $a = b + 7$
(2) $3a = 4b$

4. All working at the same constant rate, 8 bartenders can pour 96 shots per minute. At this rate, how many shots could 3 bartenders pour in 2 minutes?

○ 12
○ 24
○ 36
○ 48
○ 72

5. The average (arithmetic mean) of 2, 4, 6, and 8 equals the average of 1, 3, 5, and

○ 7
○ 9
○ 10
○ 11
○ 12

6. The latest model of space shuttle can achieve a maximum speed of 25 miles per second. This maximum speed is how many miles per hour?

○ 1,500
○ 3,600
○ 9,000
○ 15,000
○ 90,000

7. How many of the employees at Company X have life insurance?

   (1) There are 300 employees at Company X.
   (2) The ratio of employees with life insurance to employees without life insurance is 1 : 5.

8. What is x ?

   (1) The ratio of $x : y$ is 1 : 3.
   (2) The ratio of $y : z$ is 1 : 2.

9. The five starting players on a basketball team score points in the ratio of 1 : 1 : 2 : 3 : 4. If the starters score a total of 77 points in a particular game, how many points did the highest-scoring starter score?

   ◯   7
   ◯   11
   ◯   14
   ◯   21
   ◯   28

10. If $1 was invested at 4% interest, compounded quarterly, the total value of the investment, in dollars, at the end of three years would be

    ◯ $(1.4)^3$
    ◯ $(1.04)^{12}$
    ◯ $(1.04)^3$
    ◯ $(1.01)^{12}$
    ◯ $(1.01)^3$

11. Among a group of teenagers taking a driving test, 40% took a driver's education course. If 70% of the teenagers pass the driving test and all of those who took a driver's education course passed the test, what percent of the teenagers who did not take a driver's education course failed the test?

    ◯   0%
    ◯   30%
    ◯   40%
    ◯   50%
    ◯   60%

Remember!
For Data Sufficiency problems in this book, we do not supply the answer choices. The five possible answer choices are the same every time.

12. If a laser printer can print 2 pages in 10 seconds, how many pages can it print in 3 minutes at the same rate?

○ 5
○ 12
○ 18
○ 36
○ 60

13. If the average (arithmetic mean) of three positive integers is 35, how many of the numbers are greater than 10 ?

(1) The sum of two of the numbers is 75.
(2) None of the numbers is greater than 40.

14. Greg is training for a marathon by running to and from work each day, a distance of 12 miles each way. He runs from home to work at an average speed of 6 miles per hour and returns at an average speed of 4 miles per hour. What is Greg's average speed, in miles per hour, for the round trip?

○ 5.5
○ 5.0
○ 4.8
○ 2.5
○ 2.4

15. Each baseball team in a league has a roster of players in the ratio of 2 pitchers for every 3 fielders. If each team has a total of 25 players on its roster and there are 12 teams in the league, the number of pitchers in the league is how much less than the number of fielders in the league?

○ 10
○ 15
○ 60
○ 120
○ 180

16. The first-year MBA class at XYZ University is composed of 60 male students and 40 female students. How many male students from the first-year class are taking economics?

(1) Fifty percent of the first-year class is taking economics.
(2) 10 female students from the first-year class are not taking economics.

17. If the current population of country Z is 200,000 people and the population grows by 3% every year, which of the following expresses the population of Country Z in 5 years?

   ○ 200,000 × (1.03)^5
   ○ 200,000 × 5 × (1.03)
   ○ 200,000 × (0.03)^5
   ○ 200,000 × (1.3)^5
   ○ 200,000 × (1.05)^3

18. The 250 students enrolled at ABC University are taking undergraduate courses, graduate courses, or both. How many students are taking graduate courses?

   (1) 200 students are taking undergraduate courses.
   (2) 50 students are taking both undergraduate and graduate courses.

19. A total of 120 investment advisors work at a particular financial services firm, 30 in bonds and the rest in equities. Fifty percent of the investment advisors are board-certified. If one third of the equities advisors are board-certified, how many bonds advisors are not board-certified?

   ○ 0
   ○ 10
   ○ 15
   ○ 20
   ○ 30

20. How many people contributed to the Charity Y ?

   (1) The average contribution to Charity Y was $100.
   (2) Charity Y collected a total of $47,000 in contributions.

21. The average of two numbers is 108. What is the value of the greater number?

   (1) The lesser number is 72.
   (2) The ratio of the two numbers is 1 : 2.

22. A certain compound X has a ratio of 2 oxygen for every 5 carbon. Another compound Y has a ratio of 1 oxygen for every 4 carbon. If a mixture of X and Y has a ratio of 3 oxygen for every 10 carbon, what is the ratio of compound X to compound Y in the mixture?

   ○ 1 to 10
   ○ 1 to 3
   ○ 1 to 2
   ○ 2 to 5
   ○ 2 to 3

Challenge!
Take a crack at this high-level GMAT question.

ANSWERS AND EXPLANATIONS

QUIZ 1

1. **E** Start by drawing a ratio box like the one shown below. Then, fill in the numbers from the problem (shown in bold in the diagram). In the ratio, you have 3 male students and 5 female students, for a ratio total of 3 + 5 = 8 students. Given the actual total, 40 students, the multiplier is 40 ÷ 8 = 5. Multiply each of the ratio values by 5 to find the actual values. The number of female students is 5 × 5 = 25. Choose E.

	Male	Female	Total
Ratio	**3**	**5**	8
Multiplier	5	5	5
Actual	15	25	**40**

2. **C** Set up a ratio box with the numbers from the problem (shown in bold in the diagram below). The ratio total for the fruit is 5 + 3 + 2 + 6 = 16. Given the actual total of 64 pieces of fruit, you can find the multiplier, which is 64 ÷ 16 = 4 . Multiply all the ratio numbers by 4 to find all the actual numbers: 20 apples, 12 bananas, 8 cantaloupes, and 24 oranges. Now, add 4 cantaloupes for a new total of 12 cantaloupes. The new ratio of bananas to cantaloupes is 12 : 12, which reduces to 1 : 1. Choose C.

	Apples	Bananas	Cantaloupes	Oranges	Total
Ratio	**5**	**3**	**2**	**6**	16
Multiplier	4	4	4	4	4
Actual	20	12	8	24	64

3. **B** Set up a ratio box as shown below. Notice that you need to include the value of the coins as well as the number of coins. The total ratio value of the coins is $3.10 (the value of 2 nickels, 5 dimes, and 10 quarters). Given the total actual value of $15.50, you can find the multiplier, which is $15.50 ÷ $3.10 = 5. Multiply all the ratio values by 5 to get the actual values. So the number of dimes is 5 × 5 = 25. Choose B.

	# Nickles	# Dimes	# Quarters	Total #	Value of Nickles	Value of Dimes	Value of Quarters	Total Value
Ratio	**2**	**5**	**10**	17	$0.10	$0.50	$2.50	$3.10
Multiplier	5	5	5	5	5	5	5	5
Actual	10	25	50	85	$0.50	$2.50	$12.50	**$15.50**

Quiz 2

1. **D** Set up the two equivalent fractions as shown below. Notice that you need to change 2 hours to 120 minutes. You must use the same units in both fractions. Then cross-multiply to get $3 \times 120 = 20x$, which simplifies to $360 = 20x$. Divide both sides by 20 to get $x = 18$. Chris can play 18 hands of solitaire in 2 hours. Choose D.

$$\frac{3 \text{ hands}}{20 \text{ minutes}} = \frac{x \text{ hands}}{120 \text{ minutes}}$$

2. **A** Set up the equivalent fractions as shown below. Notice that the variable is in the denominator of the fraction. That's okay as long as the fractions are consistent. Cross-multiply to get $12x = 30 \times 1$ or simply $12x = 30$. Divide both sides by 12 to get $x = 2.5$. Choose A.

$$\frac{12 \text{ caps}}{1 \text{ minute}} = \frac{30 \text{ caps}}{x \text{ minutes}}$$

Quiz 3

1. **C** Draw two average circles, one for the set of four numbers and one for the set of five numbers. Fill in the numbers provided in the problem (shown in bold in the diagram below). In the set of four numbers, the total is $4 \times 5.5 = 22$. In the set of five numbers, the total is $5 \times 6 = 30$. So the additional number must be $30 - 22 = 8$. Choose C.

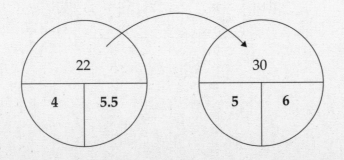

2. **D** Draw three average circles: the original set, the removed subset, and the remaining members of the original set. Fill in the numbers from the problem (shown in bold in the diagram below). In the original set, the total is $10 \times 12 = 120$. The total of the removed numbers is the difference between the totals of the original set and the remaining numbers, or $120 - 60 = 60$. Given the average of 15, the number of numbers that were removed is $60 \div 15 = 4$. So the number of remaining numbers is $10 - 4 = 6$. Choose D.

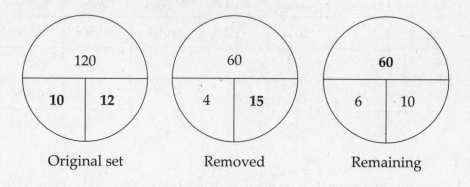

Original set   Removed   Remaining

Quiz 4

1. **A** Set up the group formula with the numbers from the problem: $2{,}000 = 1{,}500 + 700 - \text{Both} + 0$. Use the 0 for Neither because the problem states that every student takes a trip. Simplifying the equation, you get $2{,}000 = 2{,}200 - \text{Both}$, and the solution is Both = 200. Choose A.

2. **A** Set up the grid as shown. The numbers given in the problem are shown in bold. Of the 25 players, 22 took their caps, so 3 did not. You know 18 players took gloves, so 7 did not. Of the 22 players with caps, 6 forgot gloves, so 16 remembered to take gloves. Of the 18 with gloves, 16 took caps, so 2 didn't. Of the 3 who did not take caps, 2 took gloves, so 1 player took neither cap nor glove. Just where did he think he was going, anyway? Choose A.

	Gloves	No gloves	Total
Caps	16	6	22
No caps	2	1	3
Total	18	7	25

Quiz 5

1. **B** Simple interest would be $4 \times 7\% \times \$1{,}000 = \$280$. The interest compounds (more than one year), so choose the next higher answer. Choose B.

2. **D** Gilbert made his $100 withdrawal after it earned interest, not before then. Calculate the interest on $200, and then subtract $100 from the total. Simple interest for three years would be $3 \times 8\% \times 200 = \$48$, for a total of $200 + 48 - 100 = \$148$. So choose the answer that's a little higher because the interest compounds. Choose D.

Practice Set

1. **B** Set up a ratio box as shown below. The ratio total is $3 + 5 + 7 = 15$. Sharon's actual value is 15 and her ratio value is 3, so the multiplier is $15 \div 3 = 5$. Multiply all of the ratio values by 5 to get the actual values. So the actual total is $15 \times 5 = 75$. Choose B.

	Sharon	Carol	Elinor	Total
Ratio	**3**	**5**	**7**	15
Multiplier	5	5	5	5
Actual	**15**	25	35	75

2. **B** Set up a grid as shown below. The number of sales employees receiving a bonus is $30\% \times 150 = 45$, so the number of sales employees not receiving a bonus is $150 - 45 = 105$. The number of production employees receiving a bonus is $70\% \times 250 = 175$, so the number of production employees not receiving a bonus is $250 - 175 = 75$. So $105 + 75 = 180$ employees did not receive a bonus. The percent of all employees not receiving a bonus is $\dfrac{180}{150 + 250} = \dfrac{180}{400} = \dfrac{45}{100} = 45\%$. Choose B.

	Sales	Production	Total
Bonus	45	175	220
No bonus	105	75	180
Total	**150**	**250**	400

3. **B** Start with statement (1). You can't determine the ratio of a to b. If $a = 8$ and $b = 1$, the ratio of a to b is 8 : 1. If $a = 9$ and $b = 2$, the ratio is 9 : 2. You can't answer the question, so narrow your choices to B, C, and E. Try statement (2). You can rewrite this equation as $\dfrac{a}{b} = \dfrac{4}{3}$, so the ratio of a to b is 4 : 3. You can answer the question, so choose B.

4. **E** You can set up equivalent fractions for this proportion: $\dfrac{8}{96} = \dfrac{3}{x}$. Cross-multiply to get $8x = 3 \times 96$ or $8x = 288$. Solving the equation, you get $x = 36$. However, this is just the number of shots 3 bartenders can pour in 1 minute. So in 2 minutes, 3 bartenders can pour $2 \times 36 = 72$ shots. Choose E.

5. **D** Set up two average circles. In the first circle, the total is $2 + 4 + 6 + 8 = 20$. The number of things is 4, so the average is $20 \div 4 = 5$. In the second circle, the average is 5 (the same as the first circle) and the number of things is 4. Therefore, the total should be $4 \times 5 = 20$. Now you know that the total in the second circle is $1 + 3 + 5 + x = 20$. Solve for x and you get 11. Choose D.

6. **E** Set up the proportion: $\dfrac{25}{1} = \dfrac{x}{60 \times 60}$. You use 60×60 for the number of seconds because there are 60 seconds in a minute and 60 minutes in an hour. Cross-multiply to get $x = 25 \times 60 \times 60$ or $x = 90{,}000$. Choose E.

7. **C** Start with statement (1). This tells you only the total number of employees, not anything about the number that have life insurance. You can't answer the question, so narrow your choices to B, C, and E. Look at statement (2). A ratio doesn't tell you anything about actual numbers unless you have another actual number to go with it (so you can find the multiplier). You can't answer the question, so eliminate B. Try statements (1) and (2) together. Now you have the ratio as well as an actual number. You can use the actual number to find the multiplier, and then use the multiplier to find all the other actual values. You can answer the question, so choose C.

8. **E** Look at statement (1). The ratio alone won't help you find the actual values of the variables. You can't answer the question, so narrow your choices to B, C, and E. Try statement (2). This doesn't even mention x, so you can't answer the question. Eliminate B. Try statements (1) and (2) together. You could set up a ratio for x to z. But you can't find the actual value of x without another actual value to go with the ratio. You can't answer the question, so choose E.

9. **E** Set up a ratio box as shown below. The numbers from the problem are shown in bold. The ratio total is $1 + 1 + 2 + 3 + 4 = 11$. The actual total is 77, so the multiplier is $77 \div 11 = 7$. Multiply all of the ratio values by 7 to find the actual values. The actual value for the highest-scoring starter is $4 \times 7 = 28$. Choose E.

	Starter 1	Starter 2	Starter 3	Starter 4	Starter 5	Total
Ratio	**1**	**1**	**2**	**3**	**4**	**11**
Multiplier	7	7	7	7	7	7
Actual	7	7	14	21	28	77

10. **D** You just need to insert the numbers into the compound interest formula: $(1 + r)^t$. Interest compounds four times per year at a 4% rate, so $r = \dfrac{4\%}{4} = 1\% = 0.01$. The interest compounds four times per year for three years, so there are 12 interest periods. That means $t = 12$. The completed formula is $(1.01)^{12}$. Choose D.

11. **D** Set up a grid as shown below. Plug in the numbers provided in the question (bold type in the diagram below). Note that you don't have actual numbers, so just use 100% for the total and the appropriate percentages for the other boxes. Start finding the other numbers. 40% took the course, so 60% didn't. 70% passed the test, so 30% didn't. All of the course takers (40%) passed, so 0% took the course and failed. A total of 70% passed, so 70% – 40% = 30% of teenagers passed and didn't take a course. That leaves 60% – 30% = 30% who did not take the course and failed. Out of the 60% of teenagers who didn't take the course, 30% of teenagers failed, but that's $\dfrac{30\%}{60\%} = 50\%$ of those who didn't take the course. Choose D.

	Course	No course	Total
Passed	**40%**	30%	**70%**
Failed	0%	30%	30%
Total	**40%**	60%	**100%**

12. **D** Set up the proportion: $\dfrac{2}{10} = \dfrac{x}{180}$. You need to keep the units consistent in both fractions, so use 180 seconds for the 3 minutes. Cross-multiply to get

$10x = 2 \times 180$. That's $10x = 360$, so $x = 36$. Choose D.

13. **B** Start with statement (1). The sum of the three numbers is $3 \times 35 = 105$. You can calculate that the third number is $105 - 75 = 30$, definitely more than 10. However, you cannot tell whether one or two of the other numbers is more than 10. They might be 40 and 35, or they might be 1 and 74. You can't answer the question, so narrow your choices to B, C, and E. Try statement (2). This means that the smallest any number could be is $105 - 40 - 40 = 25$. If you try to make a number smaller than 25, at least one of the numbers will be greater than 40. All three numbers must be more than 10. You can answer the question, so choose B.

14. **C** On the way to work, Greg needs $\dfrac{12}{6} = 2$ hours to complete the trip. On the way home, Greg needs $\dfrac{12}{4} = 3$ hours to complete the trip. So he travels

$12 + 12 = 24$ miles in $2 + 3 = 5$ hours. That's an average speed of $\dfrac{24}{5} = 4.8$ miles

per hour. Choose C. If you chose B, you fell for the Joe Bloggs trap of averaging

the averages.

15. **C** You need to use an expanded ratio box, like the one shown below. The ratio total is 2 + 3 = 5 players. There are 25 players on a team, so the multiplier for ratio to team is 25 ÷ 5 = 5. Multiply all of the ratio values by 5 to find the actual team values. There are 12 teams in the league, so the multiplier for team to league is 12. Multiply all of the team values by 12 to get the league values. The number of fielders in the league is 3 × 5 × 12 = 180. The number of pitchers in the league is 2 × 5 × 12 = 120. So the difference is 180 − 120 = 60. Choose C.

	Pitchers	Fielders	Total
Ratio	**2**	**3**	5
Multiplier	5	5	5
Team Actual	10	15	**25**
Multiplier	**12**	**12**	**12**
League Total	120	180	300

16. **C** You should set up a group grid as shown below. Start with statement (1). This allows you to fill in 50 students for economics and 50 students not for economics. But you don't have two numbers anywhere that you can use to find a third number. You can't answer the question, so narrow your choices to B, C, and E. Try statement (2). Erase any numbers you filled in from statement (1). Now you can find that 40 − 10 = 30 female students are taking economics. But you can't find how many male students are or are not taking economics because you don't have 2 of the 3 numbers. You can't answer the question, so eliminate B. Try statements (1) and (2) together. Now you can find all the numbers because you have 2 out of every 3 numbers. Calculate all the numbers if you're unsure. Choose C.

	Male	Female	Total
Taking economics	20	30	**50**
Not taking economics	40	**10**	50
Total	**60**	**40**	100

17. **A** This is really an interest rate problem. The setup is exactly the same except that it's population growth instead of money growth. $r = 3\%$ or 0.03 and $t = 5$. So the completed formula is $200{,}000 \times (1.03)^5$. Choose A.

18. **C** Check statement (1). From the group formula, you can set up $250 = 200 + \text{Graduate} - \text{Both} + 0$, but you can't solve the equation because there are two variables. You can't answer the question, so narrow your choices to B, C, and E. Try statement (2). Now you have $250 = \text{Undergraduate} + \text{Graduate} - 50 + 0$, but you still can't solve the equation. Eliminate B. Try statements (1) and (2) together. Now you can fill in $250 = 200 + \text{Graduate} - 50 + 0$. You can solve for Graduate and answer the question. Choose C.

19. **A** Set up a group grid, as shown below, with the given information in bold. If 30 of the 120 advisors work in bonds, the other 90 work in equities. The number of board-certified advisors is $50\% \times 120 = 60$, so the number of noncertified advisors is $120 - 60 = 60$. The number of equity advisors that are certified is $\frac{1}{3} \times 90 = 30$, so the number of noncertified equities advisors is $90 - 30 = 60$. There are 60 certified advisors and 30 of them work in equities, so $60 - 30 = 30$ certified advisors work in bonds. So all 30 bond advisors are certified and none of them are noncertified. Choose A.

	Bonds	Equities	Total
Certified	30	30	60
Not certified	0	60	60
Total	**30**	90	**120**

20. **C** Start with statement (1). There are three parts to any average: the total, the number of things, and the average. You know the average contribution, but you don't know the total, so you can't find the number of things (people). You can't answer the question. Narrow your choices to B, C, and E. Try statement (2). Now you know the total contributions, but you don't know the average. You can't answer the question, so eliminate B. Try statements (1) and (2) together. You know the average and the total, so you can find the number of things. You can answer the question, so choose C.

21. **D** Start with statement (1). If the average of two things is 108, the total is
2 × 108 = 216. Now you can subtract 72 to find the other number. You can
answer the question, so eliminate B, C, and E. Try statement (2). You could set
up a ratio box. You have the ratio and one actual number, so you could find all
of the actual numbers. You can answer the question, so choose D.

22. **C** First, try putting the ratios in comparable terms. Multiple the first ratio, 2 to 5,
by 4 to get 8 to 20. Multiply the second ratio, 1 to 4, by 5 to get 5 to 20. Now you
can see that X has 8 oxygen when Y has 5 oxygen. At this point, you can plug
in the answers (using a system we call PITA—more on that in the next chapter)
on the ratios to see which one works. Start with C. If the ratio of X to Y is 1 to 2,
then for every X, you will add 2 Y. So, one X is 8 oxygen and 20 carbon, while
2 Y is 10 oxygen and 40 carbon. This amounts to 18 oxygen and 60 hydrogen,
which reduces to 3 oxygen to 10 hydrogen. This is the correct ratio for the
mixture, so choose C.

Avoiding Algebra

For many people, algebra is not fun. It can be time-consuming, and it's easy to make mistakes with algebra. If algebra isn't your favorite way to crunch numbers, fear not. In this chapter, you'll learn some powerful methods for avoiding algebra in a lot of questions on the Quantitative section of the GMAT. If you happen to like algebra, well, you're in luck, too! The next chapter is about facing algebra head-on. So no matter your preferred method for cracking math questions, these next two chapters will be of use. Use the system that you're most comfortable with, be it avoiding algebra or facing algebra. If you have time, you should get comfortable with both systems, so that you can use one system to solve the problem and the other system to check your work. For now, let's dive into strategies for algebra avoidance. You'll need some practice to be comfortable using these techniques and to be able to recognize opportunities to use them. First, however, a question: Which of the following two problems would you rather see on the GMAT?

1. Otto has a five-dollar bill. He goes to the store and buys 3 pieces of candy that cost 50 cents each. How much change, in dollars, does Otto receive?

    ○ $0.50
    ○ $1.50
    ○ $2.00
    ○ $3.00
    ○ $3.50

2. Oscar has an x-dollar bill. He goes to the store and buys y pieces of candy that cost z cents each. How much change, in dollars, does Oscar receive?

    ○ $x - yz$

    ○ $xy - z$

    ○ $x - \dfrac{yz}{100}$

    ○ $100x - yz$

    ○ $\dfrac{x - yz}{100}$

Why does the second question seem so much harder? It's identical to the first question except that it contains variables instead of numbers. For many people, the variables make this question seem harder. If that's how you feel, then you're in the right place. The techniques in this chapter will help you transform algebra questions into arithmetic questions and make the world a better place.

By the way, the answer to question 2 is *not* A. You'll see how to solve it in a short while.

PLUGGING IN

As you saw with the problem about Oscar's candy, variables can make a question considerably tougher. Wouldn't it be wonderful if there were a way to get rid of those variables? Well, there is. It's a method called Plugging In. Whenever you see a problem with variables in the answer choices, you should consider this approach.

Here's the method.

1. Replace every variable in the problem with a number. Just make one up.

2. Work the problem using the numbers you plugged in. You'll get a number for an answer. This number is your target. Circle it on your noteboard.

3. Plug your made-up numbers into the variables in the answers. Check all five and see which one matches your answer from step 2.

Try this approach with the Oscar example.

2. Oscar has an x-dollar bill. He goes to the store and buys y pieces of candy that cost z cents each. How much change, in dollars, does Oscar receive?

    ○ $x - yz$

    ○ $xy - z$

    ○ $x - \dfrac{yz}{100}$

    ○ $100x - yz$

    ○ $\dfrac{x - yz}{100}$

1. Make up numbers for the variables. Maybe $x = 10$ dollars, $y = 4$ pieces of candy, and $z = 50$ cents. You can try a different set if you like. Plugging In works with any numbers.

2. Work the problem using these numbers. If Oscar buys 4 pieces of candy for 50 cents each, he spends $4 \times 50 = 200$ cents, or 2 dollars. He started with 10 dollars, so he gets $10 - 2 = 8$ dollars in change. It's important to make sure that your answer is in the units (dollars or cents) specified by the problem. So the numerical answer (your target) is 8. Circle it on your noteboard.

3. Plug your made-up numbers into the answer choices. Using $x = 10$, $y = 4$, and $z = 50$, the answers are

○ $x - yz = 10 - (4)(50) = 10 - 200 = -190$

○ $xy - z = (10)(4) - 50 = 40 - 50 = -10$

○ $x - \dfrac{yz}{100} = 10 - \dfrac{(4)(50)}{100} = 10 - \dfrac{200}{100} = 10 - 2 = 8$

○ $100x - yz = (100)(10) - (4)(50) = 1,000 - 200 = 800$

○ $\dfrac{x - yz}{100} = \dfrac{10 - (4)(50)}{100} = \dfrac{10 - 200}{100} = \dfrac{-190}{100} = -1.90$

As you can see, C is the only answer that matches your target of 8. Note that the obvious answer choice, A, is not correct. The problem with A is that it doesn't account for the difference in units (dollars versus cents) between x and z. Many algebra problems contain one or more potential pitfalls like that, and the test writers will include trap answers to snare people who make those mistakes.

Why Use Plugging In?

Some people are initially skeptical when they learn Plugging In. "That's not the *real* way to answer the question," they might say. Or, "Why should I learn another way to solve the problem, instead of using algebra?"

Well, there are several reasons that Plugging In is superior to algebra in some cases. First, you are much more likely to make a mistake when manipulating variables than when using regular numbers. Your brain simply processes $5 + 3$ more easily than it does $x + y$. That's what makes the Oscar example tougher than the Otto example at the beginning of the chapter. In doing algebra, you have to concentrate on the variables, and that leaves you open to mistakes such as forgetting to convert units.

Second, Plugging In makes tough problems easier. Because of the adaptive nature of the test, you won't see any problems that will be easy for you. If you're good at algebra, the questions will just get tougher and tougher until working them algebraically is impractical. Plugging In is a great way to bring the difficulty of a question down a notch or two.

Third, Plugging In is faster. On some of the very easiest problems, Plugging In may not give you much of an edge when it comes to pacing. The main advantage with easier problems is the accuracy it provides. However, on the harder problems, Plugging In is simply faster. So, not only is it more accurate on the harder problems, but it also speeds you up.

Finally, it's always a good idea to have plenty of tools at your disposal. If one way of attacking a problem doesn't work, you simply try another. Plugging In is a tool that works well in a variety of situations, making it a nice option when you're uncertain how to approach a particular question.

Here's an example of a problem that is very tough to solve algebraically, but much easier to solve via Plugging In.

3. The sum of two integers is x. If the larger integer is greater than the smaller integer by 8, what is the product of x and the smaller integer, in terms of x ?

    ○ $x^2 + 12x$

    ○ $2x^2 - 8$

    ○ $\dfrac{x^2}{2} - 4x$

    ○ $x^2 - 8x$

    ○ $\dfrac{x^2}{2} + 4x - 8$

First, try to solve this problem algebraically. Go ahead, take your time....

Tough, wasn't it? Now work this problem with Plugging In. Pick numbers for the two integers. You do need to follow the restriction that one is greater than the other by 8. Suppose you choose 2 and 10. You're told that x is the sum of the integers, so $x = 2 + 10 = 12$. The question asks for the product of x and the smaller integer, so your target is 12 2 = 24.

Finally, plug $x = 12$ into the answer choices, to see which one matches your target of 24.

Choice A becomes $12^2 + 12(12) = 288$.

Choice B becomes $2(12^2) - 8 = 280$.

Choice C becomes $\dfrac{12^2}{2} - 4(12) = 24$.

Choice D becomes $12^2 - 8(12) = 48$.

Choice E becomes $\dfrac{12^2}{2} + 4(12) - 8 = 112$.

Answer choice C matches your target, so it is the correct answer.

As you can see, Plugging In was much easier than working the algebra for that problem. You should practice this method, so that you can use it effectively on tough algebra problems.

Hidden Variables

You've seen how Plugging In works when the answer choices contain variables, but sometimes the variable in the answers isn't quite so obvious. In fact, it may be invisible. If the answers contain fractions or percents, check the question. If it asks for a fraction or percent of some unknown amount, that unknown amount is the invisible variable. Plug in a number for that variable and use the steps you just learned. Here's an example.

3. Marty spends $\frac{1}{3}$ of his weekly allowance on baseball cards. He spends $\frac{1}{4}$ of the rest on bubble gum. He spends $\frac{1}{6}$ of his allowance on soda pop. If Marty has no other expenses and saves the rest of his allowance in a piggy bank, what fraction of his allowance does he save in the piggy bank?

    ○ $\frac{1}{6}$

    ○ $\frac{1}{4}$

    ○ $\frac{1}{3}$

    ○ $\frac{5}{12}$

    ○ $\frac{1}{12}$

The question asks for a fraction of Marty's allowance, so Marty's allowance is the invisible variable in the answer choices. First, make up a number, say $60, for Marty's allowance. Second, work the problem using that number. Marty spends $\frac{1}{3} \times 60 = 20$ on baseball cards. That leaves $60 - 20 = 40$ to spend. He spends $\frac{1}{4}$ *of the rest* or $\frac{1}{4} \times 40 = 10$ on bubble gum. That leaves $40 - 10 = 30$ dollars. He spends $\frac{1}{6} \times 60 = 10$ on soda pop, leaving $30 - 10 = 20$ dollars for his piggy bank. Third, you need to convert that number to match the answers. He saves 20 dollars out of the original 60 or $\frac{20}{60} = \frac{1}{3}$. The answer is C.

CHOOSING GOOD NUMBERS

When you use the Plugging In method, you should exercise some care in selecting the numbers you plug in. Although the method will work with any numbers, you'll make things easier if you follow two general guidelines.

First, plug in numbers that will work nicely with the calculations necessary to solve the problem. In the previous example, you start with Marty's allowance and multiply by the fractions $\frac{1}{3}$, $\frac{1}{4}$, and $\frac{1}{6}$. Although you could plug in an ugly number, such as $11.17, for his allowance, that would make the calculations much tougher than necessary. Instead, you should choose a number that's easily divisible by 3, 4, and 6, such as $60.

Second, avoid numbers that make more than one answer match your target. Suppose you plug in $x = 4$ for a certain question, and your target works out to be 16. If $4x$ and x^2 are both among the answer choices, you have a problem: Both match your target. How can you tell which of them is the real answer?

If you do end up with more than one answer matching your target, simply rework the problem by plugging in a different number. Then, check only the answers that seemed correct the first time.

Of course, it would be much better to prevent that problem in the first place. To do that, avoid plugging in numbers that appear in the problem or the answer choices. You should also avoid 0 and 1, because they are numbers that do weird things.

Here is a summary of guidelines to follow when selecting numbers to plug in.

Choose numbers that work nicely.

- For problems involving fractions, use a multiple of the denominators.

- For problems involving different units, use a multiple of the conversion number (for example, 120 minutes for a minutes-to-hours conversion).

- For problems involving percents, use 100 or a multiple of 100.

Avoid numbers that cause problems.

- Don't use 0 or 1.

- Don't use numbers you see in the question or answer choices.

- Don't use the same value for several variables.

- Don't use conversion numbers (although multiples of them are okay).

The next example shows how choosing a bad number can create extra work for you or possibly even lead to a wrong answer.

4. A machine can produce p fan blades in an hour. How many fan blades can this machine produce in q minutes?

- ◯ pq

- ◯ $\dfrac{60p}{q}$

- ◯ $60pq$

- ◯ $\dfrac{p}{60q}$

- ◯ $\dfrac{pq}{60}$

1. Plug in some numbers for the variables. Suppose $p = 10$ fan blades in an hour and $q = 60$ minutes.

2. Find a numerical answer. The machine produces 10 fan blades in an hour, so it produces 10 fan blades in 60 minutes, because 60 minutes is one hour. So the answer is 10. Circle it on your noteboard.

3. Plug your numbers into the answer choices to see which one matches.

   For A, you get $pq = (10)(60) = 600$. The answer should be 10, so eliminate A.

   For B, you get $\dfrac{60p}{q} = \dfrac{60 \times 10}{60} = 10$. That seems right. However, you remem-

   ber that you're supposed to check all five choices, so you keep going.

   For C, you get $60pq = (60)(10)(60) = 36,000$. That's certainly not 10, so eliminate C.

   For D, you get $\dfrac{p}{60q} = \dfrac{10}{60 \times 60} = \dfrac{10}{3,600} = \dfrac{1}{360}$. That's not 10, so eliminate D.

   For choice E, you get $\dfrac{pq}{60} = \dfrac{10 \times 60}{60} = 10$.

   Wait a second, both B and E can't be right! Now you need to try some different numbers and check B and E again.

Where did this all go wrong? The problem started with setting $q = 60$. Because 60 shows up in four of the answer choices, it's possible that $q = 60$ will make some answers equal in value. In general, you should never plug in a unit-conversion number. To avoid that problem, use a different value for q. You want to keep the calculations simple, so use a number that plays nicely with 60, such as 30 or 120. Start with these numbers so that you don't have to work the problem twice.

Try the problem with a different number for q, such as q = 120 minutes. Keep p = 10 fan blades per hour. In 120 minutes, the machine can produce 20 fan blades, because 120 minutes is 2 hours. So the answer is 20 fan blades. When you plug p = 10 and q = 120 into the answer choices, you get

○ $pq = (10)(120) = 1,200$

○ $\dfrac{60p}{q} = \dfrac{60 \times 10}{120} = 5$

○ $60pq = (60)(10)(120) = 72,000$

○ $\dfrac{p}{60q} = \dfrac{10}{60 \times 120} = \dfrac{1}{720}$

○ $\dfrac{pq}{60} = \dfrac{10 \times 120}{60} = 20$

So the correct answer turns out to be E.

There are also a couple of guidelines you should follow when using Plugging In on a problem with several variables. First, use a different number for each variable. Failure to do so can result in several answers all seeming to work. This is essentially the same problem as using a number that appears in the answer choices.

Second, if the problem contains several variables all related in an equation, you're going to make up numbers for all the variables except one. Solve the equation to find the value for that last variable.

Here's an example:

5. If $a = \dfrac{b+5}{c}$, what is the value of b in terms of a and c ?

○ $\dfrac{ac}{5}$

○ $ac - 5$

○ $c(a - 5)$

○ $(a - 5)(c - 5)$

○ $5ac$

1. Plug in numbers for the variables. There is an equation, so you'll make up numbers for only two of the three variables. If you start with $c = 3$, you probably want the top of the fraction to be a multiple of 3, such as 12. Let $b = 7$ so that the top is 12. Now, solve the equation to find the value of a, which is $a = \dfrac{7+5}{3} = \dfrac{12}{3} = 4$.

2. Find a numerical answer. In this case, the question just asks for the value of b, which is 7. Circle it on your noteboard.

3. Plug your numbers into the answer choices. You get

   ○ $\dfrac{ac}{5} = \dfrac{4 \times 3}{5} = \dfrac{12}{5}$

   ○ $ac - 5 = (4)(3) - 5 = 12 - 5 = 7$

   ○ $c(a - 5) = 3(4 - 5) = 3(-1) = -3$

   ○ $(a - 5)(c - 5) = (4 - 5)(3 - 5) = (-1)(-2) = 2$

   ○ $5ac = (5)(4)(3) = 60$

As you can see, the only answer that matches is B.

Quiz 1

1. Alice is twice as old as Brian and Cathy is 6 years younger than Brian. If Alice is a years old, how old is Cathy in terms of a ?

   ○ $a + 6$

   ○ $a - 6$

   ○ $\dfrac{a - 12}{2}$

   ○ $\dfrac{a + 12}{2}$

   ○ $2a - 6$

2. All the widgets manufactured by Company X are stored in two warehouses, A and B. Warehouse A contains three times as many widgets as does warehouse B. If $\frac{1}{15}$ of the widgets in warehouse A and $\frac{1}{20}$ of the widgets in warehouse B are defective, what fraction of all the widgets are NOT defective?

○ $\frac{1}{5}$

○ $\frac{1}{16}$

○ $\frac{15}{16}$

○ $\frac{34}{35}$

○ $\frac{74}{75}$

3. Of all the players in a professional baseball league, $\frac{1}{2}$ are foreign-born, including $\frac{1}{3}$ of the pitchers. If $\frac{3}{4}$ of the players are pitchers, what percentage of the players who are not pitchers are foreign-born?

○ 100%

○ 75%

○ $66\frac{2}{3}$%

○ 50%

○ 25%

PLUGGING IN THE ANSWERS

Plugging In The Answers is another variation of Plugging In; it also turns algebra problems into arithmetic problems. You use Plugging In when the answer choices contain variables—visible or invisible. Use Plugging In The Answers *when the answer choices are numbers*. Alternatively, if you feel the urge to write an algebraic equation, you should probably just Plug In The Answers. Essentially, you try the answer choices to see which one fits with the information in the question. Here's the step-by-step method.

1. Identify the specific number for which the question asks. In other words, what value do the answer choices represent?

2. Try answer C. Work through the problem using that number. If it works, you're done. Otherwise,

3. Try a different answer choice. If answer C was too big, try a smaller answer. If C was too small, try a bigger number. Repeat until you find the answer that fits the information in the question.

Try this example.

1. Oliver has twice as many marbles as Ted. Ted has twice as many marbles as Merrill. If the total number of marbles among the three is 28, how many marbles does Ted have?

   ○   4
   ○   8
   ○   12
   ○   14
   ○   16

1. Identify the specific number asked for in the question. The question is "how many marbles does Ted have?" so the answer choices represent Ted's marbles.

2. Using answer C, work through the question. If Ted has 12 marbles, then Oliver has twice that, or $2 \times 12 = 24$ marbles. Merrill has half as many marbles as Ted, or $\dfrac{12}{2} = 6$ marbles. The total is $12 + 24 + 6 = 42$ marbles. The total is supposed to be 28, so eliminate C.

3. Try a different answer. The total from C, 42, was too big, so you should look for a smaller number. Try B. If Ted has 8 marbles, then Oliver has $2 \times 8 = 16$ marbles. Merrill has $\dfrac{8}{2} = 4$ marbles. The total is $8 + 4 + 16 = 28$.

That matches the number in the question, so B is the correct answer.

Plugging In The Answers works when the question asks for a single number, such as "What is x?" You cannot use it when the question asks for multiple numbers, such as "What is $x + y$?" That's because you won't know how much of the answer is x and how much is y.

Plugging In The Answers offers the same advantages that regular Plugging In does. First, it helps you avoid many of the careless mistakes that people make when doing algebra. Numbers are simply easier to work with than variables. Second, it's a great tool for tackling really tough problems that are impossibly difficult to solve algebraically.

It may take a little practice to get the hang of Plugging In and Plugging In The Answers, but they are invaluable for simplifying algebra questions, particularly word problems. Take the time to get familiar with these techniques.

Quiz 2

1. Rob is twice as old as Jodie is now. In 10 years, Rob will be 20 years older than Jodie is at that time. How old is Jodie now?

    ○ 10
    ○ 20
    ○ 30
    ○ 40
    ○ 50

2. John and Mark each own a collection of baseball cards. The two collections combined contain 120 cards. If John were to trade 5 cards to Mark and receive 2 of Mark's cards in return, John would have 22 more cards than Mark does. How many cards does Mark possess before the proposed trade?

    ○ 85
    ○ 74
    ○ 52
    ○ 46
    ○ 35

Must Be Problems

Some questions ask "what must be true?" or some variation on that. They supposedly test your knowledge of the properties of various types of numbers (for example, odd, even, positive, negative, and so on). However, you can easily solve these questions with the Plugging In technique. The difference is that you need to plug in more than once.

Try numbers from both sides of whichever issue the question is testing. For example, if the question is testing odd versus even, plug in both an odd number and an even number. After you plug in an odd number, eliminate any answers that aren't true. Then plug in an even number and eliminate any answers that aren't true. In most cases, you'll be left with one answer at this point. If not, continue plugging in different numbers until you're left with one answer.

If you need to plug in more numbers, try 1 and 0. Earlier, you avoided those numbers because they did weird things. Now, however, you want the answers to do weird things so that you can eliminate them.

Look at this next example.

1. If the product xy is negative, which of the following must be true?

    ○ $x < y$

    ○ $x < 0$

    ○ $y < 0$

    ○ $\dfrac{x}{y} < 0$

    ○ $x + y < 0$

The question is testing positive versus negative, so you'll want to try both kinds of numbers. You are constrained by the fact that xy is negative. The numbers you plug in must fit that condition. You might start with $x = 2$ and $y = -3$. A is false, so you can eliminate it. B is also false, so eliminate it. C is true in this case, so keep it. D is true in this case, so keep it. E is true in this case, so keep it.

Next, try a different set of numbers. Try reversing which variables are positive and negative. Let $x = -2$ and $y = 3$. Now you need to check only C, D, and E because you've already eliminated the others. C is false, so eliminate it. D is true in this case, so keep it. E is false, so eliminate it. The correct answer must be D.

Quiz 3

1. If x is an integer, which of the following must be odd?

    ○ $3x$
    ○ $2x$
    ○ $3x + 1$
    ○ $4x$
    ○ $4x + 1$

2. If p, q, and r are nonzero numbers and $p = q - r$, which of the following must equal 0 ?

○ $p - r$

○ $\dfrac{p+r-1}{q}$

○ $\dfrac{p+q}{r} - 1$

○ $p - (q + r)$

○ $\dfrac{p+r}{q} - 1$

PRACTICE SET

1. If Joe Bob was 25 years old 5 years ago, how old was he x years ago?

   ○ $x - 30$
   ○ $x - 20$
   ○ $30 - x$
   ○ $20 - x$
   ○ $20 + x$

2. Increasing the original length of a racetrack by 15% and then increasing the new length by 10% is equivalent to increasing the original length by

   ○   30.0%
   ○   27.5%
   ○   26.5%
   ○   25.0%
   ○   12.5%

3. At a certain bakery, $\frac{1}{4}$ of the cookies sold in one week were chocolate chip and $\frac{1}{5}$ of the remaining cookies sold were oatmeal raisin. If x of the cookies sold were oatmeal raisin, how many were chocolate chip?

○ $\frac{1}{20}x$

○ $\frac{9}{20}x$

○ $\frac{4}{5}x$

○ $\frac{5}{4}x$

○ $\frac{5}{3}x$

4. If 50% of the money in a certain portfolio was invested in stocks, 20% in bonds, 15% in real estate, and the remaining $37,500 in a money market fund, what was the total amount invested in the portfolio?

○ $100,000
○ $125,000
○ $175,000
○ $250,000
○ $375,000

5. Of all the pies baked in a certain bakery, $\frac{1}{2}$ are apple pies, $\frac{1}{7}$ are cherry pies, $\frac{1}{4}$ are pecan pies, and the rest are coconut cream pies. If the combined number of pecan pies and coconut cream pies is 40, how many pies total did the bakery bake?

○ 56
○ 84
○ 91
○ 105
○ 112

6. Bill buys two types of soda. He buys *m* bottles of Brand A at $0.50 each. He buys *n* bottles of Brand B at $0.60 each. What is Bill's average cost in cents for a bottle of soda, in terms of *m* and *n* ?

$\bigcirc \quad \dfrac{0.5m + 0.6n}{m+n}$

$\bigcirc \quad \dfrac{m+n}{110}$

$\bigcirc \quad \dfrac{1.10}{m+n}$

$\bigcirc \quad \dfrac{50m + 60n}{m+n}$

$\bigcirc \quad \dfrac{50m + 60n}{mn}$

7. If *a*, *b*, and *c* are nonzero integers, which of the following must be an integer?

$\bigcirc \quad \dfrac{a+b}{c} + 1$

$\bigcirc \quad abc - 1$

$\bigcirc \quad \dfrac{ab}{c} - 1$

$\bigcirc \quad \dfrac{a}{b+c} + 1$

$\bigcirc \quad \dfrac{1}{a} + \dfrac{1}{b} + \dfrac{1}{c}$

8. In a certain school, $\dfrac{3}{5}$ of the students are boys and the rest are girls. Of the boys, $\dfrac{1}{4}$ play soccer. If the number of girls who play soccer equals the number of boys who play soccer, what fraction of the girls play soccer?

○ $\dfrac{1}{10}$

○ $\dfrac{3}{20}$

○ $\dfrac{1}{4}$

○ $\dfrac{1}{3}$

○ $\dfrac{3}{8}$

9. Jason has a handful of dimes and quarters. There are a total of 22 coins. If the total value of the coins is $3.25, how many dimes does Jason have?

○ 7
○ 8
○ 11
○ 12
○ 15

10. If both a and b are nonzero integers, which of the following must be positive?

    I. $a^2 + b^2$
   II. $a^2 - b^2$
  III. $(a - b)^2$

○ I only
○ II only
○ III only
○ I and II
○ I, II, and III

11. If $y \neq -7$, then $\dfrac{y^3 + 5y^2 - 15y - 7}{y + 7} =$

○ $y^2 - 5y + 1$
○ $y^2 - 2y - 1$
○ $y^2 + 5y - 15$
○ $2y^2 - 3y - 1$
○ $2y^2 - 5y + 1$

12. Anjeanette inserts light bulbs in a row of light sockets in the repeating pattern red bulb, white bulb, white bulb, red bulb, white bulb, and white bulb. If she inserts a total of n red bulbs in the row, including the first and last bulbs, how many white bulbs did she insert in the row?

○ $2n - 2$
○ $2n - 1$
○ $2n + 1$
○ $3n - 2$
○ $3n + 1$

13. Alex paid a $12 fee to receive a 10% discount from the list price on all books he bought in a six-month period. Victor paid a $15 fee to receive a 15% discount from the list price on all books he bought in the same period. If each bought books with a total list price of b during that period and each paid the same net amount, including the discount and the fee, what is b ?

○ $54
○ $60
○ $66
○ $100
○ $120

14. If $n > 6$ and $3m + 5n = 0$, then which of the following must be true?

○ $m > 10$
○ $m < -10$
○ $m = 10$
○ $n < 10$
○ $n > 10$

15. If x is a multiple of 5, y is a factor of 16, and z is a factor of 40, which of the following must be true?

    I. xy is a multiple of z.

    II. xy is not a factor of z.

    III. xy is a factor of z.

- ◯ None of the above
- ◯ I only
- ◯ II only
- ◯ III only
- ◯ I and II only

16. If p and q are consecutive even integers and $p < q$, which of the following must be divisible by 3 ?

- ◯ $p^2 + pq$
- ◯ $pq^2 + pq$
- ◯ $p^2q - pq$
- ◯ p^2q^2
- ◯ $pq^2 - pq$

17. A tank holds x gallons of a saltwater mixture that is 20% salt by volume. One fourth of the water is evaporated, leaving all of the salt. When 10 gallons of water and 20 gallons of salt are added, the resulting mixture is $33\frac{1}{3}$% salt by volume. What is the value of x ?

- ◯   37.5
- ◯   75
- ◯   100
- ◯   150
- ◯   175

18. Emma's piggy bank contains 12 cents more than Robert's piggy bank does, and *x* is the sum, in cents, of the money in their piggy banks. If half of the money in Emma's piggy bank is moved to Robert's and then *x* cents is added to each piggy bank, how much money, in cents, will Robert's piggy bank then contain?

○ $\dfrac{3}{4}x - 3$

○ $\dfrac{3}{4}x + 3$

○ $\dfrac{7}{4}x - 3$

○ $\dfrac{7}{4}x + 3$

○ $\dfrac{3}{2}x + 6$

19. If *u* and *v* are distinct prime numbers, which of the following CANNOT be a prime number?

○ $uv + 3v - 2$
○ $uv - u + 2v - 2$
○ $uv + 2u - v - 2$
○ $uv + 3u - 2v - 6$
○ $uv + u + v + 1$

20. If $a = x - b$ and $b = a - y$, what is the value of *ab*?

○ $\dfrac{x^2 + y^2}{4}$

○ $\dfrac{xy}{4}$

○ $\dfrac{(x - y)}{4}$

○ $\dfrac{x^2 - y^2}{4}$

○ $\dfrac{y^2 - x^2}{4}$

Challenge!
Take a crack at this high-level GMAT question.

ANSWERS AND EXPLANATIONS

Quiz 1

1. **C** First, make up a number for a, such as $a = 20$. Second, solve for a numerical answer. If Alice is 20, then Brian is 10. If Brian is 10, then Cathy is $10 - 6 = 4$. So the answer is 4. Third, plug $a = 20$ into the answers and find the one that equals 4. The only one that matches is C.

2. **C** First, make up some numbers for the number of widgets in A and B. Suppose A contains 300 widgets and B contains 100 widgets. Second, find a numerical answer. Warehouse A contains $\frac{1}{5} \times 300 = 20$ defective widgets. Warehouse B contains $\frac{1}{20} \times 100 = 5$ defective widgets. The total number of widgets is $100 + 300 = 400$ and the number of defective widgets is $20 + 5 = 25$. So the number of non-defective widgets is $400 - 25 = 375$. The fraction of widgets that are not defective is $\frac{375}{400} = \frac{15}{16}$. Choose C.

3. **A** First, plug in a number for the total number of players. The number should be compatible with $\frac{1}{2}, \frac{1}{3}$, and $\frac{3}{4}$, so try 240 players. Second, solve for a numerical answer. You may want to use a grid like the ones you learned about in Chapter 6. See the example at the end of this paragraph. If there are 240 players total, then there are $\frac{1}{2} \times 240 = 120$ foreign-born players and $240 - 120 = 120$ native-born players. There are $\frac{3}{4} \times 240 = 180$ pitchers and $240 - 180 = 60$ non-pitchers. Of the pitchers, $\frac{1}{3} \times 180 = 60$ are foreign-born, leaving $180 - 60 = 120$ native-born pitchers. Of the 120 foreign-born players, 60 are pitchers, leaving $120 - 60 = 60$ foreign-born non-pitchers. So of the 60 non-pitchers, 60 are foreign-born. That's 100%. Choose A.

	Foreign	Native	Total
Pitchers	60	120	180
Non-pitchers	60	0	60
Total	120	120	240

Quiz 2

1. **B** Start with answer C. If Jodie is 30 years old now, then Rob is $2 \times 30 = 60$ years old. In 10 years, Rob will be $60 + 10 = 70$ and Jodie will be $30 + 10 = 40$ years old. However, Rob will be $70 - 40 = 30$ years older than Jodie, not the stated 20 years. Try a different answer. In B, if Jodie is 20 years old, then Rob is $2 \times 20 = 40$. In 10 years, Rob will be $40 + 10 = 50$ and Jodie will be $20 + 10 = 30$. Rob will be $50 - 30 = 20$ years older, so B is correct.

2. **D** First, figure out what the answer represents. In this case, it is the number of cards Mark owns at the start. Second, use C and work through the problem. If Mark owns 52 cards, then John owns 120 − 52 = 68 cards. John then trades 5 cards to Mark and gets 2 back. That's a net of 3 cards to Mark. So John now has 68 − 3 = 65 and Mark has 52 + 3 = 55. That's a difference of 10 cards, not 22 cards. Eliminate C. Third, try another answer. In B, Mark starts with 74 cards, so John has 120 − 74 = 46 cards. After the trade, John has 46 − 3 = 43 cards and Mark has 74 + 3 = 77 cards. John has *fewer* cards than Mark, so that's definitely the wrong direction. Eliminate B and A and try D. Mark has 46 cards, so John has 120 − 46 = 74 cards. After the trade, John has 74 − 3 = 71 cards and Mark has 46 + 3 = 49 cards. That's a difference of 71 − 49 = 22 cards, which matches the information in the question. Choose D.

Quiz 3

1. **E** The issue is odd versus even, so plug in numbers of both types. Let $x = 2$, an even number. A is 6, an even number, so eliminate it. B is 4, an even number, so eliminate it. C is 7, an odd number, so keep it. D is 8, an even number, so eliminate it. E is 9, an odd number, so keep it. Now try an odd number, such as $x = 3$. C is 10, an even number, so eliminate it. E is 13, an odd number, so E is the correct answer.

2. **E** This question doesn't really involve an odd/even or positive/negative issue, so you'll just need to plug in different sets of numbers until you're left with one answer. Try $p = 3$, $q = 6$, and $r = 3$. Answer A is $3 - 3 = 0$. Keep it. Answer B is $\frac{3+3-1}{6} = \frac{5}{6}$. Eliminate it. C is $\frac{3+6}{3} - 1 = 3 - 1 = 2$. Eliminate it. D is $3 - (6 + 3) = -6$. Eliminate it. E is $\frac{3+3}{6} - 1 = 1 - 1 = 0$. Keep it. Try a different set of numbers, such as $p = 1$, $q = 3$, and $r = 2$. Now A is $1 - 2 = -1$. Eliminate it. E is $\frac{1+2}{3} - 1 = 1 - 1 = 0$. The correct answer must be E.

Practice Set

1. **C** Let $x = 10$. If Joe Bob was 25 years old 5 years ago, he must be 30 years old now. So 10 years ago, he was 20 years old. Plug $x = 10$ into the answers and see which one matches. The answer must be C.

2. **C** Plug in a number for the original length, say 100 yards. Increasing the length by 15% adds 15 yards for a new total of $100 + 15 = 115$ yards. Increasing this new length by 10% adds $0.10 \times 115 = 11.5$ yards, for a total length of $115 + 11.5 = 126.5$ yards. That's an overall increase of 26.5 yards or $\dfrac{26.5}{100} = 26.5\%$. Choose C.

3. **E** Suppose that the bakery sold a total of 20 cookies. Then there are $\dfrac{1}{4} \times 20 = 5$ chocolate chip cookies, leaving $20 - 5 = 15$ cookies. Of these remaining cookies, $\dfrac{1}{5} \times 15 = 3$ are oatmeal raisin, so $x = 3$. The numerical answer for the number of chocolate chip cookies is 5. Plug $x = 3$ into the answers and see which one matches. The answer is E.

4. **D** Start with C. If there is \$175,000 in the portfolio, there is
$0.5 \times \$175{,}000 = \$87{,}500$ in stocks, $0.2 \times \$175{,}000 = \$35{,}000$ in bonds,
$0.15 \times \$175{,}000 = \$26{,}250$ in real estate, and
$\$175{,}000 - \$87{,}500 - \$35{,}000 - \$26{,}250 = \$26{,}250$ left for the money market fund.
That doesn't match the \$37,500 stated in the question, so eliminate C. You need a bigger number, so try D. If the total amount is \$250,000, then there is
$0.5 \times \$250{,}000 = \$125{,}000$ in stocks, $0.2 \times \$250{,}000 = \$50{,}000$ in bonds,
$0.15 \times \$250{,}000 = \$37{,}500$ in real estate, and
$\$250{,}000 - \$125{,}000 - \$50{,}000 - \$37{,}500 = \$37{,}500$ left for the money market fund.
That matches the information in the question, so choose D.

5. **E** Normally, you'd start by checking C. However, both C and D are odd. Because apple pies are $\dfrac{1}{2}$ of the total, you can't have an odd total. Eliminate C and D. Now check the middle answer of what's left, B. If there are 84 pies total, there are $\dfrac{1}{2} \times 84 = 42$ apple pies, $\dfrac{1}{7} \times 84 = 12$ cherry pies, and $\dfrac{1}{4} \times 84 = 21$ pecan pies. That leaves $84 - 42 - 12 - 21 = 9$ coconut cream pies. The total of pecan and coconut cream pies is $21 + 9 = 30$ pies. That's too few. Eliminate B and try a bigger answer. In E, there are 112 pies total. So there are $\dfrac{1}{2} \times 112 = 56$ apple pies, $\dfrac{1}{7} \times 112 = 16$ cherry pies, and $\dfrac{1}{4} \times 112 = 28$ pecan pies. That leaves $112 - 56 - 16 - 28 = 12$ coconut cream pies. The total of pecan and coconut cream pies is $28 + 12 = 40$. That matches the information in the question, so choose E.

6. **D** Plug in numbers for m and n. Let m = 10 bottles at 50 cents each for a cost of $10 \times 50 = 500$ cents. Let n = 15 bottles at 60 cents each for a cost of $15 \times 60 = 900$ cents. Bill's total cost is $500 + 900 = 1,400$ cents for $10 + 15 = 25$ bottles of soda. So his average cost is $\frac{1,400}{25} = 56$ cents per bottle. Plug m = 10 and n = 15 into the answers to see which one equals 56. Remember that you need an answer in cents, not in dollars. A is 0.56, which is the trap answer in dollars. B is $\frac{25}{110}$. C is $\frac{1.1}{25}$. D is 56. E is $\frac{1,400}{150}$, which is about 13. Choose D.

7. **B** Plug in some numbers, such as a = 2, b = 3, and c = 4. A is $\frac{2+3}{4} + 1 = \frac{5}{4} + 1 = \frac{9}{4}$. That's not an integer, so eliminate it. B is $(2)(3)(4) - 1 = 24 - 1 = 23$. That is an integer, so keep it. C is $\frac{2 \times 3}{4} - 1 = \frac{6}{4} - 1 = \frac{2}{4} = \frac{1}{2}$. That's not an integer, so eliminate it. D is $\frac{2}{3+4} + 1 = \frac{2}{7} + 1 = \frac{9}{7}$. That's not an integer, so eliminate it. E is $\frac{1}{2} + \frac{1}{3} + \frac{1}{4} = \frac{13}{12}$. That's not an integer, so eliminate it. Choose B.

8. **E** Make up a number for the total number of students, say 200. There are $\frac{3}{5} \times 200 = 120$ boys and $200 - 120 = 80$ girls. There are $\frac{1}{4} \times 120 = 30$ soccer players among the boys, so there are also 30 soccer players among the girls. The fraction of girls that play soccer is $\frac{30}{80} = \frac{3}{8}$. Choose E.

9. **E** Start Plugging In The Answers with C. He has 11 dimes worth $11 \times 0.10 = \$1.10$. He has $22 - 11 = 11$ quarters worth $11 \times 0.25 = \$2.75$. That's a total value of $1.10 + 2.75 = \$3.85$. That doesn't match the $3.25 from the question. Eliminate C. You want less money, so you need fewer quarters and more dimes. Try D. Jason has 12 dimes worth $12 \times 0.10 = \$1.20$. He has $22 - 12 = 10$ quarters worth $10 \times 0.25 = \$2.50$. That's a total value of $1.20 + 2.50 = \$3.70$, which is still too big. Try E. Jason has 15 dimes worth $15 \times 0.10 = \$1.50$. He has $22 - 15 = 7$ quarters worth $7 \times 0.25 = \$1.75$. That's a total value of $1.50 + 1.75 = \$3.25$, which matches the information in the question. Choose E.

10. **A** Plug in numbers for a and b, such as a = 2 and b = 3. I is $4 + 9 = 13$. That's positive, so keep it. II is $4 - 9 = -5$. That's negative, so you can eliminate it. That means you eliminate B, D, and E. III is $(-1)^2 = 1$. That's positive, so keep it. Try strange numbers such as a = 2 and b = 2. I is $4 + 4 = 8$. That's positive, so keep it. III is $(0)^2 = 0$. That's not positive, so eliminate it and C. The answer must be A.

11. **B** Since there are variables in the answer choices, you should try

Plugging In. If $y = 3$, for example, the original expression becomes

$$\frac{3^3 + 5(3^2) - 15(3) - 7}{3 + 7} = \frac{27 + 45 - 45 - 7}{10} = \frac{20}{10} = 2.$$ Now, plug $y = 3$ into each

answer and see which one equals 2. Answer B becomes

$3^2 - 2(3) - 1 = 9 - 6 - 1 = 2$. None of the other answers equals 2, so choose B.

12. **A** The repeating pattern is 3 bulbs (red, white, white), and you want to start and end with a red bulb. Since there are variables in the answer choices, try Plugging In. Suppose the total is 7 bulbs, so that the sequence is red, white, white, red, white, white, red. There are 3 red bulbs, so $n = 3$. There are 4 white bulbs, so your target is 4. Plug $n = 3$ into the answer choices to see which one equals 4. A equals 4; B equals 5; C equals 7; D equals 7; and E equals 10. Choose A.

13. **B** With numerical answer choices, you should consider Plugging In The Answers. Start with C, so each person bought books totaling $66 in list price. Alex received a 10% discount, which is $0.1 \times 66 = \$6.60$ and paid a $12 fee, so his total is $66 - 6.60 + 12 = \$71.40$. Victor received a 15% discount, which is $0.15 \times 66 = \$9.90$ and paid a $15 fee, so his total is $66 - 9.90 + 15 = \$71.10$. Close, but not the same. Eliminate C and try B, in which each person buys books totaling $60 in list price. Alex's 10% discount is $0.1 \times 60 = \$6.00$, so he pays $60 - 6.00 + 12 = \$66.00$. Victor's 15% discount is $0.15 \times 60 = \$9.00$, so he pays $60 - 9.00 + 15 = \$66.00$. The two people paid the same price, as the question stipulated, so B is correct.

14. **B** It's a "must be" problem, so plug in a set of numbers. Let $n = 15$, so that $3m + 75 = 0$. That means $m = -25$. You can eliminate A, C, and D. Now try another number, such as $n = 9$. That gives the equation $3m + 45 = 0$, so $m = -15$. Although B is still true, E isn't. Cross off E and choose B.

15. **A** It's a "must be" question, so plug in one or more sets of numbers. Suppose $x = 10$, $y = 2$, and $z = 8$. Be sure the numbers you choose are consistent with the conditions described in the problem. Now, see which answers are true. Roman numeral I says that 20 is a multiple of 8. That's not true, so eliminate B and E. II says that 20 is not a factor of 8. That's true, so don't eliminate anything. III says that 20 is a factor of 8. That's not true, so eliminate D. The question is whether II is always true or only sometimes, depending on the numbers you choose. Try to find a set of numbers that disproves II. Suppose $x = 10$, $y = 2$, and $z = 20$. Now, II says that 20 is not a factor of 20, which is a false statement. Eliminate C and choose A.

16. **E** It's a "must be" problem, so plug in one or more sets of numbers. Suppose $p = 2$ and $q = 4$. Answer A becomes $2^2 + (2)(4) = 4 + 8 = 12$. That's divisible by 3, so keep it. Answer B becomes $(2)(4^2) + (2)(4) = 32 + 8 = 40$. That's not divisible by 3, so eliminate B. Answer C becomes $(2^2)(4) - (2)(4) = 16 - 8 = 8$. That's not divisible by 3, so eliminate C. Answer D becomes $(2^2)(4^2) = (4)(16) = 64$. That's not divisible by 3, so eliminate D. Answer E becomes $(2)(4^2) - (2)(4) = 32 - 8 = 24$. That is divisible by 3, so keep it. Try a new set of numbers, such as $p = 4$ and $q = 6$. Now, A becomes $4^2 + (4)(6) = 16 + 24 = 40$. That's not divisible by 3, so eliminate A. Answer E becomes $(4)(6^2) - (4)(6) = 144 - 24 = 120$. That is still divisible by 3. Choose E.

17. **D** With numerical answers to a story problem, try Plugging In The Answers. Start with C, which is 100 gallons of mixture. It's 20% salt, so there are 20 gallons of salt and 80 gallons of water. Take away one fourth of the water, or 20 gallons, leaving 60 gallons of water and 20 gallons of salt. Finally, add 10 gallons of water and 20 gallons of salt to get 40 gallons of salt and 70 gallons of water, or $40 + 70 = 110$ gallons of the mixture. The salt percentage is $\dfrac{40}{110} = 36.36...\%$, not $33\dfrac{1}{3}\%$, so eliminate C and try a different answer. With D, you start with 150 gallons, including $0.2 \times 150 = 30$ gallons of salt and 120 gallons of water. Evaporating one fourth of the water leaves 30 gallons of salt and 90 gallons of water. Adding new salt and water gives you $30 + 20 = 50$ gallons of salt and $90 + 10 = 100$ gallons of water, or $50 + 100 = 150$ gallons total. The salt percentage is $\dfrac{50}{150} = \dfrac{1}{3} = 33\dfrac{1}{3}\%$, so D is correct.

18. **C** It's easier to plug in the numbers for Emma and Robert and then find x than vice versa. Suppose Robert has 10 cents and Emma has $10 + 12 = 22$ cents. That makes $x = 10 + 22 = 32$. Taking half of Emma's money, 11 cents, and giving it to Robert gives him $10 + 11 = 21$ cents. Now, $x = 32$ cents is given to each child, so Robert has $21 + 32 = 53$ cents. That's your target. Plug $x = 32$ into the answers to see which one equals 53. Answer choice C becomes $\dfrac{7}{4}(32) - 3 = 56 - 3 = 53$. None of the other answers equal 53, so choose C.

19. **E** This is similar to a "must be" problem. Plug in several sets of numbers and eliminate answer choices that are prime. Suppose $u = 2$ and $v = 3$.

Choice A becomes $(2)(3) + 3(3) - 2 = 13$; that's prime, so eliminate it.

B becomes $(2)(3) - 2 + 2(3) - 2 = 8$; that's not prime, so keep it.

C becomes $(2)(3) + 2(2) - 3 - 2 = 5$; that's prime, so eliminate it.

D becomes $(2)(3) + 3(2) - 2(3) - 6 = 0$; that's not prime, so keep it.

E becomes $(2)(3) + 2 + 3 + 1 = 12$; that's not prime, so keep it. Try switching the numbers, so that $u = 3$ and $v = 2$. B becomes $(3)(2) - 3 + 2(2) - 2 = 5$; that's prime, so eliminate it. D becomes $(3)(2) + 3(3) - 2(2) - 6 = 5$; that's prime, so eliminate it. E becomes $(3)(2) + 3 + 2 + 1 = 12$; that's not prime, so keep it. You've eliminated A, B, C, and D, so choose E.

20. **D** If you attempted the typical algebraic solution for this question, you are likely surprised by this answer. Instead of spending time trying to manipulate the equations to yield the correct answer, you should Plug In! Pick a number for x and b. Make $x = 5$ and $b = 2$. Therefore, $a = 3$, and $y = 1$. The target for this question is ab, or $(3)(2) = 6$. Now, plug $x - 5$ and $y - 1$ into the answers until one works. Only D yields 6. Choose D.

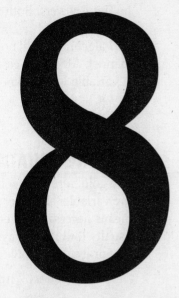

Facing Algebra

In the last chapter, you learned how to avoid algebra by using Plugging In and Plugging In The Answers. Both are useful strategies if you are a bit algebra-phobic. This chapter is for the pro-algebra contingent of GMAT test takers (or at least the test takers who aren't anti-algebra). You'll notice that many of the GMAT math problems involve algebra in some manner. Algebra is essentially arithmetic with one or more variables thrown into the mix. A variable is an unknown number and is usually indicated by an italicized letter, such as x or n.

SOLVING EQUATIONS

The golden rule for solving equations is "Do the same thing to both sides until you isolate the variable." In other words, add, subtract, multiply, and divide both sides by whatever means necessary to get the variable all by itself on one side of the equals sign. You should usually (but not always) add and subtract before you multiply and divide.

For example, solve for x in the equation $3x + 7 = 19$.

Subtract 7 from both sides to get $\qquad$ $3x = 12$

Divide both sides by 3 to get $\qquad$ $x = 4$

You should also know how to deal with numbers in parentheses, such as $5(x + 3)$. In this case, just multiply each number in the parentheses by 5. So $5(x + 3) = 5x + 15$. You may also need to reverse this process by factoring. Just find the common factor of the numbers and put that outside the parentheses. For example, factor $6x + 12$. Both numbers are divisible by 6, so factor out the 6 and put it in front of parentheses. So $6x + 12 = 6(x + 2)$.

Factoring is often required in problems with complicated fractions, such as $\dfrac{7x + 14}{x + 2}$.

To simplify the fraction, you could try factoring out a number so that something on the top cancels with something on the bottom. This could let you reduce the fraction to a simpler

form. If you factor out a 7 on the top to get $\dfrac{7x + 14}{x + 2} = \dfrac{7(x + 2)}{x + 2}$, then you can cancel the

$x + 2$ on the top with the $x + 2$ on the bottom. So $\dfrac{7x + 14}{x + 2} = \dfrac{7}{1} = 7$.

QUIZ 1

1. If $\dfrac{1}{2}x + 12 = 4$, then $x =$

   - ○ −16
   - ○ −8
   - ○ −4
   - ○ 8
   - ○ 6

2. If $x \neq -2$, then $\dfrac{5x+10}{x+2} =$

   ○ 2
   ○ 3
   ○ 4
   ○ 5
   ○ 6

3. If $\dfrac{2}{x+1} = \dfrac{1}{x-1}$, for $x \neq 1$ and $x \neq -1$, then $x =$

   ○ −3
   ○ −2
   ○ 0
   ○ 2
   ○ 3

4. If $\dfrac{1}{1+\dfrac{1}{y-1}} = \dfrac{3}{4}$ and $y \neq 1$, then $y =$

   ○ 4

   ○ 3

   ○ 2

   ○ $\dfrac{4}{3}$

   ○ $\dfrac{1}{4}$

MORE THAN ONE VARIABLE (SIMULTANEOUS EQUATIONS)

You've seen how to solve an equation that contains one variable. What can you do if an equation has more than one variable, such as $2x + y = 7$? Well, you can't actually solve that equation without more information in the form of another equation. The general rule is that the number of different variables equals the number of different equations necessary to solve for those variables.

If you have two variables in two equations, such as $2x + y = 7$ and $x - y = -1$, you can solve for the variables. The method is often referred to as simultaneous equations. Line up the two equations, as shown below, and then add the equations and eliminate one variable. This will leave you with an equation with one variable.

$$2x + y = 7$$
$$\underline{+\ x - y = -1}$$
$$3x = 6$$

Solve that equation as you learned to do earlier in the chapter. $3x = 6$ becomes $x = 2$. Now you can find y by plugging the value for x into one of the original equations (it doesn't matter which). The first equation would become $2(2) + y = 7$. That gives you a one-variable equation, which you can then solve for y. In this case, $y = 3$.

What if simply adding the equations doesn't eliminate a variable, as with $x + y = 9$ and $2x + y = 12$? In such cases, you need to multiply one or both of the equations to set up one of the variables for elimination. Multiply every term in the equation by the same number. In this example, you can multiply the first equation by -1. So $x + y = 9$ becomes $-x - y = -9$. Now you can add the equations and eliminate the y variable. The resulting equation is $x = 3$. Plug that back into one of the equations. Using the first equation, you get $3 + y = 9$. Now you can determine that $y = 6$.

Look at a slightly more complex example: $3x + y = 11$ and $2x + 3y = 19$. In this case, you can multiply the first equation by -3 to eliminate the y variable. Combining $-9x - 3y = -33$ with $2x + 3y = 19$, you get $-7x = -14$. So $x = 2$. Plug that into the first equation to get $3(2) + y = 11$ and solve to get $y = 5$.

QUIZ 2

1. If $x + 2y = 13$ and $5x - y = 21$, what is $x + y$?

- ◯ 1
- ◯ 4
- ◯ 5
- ◯ 8
- ◯ 9

2. If $2a + 3b = 7$, what is the value of b ?

    (1) $a - b = -4$
    (2) $4a = 14 - 6b$

Remember!
For Data Sufficiency problems in this book, we do not supply the answer choices. The five possible answer choices are the same every time.

INEQUALITIES

Inequalities are very similar to equations. Whereas equations use equals signs (=), inequalities use inequality signs (>, <, ≥, or ≤). Those symbols mean "greater than," "less than," "greater than or equal to," and "less than or equal to," respectively. Solving an inequality is very much like solving an equality. You add, subtract, multiply, and divide to isolate the variable. For example, solve $2x + 4 > 6$.

Subtract 4 to get $\qquad\qquad\qquad\qquad\qquad\qquad\qquad$ $2x > 2$

Divide by 2 to get $\qquad\qquad\qquad\qquad\qquad\qquad\qquad$ $x > 1$

However, there is one critical difference between equalities and inequalities. When you multiply or divide an inequality by a negative number, you must reverse the inequality sign. For example, try $-3x + 4 < -2$.

Subtract 4 to get $\qquad\qquad\qquad\qquad\qquad\qquad\qquad$ $-3x < -6$

Divide by –3 (and reverse the inequality) to get $\qquad$ $x > 2$

Sometimes a problem provides two inequalities and ask you to combine them in some way. Plug in the highest and lowest values for each variable and list all of the results. You'll have four numbers if there are two variables. From this list, choose the highest and lowest values and match the answer that includes those as the minimum and maximum values. Look at this next example.

1. If $2 < x < 5$ and $3 < y < 10$, which of the following expresses the possible range of values for $x - y$?

   ○ $-1 < x - y < 5$
   ○ $-1 < x - y < 2$
   ○ $-5 < x - y < 2$
   ○ $-8 < x - y < 2$
   ○ $-8 < x - y < -1$

Try all four combinations of the highest and lowest values for x and y. If $x = 2$ (well, obviously it couldn't be 2, because $2 < x$, but it could be very close, for instance 2.01; here we'll use 2 as the closest approximation) and $y = 3$, then $x - y = 2 - 3 = -1$. If $x = 2$ and $y = 10$, then $x - y = 2 - 10 = -8$. If $x = 5$ and $y = 3$, then $x - y = 2$. Finally, when $x = 5$ and $y = 10$, then $x - y = -5$. The highest value for $x - y$ is 2 and the lowest value is –8. Those are the numbers you want in the answer, so choose D.

The following diagram shows this process visually. Perform the operation $x - y$ with two vertical pairs and two diagonal pairs.

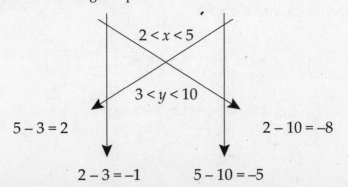

$2 < x < 5$

$3 < y < 10$

$5 - 3 = 2 \qquad\qquad\qquad\qquad\qquad\qquad 2 - 10 = -8$

$2 - 3 = -1 \qquad\quad 5 - 10 = -5$

Quiz 3

1. If $5 - 3x > 3$, which of the following expresses the possible values of x ?

   ○ $x < -\dfrac{2}{3}$

   ○ $x > -\dfrac{2}{.3}$

   ○ $x < \dfrac{2}{3}$

   ○ $x > \dfrac{2}{3}$

   ○ $x > \dfrac{3}{2}$

2. If $-2 < p < 3$ and $-1 < q < 10$, which of the following expresses the possible values of $p - q$?

   ○ $-12 < p - q < 4$
   ○ $-12 < p - q < 7$
   ○ $-3 < p - q < 4$
   ○ $-3 < p - q < 7$
   ○ $-1 < p - q < 4$

EXPONENTS

Exponents are just a shorthand expression for multiplication. For example, 4^5 simply means $4 \times 4 \times 4 \times 4 \times 4$. If you ever get confused by exponents, rewriting them as multiplication can demystify the problem. In the expression 4^5, the number 4 is the base and 5 is the exponent.

When two exponents have the same base, you can combine them in several ways. Here are the rules for manipulating exponents.

To multiply, add the exponents.	$3^2 \times 3^5 = 3^{2+5} = 3^7$
To divide, subtract the exponents.	$\dfrac{7^5}{7^2} = 7^{5-2} = 7^3$
To raise to a power, multiply the exponents.	$\left(5^2\right)^3 = 5^{2 \times 3} = 5^6$
To find a root, divide the exponent by the root.	$\sqrt[3]{5^9} = 5^{\frac{9}{3}} = 5^3$

If you forget these rules, you can also rewrite the exponents as multiplication.

$$3^2 \times 3^5 = 3 \times 3 \times 3 \times 3 \times 3 \times 3 \times 3 = 3^7$$

$$\frac{7^5}{7^2} = \frac{7 \times 7 \times 7 \times 7 \times 7}{7 \times 7} = 7 \times 7 \times 7 = 7^3$$

$$\left(5^2\right)^3 = \left(5 \times 5\right)\left(5 \times 5\right)\left(5 \times 5\right) = 5^6$$

$$\sqrt[3]{5^9} = \sqrt[3]{5 \cdot 5 \cdot 5 \cdot 5 \cdot 5 \cdot 5 \cdot 5 \cdot 5 \cdot 5} = 5^3$$

There are a few special cases for exponents that you should know.

Any number to the zero power equals 1.	$x^0 = 1$
Any number to the first power equals itself.	$x^1 = x$
1 to any power equals 1.	$1^x = 1$

NEGATIVE EXPONENTS

You may also see a negative exponent. The negative sign simply means the reciprocal of the positive exponent. For example

$$x^{-3} = \frac{1}{x^3}$$

People frequently make the mistake of assuming that negative exponents have something to do with negative numbers. That is *not* the case. For example, $5^{-2} = \frac{1}{5^2} = \frac{1}{25}$, *not* –25.

Also remember:

$$\boxed{x^{-2} \neq -x^2}$$

EXPONENTS OF NEGATIVE NUMBERS

A negative number raised to a power can become either positive or negative, depending on whether the exponent is even or odd. A negative number to an even exponent becomes positive; for example, $(-3)^2 = (-3)(-3) = 9$. A negative number to an odd exponent becomes negative; for example, $(-3)^3 = (-3)(-3)(-3) = -27$. Just remember that the exponent tells you how many times to multiply the number by itself. With an even exponent, the negative signs all pair up and cancel each other. With an odd exponent, most of the negative signs pair up, but there will be one left over that makes the resulting number negative.

- Negative number to an even exponent = positive

- Negative number to an odd exponent = negative

SCIENTIFIC NOTATION

Scientific notation is a way to express very small and very large numbers (such as the number of inches between the earth and the sun) in a readable format. To express a number in scientific notation, move the decimal point so that there's one digit to the left of the decimal point and then multiply by a power of 10. The exponent represents the number of places you moved the decimal point. A positive exponent means the original number was big (more than 1) and a negative exponent means the original number was small (less than 1). For example

$$1,200,000 = 1.2 \times 10^6$$

$$0.0000567 = 5.67 \times 10^{-5}$$

QUIZ 4

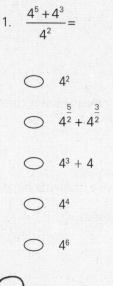

1. $\dfrac{4^5 + 4^3}{4^2} =$

    ○ 4^2

    ○ $4^{\frac{5}{2}} + 4^{\frac{3}{2}}$

    ○ $4^3 + 4$

    ○ 4^4

    ○ 4^6

2. If $x = -3$, then $\dfrac{x^3 - x^2 - x}{x+1} =$

    ○ $-\dfrac{33}{2}$

    ○ $-\dfrac{39}{4}$

    ○ $\dfrac{33}{4}$

    ○ $\dfrac{33}{2}$

    ○ $\dfrac{39}{2}$

3. The number of people surfing the Internet doubles every three months. If the number of people surfing the Internet today is 10^3, how many people will be surfing the Internet in one year?

○ 4×10^3
○ $10^3 \times 2^4$
○ 10^7
○ $10^7 \times 2^4$
○ 10^{11}

ROOTS

A root is like an exponent in reverse. For example, $5^3 = 125$ and $\sqrt[3]{125} = 5$. So the square root of x is the number that you would square to get x. Almost all of the roots on the GMAT are square roots (as opposed to cube roots and so forth). Square roots are generally indicated by a radical sign $\left(\sqrt{}\right)$; other roots will include a small number over the left side of the radical sign that tells you what kind of root it is. For example, the 3 in $\sqrt[3]{125}$ tells you to find the third root (or cube root).

Adding and subtracting roots is just like adding and subtracting variables. If the roots are the same, you can add and subtract. If they're different, you can't add or subtract. Just as you can add $x + 4x = 5x$, you can add $\sqrt{3} + 4\sqrt{3} = 5\sqrt{3}$. Just as you can't do anything with $x + y$, you can't combine $\sqrt{2} + \sqrt{3}$. You can add or subtract only if the roots are the same.

If you're multiplying or dividing several roots, it's usually easiest to combine them under one radical sign and then do the calculation. Look at these examples.

$$2\sqrt{2} \times \sqrt{8} = 2 \times \sqrt{2 \times 8} = 2\sqrt{16} = 2 \times 4 = 8$$

$$\frac{\sqrt{12}}{\sqrt{3}} = \sqrt{\frac{12}{3}} = \sqrt{4} = 2$$

Sometimes you need to take a single root and split it up into several roots. Try to factor out perfect squares so that you can simplify them to integers. Look at these examples.

$$\sqrt{\frac{1}{4}} = \frac{\sqrt{1}}{\sqrt{4}} = \frac{1}{2}$$
$$\sqrt{48} = \sqrt{16 \times 3} = \sqrt{16} \times \sqrt{3} = 4\sqrt{3}$$

Sometimes your answer will have a root in the denominator of a fraction. If it does, that answer won't be in the answer choices. On the GMAT, you can't have a radical in the denominator of a fraction, so you'll need to convert it to something that's acceptable. Just multiply both the numerator and denominator of the fraction by that root. It will get rid of the root in the denominator. You haven't changed the value of the number, just what it looks like. Look at this example.

$$\frac{3\sqrt{2}}{\sqrt{5}} = \frac{3\sqrt{2}}{\sqrt{5}} \times \frac{\sqrt{5}}{\sqrt{5}} = \frac{3\sqrt{10}}{5}$$

EXPONENTS AND SQUARE ROOTS

At The Princeton Review, we teach you the math that you need to know to crack the test. We don't review every facet of theoretical math—just what you must know to crack the GMAT. To that end, let's review a seeming contradiction in exponents and square roots.

For the purposes of the GMAT, $\sqrt{9} = 3$ means that the square root of 9 is 3. Technically, a square root can be positive or negative and the square root that's positive is called the *principal square root*. For test-taking purposes, though, we're always talking about the principal square root, so $\sqrt{9} = 3$, never –3. Things on the flip side of that aren't quite as cut-and-dry, though.

On the GMAT, you might also see $x^2 = 9$, but in this case, unlike what we saw above, $x = 3$ or –3. Confusing, huh? Just remember: For the purposes of test taking, a radical sign always indicates a positive number, but a variable that is raised to an exponent can be reduced to positive or negative.

ESTIMATING ROOTS

In some calculations involving square roots, your final answer will have a root in it. In these cases, you may want to know the approximate value of the number, so that you can use Ballparking or other elimination strategies.

You should memorize the easier perfect squares and their roots, such as $\sqrt{1} = 1$, $\sqrt{4} = 2$, and $\sqrt{100} = 10$. Learn the perfect squares at least up to $10^2 = 100$; preferably, you should know them up to $15^2 = 225$ or $20^2 = 400$. You can use these perfect squares as guideposts for estimating the value of other roots. For example, you know that $\sqrt{16} = 4$ and $\sqrt{25} = 5$. Since $\sqrt{20}$ is between $\sqrt{16}$ and $\sqrt{25}$, its value should be somewhere between 4 and 5.

Two particular roots that you will see frequently are $\sqrt{2}$ and $\sqrt{3}$. They often crop up in geometry problems, especially those involving right triangles, so you should learn their approximate values: $\sqrt{2} \approx 1.4$ and $\sqrt{3} \approx 1.7$.

FRACTIONAL EXPONENTS

It's possible that you'll see a fractional exponent on the GMAT. While they appear strange, they're not really that tough. A fractional exponent is just a way of expressing both an exponent and a root at the same time. Use the numerator as the exponent and the denominator as the root. Here are some examples.

$$x^{\frac{1}{2}} = \sqrt[2]{x^1} \text{ or } \sqrt{x}$$

$$x^{\frac{1}{3}} = \sqrt[3]{x^1} \text{ or } \sqrt[3]{x}$$

$$x^{\frac{3}{4}} = \sqrt[4]{x^3}$$

This ties in with the rule you learned earlier: To find a root, divide the exponent by the root.

$$\sqrt{5^8} = 5^{\frac{8}{2}} = 5^4$$

QUIZ 5

1. $\sqrt{10} \times \sqrt{2} + \dfrac{\sqrt{10}}{\sqrt{2}}$

   ◯ $\sqrt{2} + \sqrt{5}$

   ◯ $2\sqrt{5}$

   ◯ $3\sqrt{5}$

   ◯ $4\sqrt{5}$

   ◯ $3\sqrt{10}$

2. What is n ?

   (1) $n = \sqrt{25}$

   (2) $n^2 = 25$

QUADRATIC EQUATIONS

On the GMAT, you will most likely see some problems that involve quadratic equations and polynomials. The good news is you don't really have to know what either of those terms mean (or even how to spell them). Just follow a few guidelines to get you through these problems.

One issue that will probably come up is multiplying two sets of parentheses, such as $(x + 2)(x + 3)$. To do this, remember FOIL. It stands for First, Outer, Inner, Last. Those are the pairs of numbers you need to multiply. Check out the diagram below.

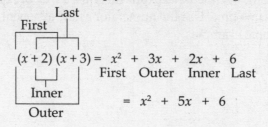

$$(x + 2)(x + 3) = x^2 + 3x + 2x + 6$$
$$\text{First} \quad \text{Outer} \quad \text{Inner} \quad \text{Last}$$
$$= x^2 + 5x + 6$$

Notice that you can usually combine the inner and outer terms into one term.

Sometimes you'll be given an equation that you need to factor out. Start by looking at the first number. That will tell you the first number in each set of parentheses. Then look at the signs (positive or negative) of the middle number and last number of the original equation. These tell you the signs of the second numbers inside the parentheses. Then find the factors of that last number because those are the potential choices for the second numbers in each set of parentheses. Last, look at the middle number of the original equation to help choose which pair of factors is appropriate. Choose the numbers that add up to this middle number. Be very careful with positive and negative signs.

Suppose you need to factor $x^2 - 4x + 4$. From the x^2, you can tell that the first numbers in the parentheses are x and x. From the sign of the last number (+4), you can tell that you need two positives or two negatives because the product must be positive. The negative sign of $-4x$ tells you it must be two negatives. The factors of the 4 are -1 and -4 or -2 and -2 (you already know that they're negative). To add up to $-4x$, you need -2 and -2. So the equation $x^2 - 4x + 4$ factors out to $(x - 2)(x - 2)$.

$$x^2 - 4x + 4 = (x \quad)(x \quad)$$
$$= (x -)(x -)$$
$$= (x - 2)(x - 2)$$

There are three patterns of quadratic equations that the GMAT writers love to use. You should memorize these and look for them whenever you see a problem with quadratic equations. You'll be able to avoid the tedious calculations if you recognize the patterns. Here are the three patterns:

$$(x + y)(x + y) = x^2 + 2xy + y^2$$
$$(x - y)(x - y) = x^2 - 2xy + y^2$$
$$(x + y)(x - y) = x^2 - y^2$$

The final thing you need to know about quadratic equations is how to solve one for the value(s) of the variable. Suppose you're told to find the value of x in the equation $x^2 - 2x = 35$. First, move everything to one side of the equation, so that you have a zero on the other side. In the example, you should get $x^2 - 2x - 35 = 0$. Next, factor the non-zero side using the method you learned. In the example, you get $(x - 7)(x + 5) = 0$.

Now for the tricky part. The only way to multiply two things together and get zero is for one of the things to equal zero. So if $(x - 7)(x + 5) = 0$, then either $x - 7 = 0$ or $x + 5 = 0$. Solve both of these mini-equations to get $x = 7$ and $x = -5$. Note that you will get two answers (unless the two mini-equations are the same). You can tell that x is either 7 or –5, but you can't pin it down to one value. That's the best you can do with a quadratic equation. The possible values are often referred to as the solutions or roots of the equation, so learn to recognize those terms.

Note that the mini-equations are pretty easy to solve. If there is no coefficient in front of the x, simply take the number in each parentheses and reverse the positive/negative sign. Suppose you have $x^2 - 4x + 7 = 4$. First, subtract 4 from each side to get $x^2 - 4x + 3 = 0$. Then, factor the left side to get $(x - 3)(x - 1) = 0$. Take the –3 and the –1 and reverse the signs, so $x = 3$ or $x = 1$. Note that this method works only if there is no coefficient in front of the x^2 in the original equation.

QUIZ 6

1. If $\dfrac{x^2 + 5x + 6}{x + 2} = 5$, what is the value of $x + 5$?

   ○ 2
   ○ 3
   ○ 5
   ○ 7
   ○ 10

2. If $x^2 - 5x - 6 = 0$, which of the following could be x?

   ○ –2
   ○ –1
   ○ 1
   ○ 2
   ○ 3

PRACTICE SET

1. Which one of the following equations has a root in common with $m^2 + 4m + 4 = 0$?

   ○ $m^2 - 4m + 4 = 0$
   ○ $m^2 + 4m + 3 = 0$
   ○ $m^2 - 4 = 0$
   ○ $m^2 + m - 6 = 0$
   ○ $m^2 + 5m + 4 = 0$

2. If $\dfrac{3}{1+\dfrac{3}{x}} = 2$, then $x =$

   ○ −6

   ○ $-\dfrac{3}{2}$

   ○ $\dfrac{1}{2}$

   ○ $\dfrac{3}{2}$

   ○ 6

3. If $3^{n+1} = 9^{n-1}$, then $n =$

   ○ −1
   ○ 0
   ○ 1
   ○ 2
   ○ 3

4. If $7 < m < 11$ and $-2 < n < 5$, then which of the following expresses the possible values of mn ?

   ○ $-14 < mn < 35$
   ○ $-14 < mn < 55$
   ○ $-22 < mn < 35$
   ○ $-22 < mn < 55$
   ○ $5 < mn < 16$

5. Which of the following most closely approximates $\sqrt{\dfrac{(3.97)(50.02)}{1.84}}$?

   ○ 1
   ○ 5
   ○ 10
   ○ 20
   ○ 100

6. If $x + 3y = 15$ and $y - x = 5$, then $y =$

   ○ −5
   ○ 0
   ○ 3
   ○ 5
   ○ 15

7. If $n = \dfrac{n-6}{n+6}$, what is the value of $n^2 + 5n + 6$?

   ○ −3
   ○ −2
   ○ 0
   ○ 2
   ○ 3

8. If $\dfrac{2.25 \times 10^a}{0.15 \times 10^b} = 1.5 \times 10^3$, then $a - b =$

   ○ 1
   ○ 2
   ○ 3
   ○ 4
   ○ 5

9. $\left(3 + \sqrt{11}\right)\left(3 - \sqrt{11}\right) =$

   ○ −2
   ○ $6 - 2\sqrt{11}$
   ○ 2
   ○ $9 - 2\sqrt{11}$
   ○ 8

10. If $(x - 2)^2 = 100$, which of the following could be the value of $x + 2$?

    ○ −10
    ○ −8
    ○ −6
    ○ 10
    ○ 12

11. What is the value of z ?

    (1) $6z = z^2 + 9$
    (2) $z^2 = -z + 12$

12. If $y^c = y^{d+1}$, what is the value of y ?

    (1) $y < 1$
    (2) $d = c$

13. If 3 is one value of x for the equation $x^2 - 7x + k = -5$, where k is a constant, what is the other solution?

    ⚬   2
    ⚬   4
    ⚬   5
    ⚬   6
    ⚬   12

14. $\dfrac{19^2 + 19}{20} =$

    ⚬ $\dfrac{19}{10}$

    ⚬ $\dfrac{57}{20}$

    ⚬   19

    ⚬   38

    ⚬   361

15. $\dfrac{(0.2)^2}{(0.2)^4} =$

    ⚬   0.04
    ⚬   0.25
    ⚬   0.4
    ⚬   4.0
    ⚬   25.0

16. $\sqrt{25 + 25} =$

   ○ $2\sqrt{5}$
   ○ $5\sqrt{2}$
   ○   10
   ○   20
   ○   25

17. What is the value of t?

   (1) $2t - 1 \geq 5$
   (2) $3t + 2 \leq 11$

18. Which of the following expresses $3^4 \times 25^6 \times 2^{12}$ in scientific notation?

   ○ 1.2×10^{12}
   ○ 8.1×10^{12}
   ○ 8.1×10^{13}
   ○ 1.5×10^{22}
   ○ 1.2×10^{24}

19. What is the value of $x - y$?

   (1) $x = y + 3$
   (2) $x^2 - 2xy + y^2 = 9$

20. If $\dfrac{4^7 + 4^8 + 4^9 + 4^{10}}{5}$ is x times 4^7, what is the value of x?

   ○ $\dfrac{1}{5}$

   ○ $\dfrac{4}{5}$

   ○   5

   ○   13

   ○   17

ANSWERS AND EXPLANATIONS

QUIZ 1

1. **A** Subtract 12 from both sides to get $\frac{1}{2}x = -8$. Then multiply both sides by 2 to get $x = -16$. Choose A.

2. **D** First, factor out 5 in the top of the fraction. That gives you $\frac{5(x+2)}{x+2}$. Now you can cancel the $x + 2$ on the top with the one on the bottom to get $\frac{5}{1} = 5$. Choose D.

3. **E** The variable in the denominator of the fractions is hard to work with, unless you move it to the top. Multiply both sides by $x + 1$ to get $2 = \frac{x+1}{x-1}$. Next, multiply both sides by $x - 1$ to get $2(x - 1) = x + 1$ or $2x - 2 = x + 1$. You can also get this by cross-multiplying the original two fractions. Subtract x from both sides to get $x - 2 = 1$. Finally, add 2 to both sides to get $x = 3$.

4. **A** Again, move the variable to the numerator by multiplying by the denominator.

   Multiply both sides by $1 + \frac{1}{y-1}$ to get $1 = \frac{3}{4}\left(1 + \frac{1}{y-1}\right)$, which becomes

   $1 = \frac{3}{4} + \frac{\frac{3}{4}}{y-1}$. Subtract $\frac{3}{4}$ from both sides to get $\frac{1}{4} = \frac{\frac{3}{4}}{y-1}$. Multiply both sides

   by 4 to simplify some of the fractions: $1 = \frac{3}{y-1}$. Now multiply both sides by

   $y - 1$ to get $y - 1 = 3$. Add 1 to each side to get $y = 4$. *Note:* You might also try

   PITA on this question.

QUIZ 2

1. **E** You can't eliminate a variable by adding the equations as they are. So multiply the second equation by 2 to eliminate the y variable. Adding the equations, you get $11x = 55$. Divide both sides by 11 to get $x = 5$. Plug that back into the first equation to get $5 + 2y = 13$. Subtract 5 from each side to get $2y = 8$. Now divide by 2 to get $y = 4$. So $x + y = 5 + 4 = 9$. Choose E.

2. **A** Start with statement (1). This gives you two different equations, so you can solve for the two variables. You can answer the question, so eliminate B, C, and E. Look at statement (2). This does not give you two different equations. The equation from the statement is the same as the equation from the question. Take the question equation and multiply by 2 to get $4a + 6b = 14$. Then subtract $6b$ to get $4a = 14 - 6b$. If you tried to solve for the variables by adding the equations, you would find that everything was eliminated, leaving you with $0 = 0$. The key is that you need two *different* equations. You can't answer the question, so choose A.

QUIZ 3

1. **C** Subtract 5 from each side of the inequality to get $-3x > -2$. Then, divide each side by -3 to get $x < \dfrac{2}{3}$. *Remember:* You need to flip the inequality sign when you divide (or multiply) by a negative number. Choose C.

2. **A** To combine the inequalities, calculate $p - q$ using all four numbers. When $p = -2$ and $q = -1$, then $p - q = -2 - (-1) = -2 + 1 = -1$. When $p = -2$ and $q = 10$, then $p - q = -2 - 10 = -12$. When $p = 3$ and $q = -1$, then $p - q = 3 - (-1) = 3 + 1 = 4$. Finally, when $p = 3$ and $q = 10$, then $p - q = 3 - 10 = -7$. The greatest value of $p - q$ is 4 and the least value is -12, so $-12 < p - q < 4$. Choose A.

QUIZ 4

1. **C** First, factor out 4^2 in the numerator of the fraction. That gives you $\dfrac{4^2\left(4^3 + 4\right)}{4^2}$. Cancel the 4^2 in the numerator with the one in the denominator. That gives you $4^3 + 4$. Choose C.

2. **D** Plug $x = -3$ into the fraction to get $\dfrac{-27 - 9 - (-3)}{-3 + 1} = \dfrac{-27 - 9 + 3}{-2} = \dfrac{-33}{-2} = \dfrac{33}{2}$. Don't forget about the positive/negative rules for multiplication. A negative number to an even exponent will be positive and a negative number to an odd exponent will be negative. Choose D.

3. **B** Every time the number of Internet surfers doubles, you're just multiplying by 2. It will double four times in a year, so that's $2 \times 2 \times 2 \times 2$, or 2^4. You need to multiply that by the original 10^3 to get $10^3 \times 2^4$. Choose B.

Quiz 5

1. **C** When you multiply and divide roots, you can combine them under one radical sign. But you can't do that with adding or subtracting roots. So you can combine $\sqrt{10} \times \sqrt{2} = \sqrt{10 \times 2} = \sqrt{20}$. You can also combine $\dfrac{\sqrt{10}}{\sqrt{2}} = \sqrt{\dfrac{10}{2}} = \sqrt{5}$. Putting this together, you get $\sqrt{20} + \sqrt{5}$. You can factor the perfect square 4 out of 20 to get $\sqrt{20} + \sqrt{5} = \sqrt{4 \times 5} + \sqrt{5} = \sqrt{4} \times \sqrt{5} + \sqrt{5} = 2\sqrt{5} + \sqrt{5}$. Since the base is the same, you can add $2\sqrt{5} + \sqrt{5} = 3\sqrt{5}$. Choose C.

2. **A** Start with statement (1). You know that the radical sign refers only to the positive root. So $n = 5$. You can answer the question. Eliminate B, C, and E. Try statement (2). In this case, n could be either the positive root (5) or the negative root (–5). You have more than one value, so you can't answer the question. Choose A.

Quiz 6

1. **D** First, factor the numerator of the fraction. The x^2 tells that you have x and x for the first numbers inside the parentheses. The signs of the middle (+ 5x) and last numbers (+ 6) tell you that you're adding in both of the parentheses. The factors of 6 are 1 and 6 or 2 and 3. To add up to 5, you need 2 and 3. So $x^2 + 5x + 6$ factors into $(x + 2)(x + 3)$ to give you $\dfrac{(x+2)(x+3)}{x+2} = 5$. You can cancel the $x + 2$ in the numerator and the denominator of the fraction to get $x + 3 = 5$, so $x = 2$. However, the question asks for $x + 5$. So $x + 5 = 2 + 5 = 7$. Choose D.

2. **B** If you're a little nervous about factoring, this is an easy place to Plug In The Answer choices. Start with C: $1^2 - 5(1) - 6 = 0$, or $10 = 0$. That obviously doesn't work, so now you need to decide whether to try a bigger or smaller number. It doesn't take much time to substitute the values into the equation, so if you don't know whether you need a bigger or smaller number, experiment. Eventually, when you test B, you'll get: $1^2 - 5(1) - 6 = 0$, which can be simplified to $1 + 5 - 6 = 0$, or $0 = 0$. B is the right answer.

PRACTICE SET

1. **C** Find the factors of the equation in the question and then factor the answer choices until you find one that matches. The equation in the question factors to $(m + 2)(m + 2) = 0$. Answer A factors to $(m - 2)(m - 2) = 0$. Answer B factors to $(m + 3)(m + 1) = 0$. Answer C factors to $(m + 2)(m - 2) = 0$. Answer D factors to $(m + 3)(m - 2) = 0$. Answer E factors to $(m + 4)(m + 1) = 0$. The only one that matches is the $(m + 2)$ from C.

2. **E** First, multiply both sides by $1 + \dfrac{3}{x}$. This gives you $3 = 2 + \dfrac{6}{x}$. Next, multiply both sides by x to get $3x = 2x + 6$. Subtract $2x$ from both sides to get $x = 6$. Choose E.

3. **E** You can't combine exponents unless the bases are the same. So translate the 9 into 3^2. That gives you $3^{n+1} = \left(3^2\right)^{n-1}$. To raise an exponent to a power, just multiply the exponents. That gives you $3^{n+1} = 3^{2n-2}$. So $n + 1 = 2n - 2$. Add 2 to both sides to get $n + 3 = 2n$. Subtract n from each side to get $3 = n$. Choose E.

   Note: You might also try PITA on this question.

4. **D** Plug in both of the values for m and both of the values for n to get the four possible numbers. They are –14, 35, –22, and 55. The greatest value is 55 and the least value is –22, so $-22 < mn < 55$. Choose D.

5. **C** The problem says "approximates," so round off the numbers and Ballpark. The problem becomes $\sqrt{\dfrac{4 \times 50}{2}} = \sqrt{\dfrac{200}{2}} = \sqrt{100} = 10$. Choose C.

6. **D** If you didn't see the opportunity to solve the simultaneous equations here, you could also have solved by Plugging In The Answer choices. By plugging in values for y, you can derive a value for x. Then you simply substitute those numbers into the original equation to test them. Start with C. If $y = 3$, then $3 - x = 5$. So, x would equal –2. Next, plug those values for x and y into the original equation: $-2 + 3(3) = 15$. Since 7 is obviously not equal to 15, C isn't your answer. If you can't tell whether you need a bigger or smaller value for y, take a guess and find out. If you choose D, $y = 5$, which means that $x = 0$. Next plug those values into the original equation: $0 + 3(5) = 15$. True.

7. **C** Multiply both sides of the equation by $n + 6$ to get $n^2 + 6n = n - 6$. Subtract n and add 6 to both sides to get $n^2 + 5n + 6 = 0$. Surprisingly enough, that's the value you need. Choose C.

8. **B** Split the decimals and the powers of 10 into separate fractions to get

   $\dfrac{2.25}{0.15} \times \dfrac{10^a}{10^b} = 1.5 \times 10^3$. When you do the division, you get

   $15 \times \dfrac{10^a}{10^b} = 1.5 \times 10^3$. When you divide numbers with exponents, just subtract

   the exponents. So the equation becomes $15 \times 10^{a-b} = 1.5 \times 10^3$. Divide both sides

   by 15 to get $10^{a-b} = 0.1 \times 10^3$, which becomes $10^{a-b} = 10^2$. So $a - b = 2$. Choose B.

9. **A** Use FOIL to multiply these terms. You get $9 - 3\sqrt{11} + 3\sqrt{11} - 11 = 9 - 11 = -2$.
Notice that this is one of the three common patterns for quadratic equations.
Choose A.

10. **C** If you take the square root of both sides, you get $x - 2 = 10$ or $x - 2 = -10$.
Solving both of these equations, you get $x = 12$ and $x = -8$. However, the
question asks for $x + 2$, which will be $12 + 2 = 14$ or $-8 + 2 = -6$. The only answer
that matches is C.

11. **A** In statement (1), rearrange the equation to $z^2 - 6z + 9 = 0$. You can factor that
into $(z - 3)(z - 3) = 0$. Although many quadratic equations have two solutions,
this is one with only one solution, $z = 3$. The tipoff is that the two factors
(the parts in parentheses) are the same. Narrow the choices to A and D. With
statement (2), you can rearrange the equation to $z^2 + z - 12 = 0$, which factors
into $(z + 4)(z - 3) = 0$. With this equation, there are two possible solutions, $z = 3$
and $z = -4$. Since you can't determine just one value, statement (2) is insufficient.
Choose A.

12. **C** With statement (1), you don't know anything about the values of c and d. If
$c = d + 1$, so that the two exponents are equal, y could be almost anything (limited
by $y < 1$, of course), so statement (1) is insufficient. Narrow the choices to B, C, and E.
With statement (2), you can substitute $c = d$ into the equation to get $y^c = y^{c+1}$. It may
be helpful to make up some values for c to get $y^2 = y^3$ or $y^5 = y^6$. Most potential
numbers for y won't fit those equations, but two will: $y = 0$ and $y = 1$. With
two possible solutions, statement (2) is insufficient. Eliminate B. With both
statements, you can find a single value for y. From statement (2) you know that
y is either 0 or 1, and statement (1) eliminates 1 as a possible value, so $y = 0$.
Choose C.

13. **B** The question tells you that x can equal 3. So plug that into the equation to solve
for k. You get $3^2 - 7(3) + k = -5$, which becomes $9 - 21 + k = -5$. So $-12 + k = -5$,
or $k = 7$. Now you can plug the value of k into the original equation to solve for
the other possible value of x. You get $x^2 - 7x + 7 = -5$. Add 5 to each side to get
$x^2 - 7x + 12 = 0$. That factors into $(x - 4)(x - 3) = 0$. Set up the two mini-equations
$x - 4 = 0$ and $x - 3 = 0$. Solving them, you get $x = 4$ or $x = 3$. So the two possible
values for x are 4 (the new one) and 3 (which you already had). Choose B.

14. **C** Factor out a 19 in the numerator of the fraction to get $\dfrac{19(19+1)}{20} = \dfrac{19(20)}{20} = 19$.
Choose C.

15. **E** You can cancel a $(0.2)^2$ from the numerator and denominator of the fraction,
leaving you with $\dfrac{1}{(0.2)^2} = \dfrac{1}{0.04} = 25$. Choose E.

16. **B** Don't fall for the Joe Bloggs trap of 25. Add the numbers to get $\sqrt{25 + 25} = \sqrt{50}$.
Then factor out the perfect square to get $\sqrt{50} = \sqrt{25 \times 2} = \sqrt{25} \times \sqrt{2} = 5\sqrt{2}$.
Choose B.

17. **C** If you solve the inequality in statement (1), you find that $t \geq 3$. Since there are many possible values for t, that is insufficient. Narrow the choices to B, C, and E. With statement (2), you can find that $t \leq 3$. Again, there are many possible values for t. Eliminate B. With both statements, you can find the value of t. Only $t = 3$ fits both inequalities. Choose C.

18. **C** The best way to solve this problem is to work with the factors, rather than combine them into a single number and convert that to scientific notation. You know that you need some factors of 10, because it's in all of the answer choices. Split 25^6 into $(5 \times 5)^6 = 5^6 \times 5^6 = 5^{12}$. Next, combine that with the 2^{12}: The result is $5^{12} \times 2^{12} = (5 \times 2)^{12} = 10^{12}$. Since $3^4 = 81$, the overall expression is 81×10^{12} or 8.1×10^{13}, so the answer is C.

19. **A** With statement (1), you can subtract y from both sides to get $x - y = 3$. Even though you don't know the individual values of x and y, you can answer the question. Narrow the choices to A and D. With statement (2), you can factor the quadratic term to get $(x - y)(x - y) = 9$ or $(x - y)^2 = 9$. However, if you take the square root of both sides, you get two possible solutions: $x - y = 3$ and $x - y = -3$. That's not sufficient, so choose A.

20. **E** First, factor the expression in the numerator. You can take the common factor, 4^7, out of the expression, leaving $\dfrac{4^7(1 + 4 + 4^2 + 4^3)}{5}$. Next, simplify the expression in the parenthesis to $1 + 4 + 16 + 64 = 85$. So, now the expression reads $\dfrac{4^7(85)}{5}$, which reduces to $4^7(17)$. So, x must equal 17. Choose E.

9 Geometry

Although you probably studied geometry in high school, the geometry tested on the GMAT is very different. There are no proofs to memorize and regurgitate. However, there are some rules that you need to know and, as always, the GMAT writers will try to trick and confuse you.

The diagrams on problem-solving geometry questions are drawn roughly to scale, unless they say otherwise. This means that an angle that looks significantly bigger than another angle probably is. However, you should know that the computer screen may occasionally distort the diagrams a bit. Don't assume that an angle that looks like a 90-degree angle really is one. It might be 89 or 91 degrees. Also, straight lines sometimes look jagged on the screen.

The diagram on a data sufficiency question is a different story. *Never* assume that a data sufficiency diagram is drawn to scale.

Note: A significant number of GMAT questions don't provide diagrams of the figures described in the questions. Don't worry; in these cases, the questions supply the information you need to simply draw them yourself.

ANGLES AND LINES

Angles come in three flavors. Acute angles are angles of less than 90 degrees. Obtuse angles are angles of more than 90 degrees. Right angles are angles of exactly 90 degrees. A straight line makes an angle of 180 degrees.

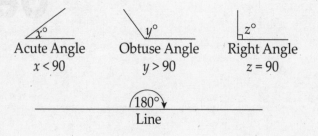

When two lines intersect, they form two kinds of angles. Supplementary angles are angles that combine to form a line. Therefore, they must add up to 180 degrees. Vertical angles are the angles across from each other. They are equal. See the diagram below.

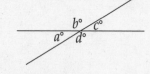

Supplementary Angles	Vertical Angles
$a + b = 180$	$a = c$
$b + c = 180$	$b = d$

Parallel lines are lines that never intersect. When two parallel lines are intersected by a third line, called a transversal, eight angles are created. However, these angles come in only two sizes. All of the big angles are equal and all of the small angles are equal. See the diagram below.

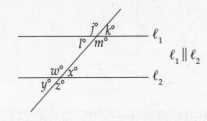

Big Angles	Small Angles
$j = m = w = z$	$k = l = x = y$

Any big angle + any small angle = 180°

QUADRILATERALS

The term quadrilateral refers to any four-sided figure. The only important rule that all quadrilaterals follow is that their four inside angles must add up to 360 degrees. There are three specific types of quadrilaterals that do follow other rules: the parallelogram, the rectangle, and the square.

Parallelograms are composed of two sets of parallel lines. Because they involve parallel lines, parallelograms follow the rule about two sizes of angles: The big angles are equal and the small angles are equal. A big angle and a small angle must add up to 180 . Additionally, each side is equal in length to the side opposite it.

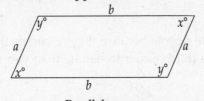

Parallelogram

Rectangles are quadrilaterals with four right angles. This also means that their opposite sides are equal. Every rectangle is also a parallelogram.

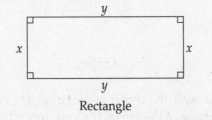

Rectangle

Squares are quadrilaterals that have four right angles and four equal sides. Every square is also a rectangle and a parallelogram.

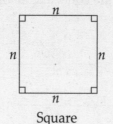

Square

The perimeter of a quadrilateral is simply the sum of all four sides. The area of a parallelogram, rectangle, or square is calculated by the following formula: *Area = Base × Height*. For rectangles, the area is sometimes expressed as *Area = Length × Width*. For squares, the area is sometimes expressed as *Area = Side²*. However, these are just different ways of saying the same thing. The one important thing to remember is that the base and height must be perpendicular (forming a right angle). This is most important with parallelograms, because the sides are not necessarily perpendicular. In that case, the height is a line from the top to the base that forms a right angle to the base. See the diagram below.

Area = Base × Height

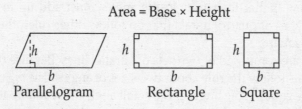

Parallelogram   Rectangle   Square

CIRCLES

Circles sometimes intimidate people because they're curves that you can't measure with a ruler. However, circles are much easier to handle than you might think. Take a look at the parts of a circle.

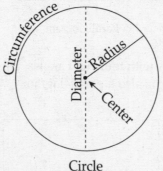

Circle

The center is the point at, well, the center of the circle. The circumference of the circle is the distance around the outside of the circle. It's very much like the perimeter of a quadrilateral or triangle. Each point on the circumference is the same distance from the center of the circle. The distance from the center of the circle to the circumference is the radius. It's a very important part of the circle because it plays a role in measuring all the other parts of the circle.

A diameter is a line that runs from the edge of the circle, through the center, to the edge on the other side. The diameter is twice the length of the radius, and it is the longest possible distance within a circle. All circles measure 360 degrees.

A chord is a line that runs from one edge of a circle to another. A diameter is a special kind of chord because it runs through the center of a circle. However, not all chords run through the center of the circle.

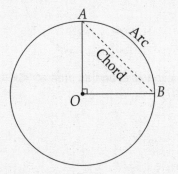

The formula for the area of a circle is $Area = \pi r^2$, where r is the radius of the circle. π is the symbol for pi, a constant. You don't need to know the exact value of pi, just that it's a little more than 3. For example, if the radius of a circle is 3, the area is $\pi(3^2) = 9\pi$, which is roughly 27. The formula for the circumference of circle is $Circumference = 2\pi r$, where r is the radius of the circle. For example, if the radius of a circle is 3, the circumference is $(2)(\pi)(3) = 6\pi$. As you can imagine, finding the radius of the circle is usually the first step in solving a circle problem.

Sometimes a geometry question will ask about a piece of a circle, like a slice of a pie.

The rule for these situations is that all the characteristics of the slice are proportional to the size of the slice. For example, if the slice is $\frac{1}{4}$ of the circle (like AOB in the diagram above), then the area of the slice is $\frac{1}{4}$ of the area of the whole circle. The arc of the slice (the piece of the circumference) is $\frac{1}{4}$ of the circumference of the whole circle. The angle of the slice is $\frac{1}{4}$ of the 360 degrees in a circle, or 90 degrees. If it's a pie, the slice has $\frac{1}{4}$ of the calories of the whole pie.

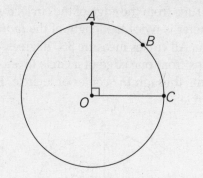

1. If the circle above has center O and an area of 36π, what is the perimeter of sector $ABCO$?

   ⬭ 6π
   ⬭ 9π
   ⬭ $6 + 3\pi$
   ⬭ $9 + 3\pi$
   ⬭ $12 + 3\pi$

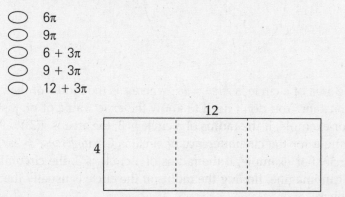

2. If a rectangle measuring 4 inches by 12 inches is cut into 3 equal rectangles, as shown above, what is the perimeter, in inches, of each of the three new rectangles?

   ⬭ $\dfrac{16}{3}$

   ⬭ $\dfrac{32}{3}$

   ⬭ 16

   ⬭ 24

   ⬭ 32

TRIANGLES

A triangle is any three-sided figure. The three angles in a triangle must add up to 180 degrees. The size of the sides corresponds to the size of the angles. The bigger sides are opposite the bigger angles, and vice versa. There are a couple of special triangles that you should know: isosceles and equilateral.

In an isosceles triangle, two of the sides are equal. Also, the two angles opposite those sides are equal. See the diagrams below.

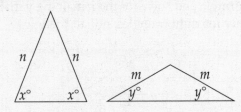

Isosceles Triangles

In an equilateral triangle, all three sides are equal. Also, all three angles are equal. Because there are 180 degrees in a triangle, each angle in an equilateral triangle measures $\frac{180}{3} = 60$ degrees. See the diagram below.

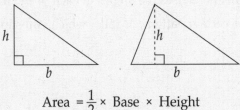

Equilateral Triangle

The perimeter of a triangle is simply the sum of the three sides. The area of a triangle is calculated by this formula: $Area = \frac{1}{2} \times Base \times Height$. As with quadrilaterals, the base must be perpendicular to the height. If two sides form a right angle, you can use those sides as the base and height. Otherwise, you'll have to draw in a line to serve as the height. See the diagrams below.

Area $= \frac{1}{2} \times$ Base $\times$ Height

RIGHT TRIANGLES

If one of the angles in a triangle is a right angle, that triangle is called a right triangle. The two short sides that form the right angle are called legs, and the longest side (the side opposite the right angle) is called the hypotenuse. The lengths of the sides of a right triangle are related by a formula called the Pythagorean theorem: $a^2 + b^2 = c^2$, in which a and b are the legs and c is the hypotenuse. If you know the length of two sides, you can use this formula to calculate the length of the third side. Just plug the two known numbers into the appropriate places in the formula and solve for the remaining variable. Remember that the Pythagorean theorem is only for right triangles, not all triangles.

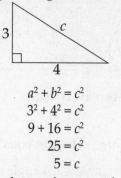

$$a^2 + b^2 = c^2$$
$$3^2 + 4^2 = c^2$$
$$9 + 16 = c^2$$
$$25 = c^2$$
$$5 = c$$

For example, in the figure above, the two known sides are 3 and 4. They go in the a and b spots in the formula because the other side, c, is the hypotenuse. Filled in, the formula now reads $3^2 + 4^2 = c^2$. When you solve the equation, you get $c = 5$.

The GMAT writers have a couple of favorite versions of the right triangle. They are the 3 : 4 : 5 right triangle and the 5 : 12 : 13 right triangle. These are nothing more than some numbers that happen to work nicely with the Pythagorean theorem to result in integers. They're just shortcuts to avoid actually making the calculation with the formula. For example, if you see a right triangle with a side of 3 and a hypotenuse of 5, you can fill in 4 for the other side without needing to do the calculation. If you see a right triangle with sides of 5 and 12 with the hypotenuse missing, you can fill in 13 for the hypotenuse. It's important to realize that 3 : 4 : 5 and 5 : 12 : 13 are ratios. So a 30 : 40 : 50 triangle works just as well. If you see a right triangle with sides of 10 and 24 with the hypotenuse missing, you can fill in 26 because it's just a 5 : 12 : 13 right triangle with everything doubled.

45-45-90 AND 30-60-90 RIGHT TRIANGLES

The GMAT frequently tests two other special cases of right triangles: the 45-45-90 and 30-60-90 right triangles. The numbers refer to the angles in each of the triangles. For each of the triangles, the sides follow a certain pattern, or ratio, which you should memorize.

The sides in a 45-45-90 right triangle (also known as an isosceles right triangle) fit the ratio $x : x : x\sqrt{2}$, in which x is the length of each leg. Use the information given to find x; then use that to find the remaining sides.

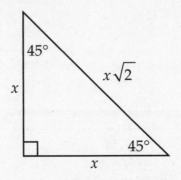

45-45-90 Right Triangle

For example, suppose you're given an isosceles right triangle with one leg having a length of 3, as shown below. That 3 corresponds to one of the x sides, so $x = 3$. That means the other two sides are 3 and $3\sqrt{2}$. Just plug in 3 for x on each side.

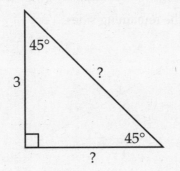

Suppose you know that the hypotenuse of a 45-45-90 triangle is $6\sqrt{2}$, as shown below. The hypotenuse is the $x\sqrt{2}$ side, so solve the equation $x\sqrt{2} = 6\sqrt{2}$ to get $x = 6$. Then plug 6 in for x on the other sides. Both will be 6.

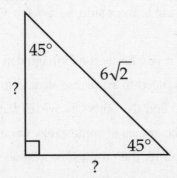

The sides of a 30-60-90 right triangle also fit a certain ratio, $x : x\sqrt{3} : 2x$.

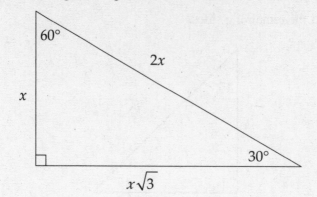

30-60-90 Right Triangle

With this pattern, it's important to be careful about which side is which. The $x, x\sqrt{3}$, and $2x$ lengths correspond to the sides across from the 30°, 60°, and 90° angles, respectively. Remember that the smallest side is across from the smallest angle and the largest side (the hypotenuse) is across from the largest angle. Use the given information to find x, and then plug that into the ratio to find the remaining sides.

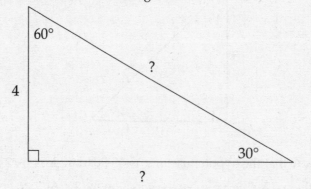

Suppose you're given a 30-60-90 triangle in which the shortest side has a length of 4, as shown above. The shortest side is the x side, so $x = 4$. The other leg is $x\sqrt{3}$, or $4\sqrt{3}$, and the hypotenuse is $2x$, or 8.

Do you need these patterns if you know the Pythagorean theorem? Yes. With the standard Pythagorean theorem, you need to know *two sides* to find the third. With the special ratios, you need only *one side* to find the others, provided the angles fit the patterns. Also, you can use the sides to find the angles in some cases. For example, if you see a triangle with sides of length 5, $5\sqrt{3}$, and 10, then it must be a 30-60-90 triangle.

THE THIRD SIDE RULE

Some GMAT questions will tell you the lengths of two sides of a triangle and ask you about the length of the third. If the triangle is a right triangle, you simply apply the Pythagorean theorem or one of the special right triangle patterns. However, these apply only to right triangles. With a non-right triangle, you cannot find the exact length of the third side using only the lengths of the other two sides, but you can determine a range for its length by using the third side rule.

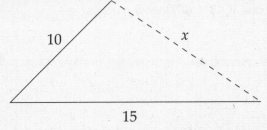

The third side rule says that the length of an unknown side of a triangle must be less than the sum of the two known sides but more than their difference. In the figure above, that means $(15 - 10) < x < (15 + 10)$, so the missing side is between 5 and 25.

Pretend that the known sides are connected by a hinge, so that they can be opened and closed like the cover of a book. The unknown side is a rubber band that expands and contracts as the known sides are opened and closed. If the known sides are fully opened so that they form a 180 angle, the unknown side will be as long as both of the known sides put together. However, that's not a triangle. To make a triangle, you must close the known sides just a bit, making the unknown side a little less than the sum of the known sides.

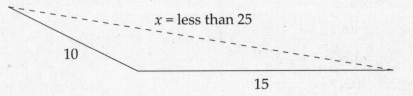

Now, completely close the known sides so that they overlap. The unknown side is the distance between their ends, or the difference in their lengths. Again, this isn't a triangle; you must open the known sides slightly. Now, the length of the unknown side is a bit more than the difference in length of the known sides.

10   x = more than 5

15

The third side rule doesn't provide an exact number for the length of the unknown side, but it does put limits on the possible length. Tough data sufficiency questions often test this sort of partial fact.

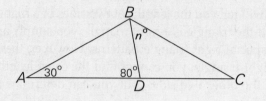

1. In the figure above, if $AB = BC$, then $n =$

   ⭕ 30°
   ⭕ 40°
   ⭕ 50°
   ⭕ 60°
   ⭕ 70°

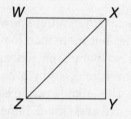

2. If square $WXYZ$ above has an area of 100, what is the length of diagonal XZ?

   ⭕ 10
   ⭕ $10\sqrt{2}$
   ⭕ $10\sqrt{3}$
   ⭕ $100\sqrt{2}$
   ⭕ $100\sqrt{3}$

OVERLAPPING FIGURES

Many geometry problems on the GMAT involve more than one geometric shape. For example, you might see a circle drawn inside a square. The key to solving these problems is to find the link between the two figures. You can see this in the following example.

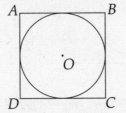

1. In the figure above, the circle with center *O* has an area of 25π. What is the area of square *ABCD* ?

    ○   5
    ○   10
    ○   25
    ○   50
    ○   100

   If the circle has an area of 25π, you can determine that the radius is 5, which makes the diameter 10. The link between the two shapes is that the diameter of the circle equals the side of the square. Try drawing a vertical diameter for the circle and seeing how it matches the vertical side of the square. So the side of the square is 10, which means that the area of the square is 10 × 10 = 100. The correct answer is E.

SHADED REGIONS

Some geometry problems deal with the area of a shaded region. Instead of treating the shaded region as a separate shape and trying to calculate its area directly, you should treat it as something formed by two overlapping shapes. Typically, its area is the remainder when you subtract the area of a smaller shape from that of a larger shape.

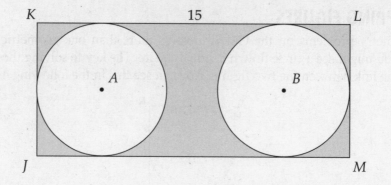

2. In the figure above, circles with centers *A* and *B* are inscribed in rectangle *JKLM*. If the area of *JKLM* is 90, what is the area of the shaded region?

- ◯ $90 - 9\pi$
- ◯ $90 - 15\pi$
- ◯ $90 - 18\pi$
- ◯ $90 - 36\pi$
- ◯ $90 - 72\pi$

The shaded region is formed by subtracting the two circles from the rectangle. Plug the rectangle's area, 90, and its length, 15, into the area formula: $A = l \times w$, or $90 = 15 \times w$. Solving, you find the width is $w = 6$. The radius of each circle is half of the rectangle's width, or 3. Plug that into the area formula for a circle: $A = \pi r^2 = \pi 3^2 = 9\pi$. The area of the shaded region is the area of the rectangle minus the area of the two circles: $90 - 9\pi - 9\pi$ or $90 - 18\pi$. The correct answer is C.

SOLIDS

Solids are three-dimensional geometric shapes, including cubes, cylinders, spheres, and so on. You may be asked to find the volume or the surface area of a solid.

VOLUME

Finding the volume of a solid is very similar to finding the area of a shape. In fact, if you think of a solid as a flat shape times one more dimension, that's how you find the volume. Just multiply the area by the extra number, which is the third dimension.

Suppose you have a rectangle with measurements of 3 by 5. The area is $3 \times 5 = 15$. If you have a rectangular solid with measurements of 3 by 5 by 6, the volume is $3 \times 5 \times 6$. A cube is just a rectangular solid with the same measurement in all three dimensions.

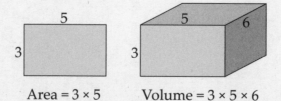

Area = 3 × 5   Volume = 3 × 5 × 6

The volume of a cylinder follows a similar pattern. Start with the area of a circle. Then, multiply by the height of the cylinder. Officially, the formula is $V = \pi \times r^2 \times h$, but that's just the area of the circle times h. In the cylinder shown on the previous page, the area of the circle is $\pi r^2 = \pi \times 3^2 = 9\pi$. To find the volume of the cylinder, multiply that area by the height of the cylinder: $9\pi \times 10 = 90\pi$. For any other solid, such as a sphere, the question will provide the formula.

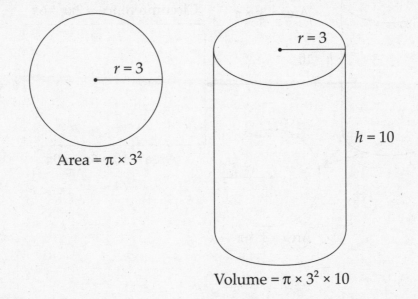

Area = $\pi \times 3^2$

$h = 10$

Volume = $\pi \times 3^2 \times 10$

SURFACE AREA

To calculate the surface area of a solid, break it up into several flat figures and find the area of each. For example, the 3 by 5 by 6 rectangular solid mentioned earlier has six faces: two are 3 by 5, two are 3 by 6, and two are 5 by 6. So the total surface area is $(3 \times 5) + (3 \times 5) + (3 \times 6) + (3 \times 6) + (5 \times 6) + (5 \times 6) = 15 + 15 + 18 + 18 + 30 + 30 = 126$.

The cylinder discussed earlier has two circular surfaces, the top and the bottom. Each circle has an area of $3^2 \times \pi = 9\pi$. When you "unroll" the vertical part of the cylinder, you get a rectangle, as shown below. (Think of unwrapping a paper towel from the roll.) The top edge of the rectangle is equal to the circumference of the circle: $2\pi r = 2 \times \pi \times 3 = 6\pi$. The vertical edge of the rectangle is the height of the cylinder: $h = 10$. Thus, the area of the rectangle is $6\pi \times 10 = 60\pi$, and the total surface area of the cylinder is $9\pi + 9\pi + 60\pi = 78\pi$.

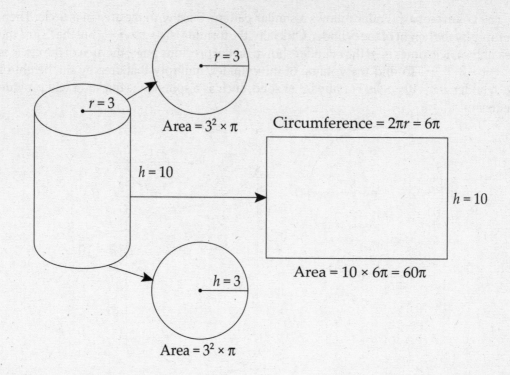

Area = $3^2 \times \pi$

Circumference = $2\pi r = 6\pi$

$r = 3$

$r = 3$

$h = 10$

$h = 10$

$h = 3$

Area = $10 \times 6\pi = 60\pi$

Area = $3^2 \times \pi$

DISTANCE

Occasionally, the GMAT will test you on the distance between two points in a three-dimensional space. This often takes the form of a diagonal line between opposite corners of a rectangular box. The formula for this is sometimes called the Super Pythagorean formula, because it is closely related to the formula for right triangles.

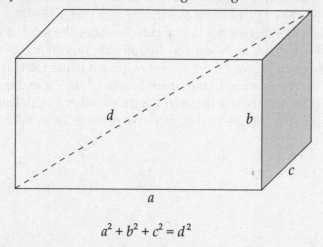

$$a^2 + b^2 + c^2 = d^2$$

The length of the diagonal line is d, and the dimensions of the box are a, b, and c. Note that it doesn't matter which dimension is called a, b, or c. Plug in the numbers for a, b, and c, and then solve for d.

1. A cube has a volume of 125 cubic inches. What is the length, in inches, of the longest line that can be drawn between any two points on the cube?

○ $5\sqrt{5}$

○ $5\sqrt{3}$

○ $5\sqrt{2}$

○ 5.5

○ 5

Start by drawing a picture of a cube. The formula for the volume of a cube is $V = s^3$, so $125 = s^3$, or $s = 5$. The longest possible line will be a diagonal between two opposite corners. That's the d in the Super Pythagorean formula. The dimensions of a cube are all equal, so plug 5 in for a, b, and c to get $5^2 + 5^2 + 5^2 = d^2$ or $25 + 25 + 25 = d^2$. Since $d^2 = 75$, then $d = \sqrt{75} = \sqrt{25} \times \sqrt{3} = 5\sqrt{3}$. So answer choice B is correct.

COORDINATE GEOMETRY

The coordinate grid is made up of an x-axis and a y-axis. When a coordinate is listed, it will be in the format of (x,y). The x number indicates the position on the x-axis and the y indicates the position on the y-axis. It's very easy to get your x and y confused. Be careful, because those reversed answers will usually be there to trap you. The following diagram demonstrates the coordinate grid and the position of a point.

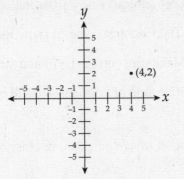

Some geometry questions provide a line on a coordinate grid and ask you to determine its length. This is really just a triangle question in disguise. To solve a problem like this, draw a right triangle, making the line in question the hypotenuse. Make each of the other sides parallel to either the *x*-axis or the *y*-axis. Look at the example below.

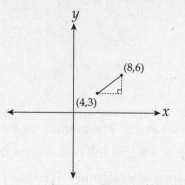

The horizontal side goes from $x = 4$ to $x = 8$, so its length is 4. The vertical side goes from $y = 3$ to $y = 6$, so its length is 3. Once you know these two values, you can use the Pythagorean theorem to find the length of the third side. In this case, it's the hypotenuse of a $3 : 4 : 5$ right triangle, so the length is 5.

SLOPE

Some questions may ask you to find the slope (*m*) of a line. The easy definition of slope is "rise over run" or $\dfrac{\text{rise}}{\text{run}}$. Rise is the change in the value of *y* between two points on the line, and run is the change in *x*. Thus, the slope formula is $\dfrac{\text{rise}}{\text{run}} = \dfrac{\text{change in } y}{\text{change in } x} = \dfrac{y_2 - y_1}{x_2 - x_1}$. Just find two points on the line, subtract one *y* from the other, and put the result in the numerator of the fraction. Then subtract one *x* from the other and put that in the denominator of the fraction. Make sure you start with the same point for both subtractions. Otherwise, the positive/negative sign of your answer will be wrong.

Here's an example.

1. If the points (5,7) and (8,13) are on a line, what is the slope of that line?

    ○   –2

    ○ $-\dfrac{1}{2}$

    ○ $\dfrac{1}{2}$

    ○   2

    ○   8

To find the slope, substitute the known values in the slope formula:

$$m = \frac{y_2 - y_1}{x_2 - x_1} = \frac{13 - 7}{8 - 5} = \frac{6}{3} = 2$$

The slope of the line is 2, which means that the line goes up two units for every one unit it goes to the right. The answer is D.

A line with a positive slope goes up to the right. A line with a negative slope goes down to the right. A horizontal line has a slope of 0 (rise is 0), and a vertical line's slope is undefined (0 in the denominator). The diagrams below illustrate each of these conditions.

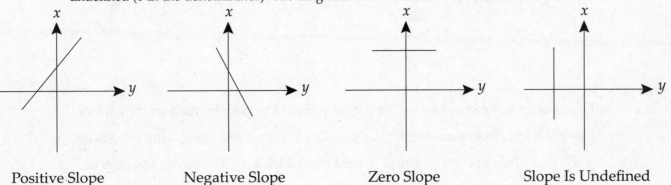

| Positive Slope | Negative Slope | Zero Slope | Slope Is Undefined |

LINE EQUATION

$$y = mx + b$$
m is the slope of the line
b is the y-intercept of the line

The equation of a line is usually expressed in the slope-intercept form $y = mx + b$, in which m and b are particular numbers defining the line. The m is the slope of the line, which you just learned to calculate. The b is called the y-intercept, and the line crosses the y-axis at the point $(0,b)$. For example, the line $y = -2x + 3$ has a slope of -2 (i.e., it goes down two units for every one unit to the right) and crosses the y-axis at the point $(0,3)$. The line $y = \frac{2}{3}x - 4$ has a slope of $\frac{2}{3}$ (i.e., goes up two units for every three units to the right) and crosses the y-axis at $(0,-4)$. If the equation for a line is not in $y = mx + b$ format, you simply need to solve the equation for y, moving all coefficients and constants to the right side of the equation.

2. What is the slope of the line defined by the equation
   $2x - 3y = 9$?

   ○ -2

   ○ $-\dfrac{2}{3}$

   ○ $\dfrac{2}{3}$

   ○ $\dfrac{3}{2}$

   ○ 2

The equation is not in $y = mx + b$ format, so you need to get y by itself on the left side.

First, subtract $2x$ from each side to get $-3y = -2x + 9$. Then, divide everything by -3 to get $y = \dfrac{2}{3}x - 3$. The slope is the number in front of x, which is $\dfrac{2}{3}$. The correct answer is C.

Every point on the line must fit the equation for that line. That means you could plug the x- and y-coordinates into the equation and everything will fit. For example, the point $(2,5)$ is on the line $y = x + 3$ because $5 = 2 + 3$. Try this example.

3. Which of the following points is the intersection between the
   lines $y = 3x + 6$ and $y = -2x - 4$?

   ○ (2,0)
   ○ (0,−2)
   ○ (−2,0)
   ○ (0,2)
   ○ (1,5)

To be the intersection of the lines, the correct answer must fit both equations. The easiest way to check this is to plug the coordinates into each equation to see whether they fit. Plugging A into the first equation, you get $0 = 3(2) + 6$, or $0 = 12$. That won't work. You don't even need to check the second equation. Plugging B into the first equation, you get $-2 = 3(0) + 6$, or $-2 = 6$. That won't work. Plugging C into the first equation, you get $0 = 3(-2) + 6$, which simplifies to $0 = -6 + 6$, or $0 = 0$. That works. Try that point in the second equation. You get $0 = -2(-2) - 4$, or $0 = 4 - 4$. That also works. C fits both equations, so it must be the right answer.

Quiz 3

1. A cylinder of wax is 20 inches tall with a radius of 1 inch. If this cylinder is melted and poured into a new cylindrical mold with a radius of 2 inches, what will be the height of the new cylinder in inches?

    ○   5
    ○   10
    ○   15
    ○   20
    ○   40

2. A line that passes through the point (2,5) has a slope of $-\dfrac{2}{3}$. Which of the following points is *not* on the line?

    ○   (11,–1)
    ○   (8,1)
    ○   (4,7)
    ○   (–1,7)
    ○   (5,3)

PRACTICE SET

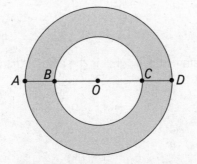

Note: Figure not drawn to scale.

1. The figure above contains two circles with center O. If $OD = 10$ and the area of the shaded region is 36π, what is the area of the smaller circle?

    ○ 6π
    ○ 10π
    ○ 36π
    ○ 64π
    ○ 100π

2. If the length of a rectangle is decreased by 10% and its width is decreased by 20%, by what percent does its area decrease?

    ◯ 30%
    ◯ 28%
    ◯ 25%
    ◯ 23%
    ◯ 15%

3. Freddy has a piece of string that is 20 inches long. He wants to use the string as the perimeter of a rectangle. What is the greatest area that rectangle could have?

    ◯   5
    ◯ 10
    ◯ 20
    ◯ 25
    ◯ 40

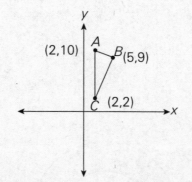

4. In the coordinate system above, what is the area of triangle *ABC* ?

    ◯ 10
    ◯ 12
    ◯ 24
    ◯ 25
    ◯ 50

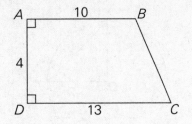

5. What is the area of quadrilateral *ABCD* above?

    ◯ 52
    ◯ 46
    ◯ 40
    ◯ 26
    ◯ 20

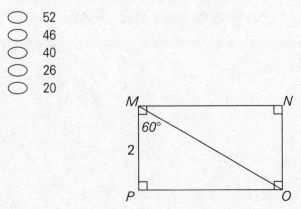

6. In rectangle *MNOP* above, if *MP* = 2, what is the length of *MO* ?

    ◯ $2\sqrt{2}$

    ◯ $2\sqrt{3}$

    ◯ 4

    ◯ 5

    ◯ 6

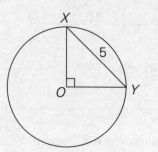

7. In the figure above, if $XY = 5$, what is the area of the circle with center O ?

○ $\dfrac{5\sqrt{2}}{2}\pi$

○ $\dfrac{25}{4}\pi$

○ $5\sqrt{2}\pi$

○ $\dfrac{25}{2}\pi$

○ 25π

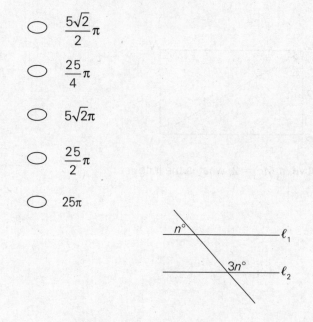

8. If ℓ_1 is parallel to ℓ_2 in the figure above, what is the value of n ?

○   30
○   45
○   60
○   105
○   135

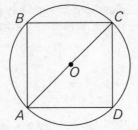

9. In the figure above, square *ABCD* has an area of 25. What is the area of the circle with center *O* ?

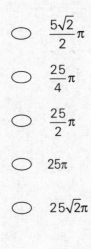

○ $\dfrac{5\sqrt{2}}{2}\pi$

○ $\dfrac{25}{4}\pi$

○ $\dfrac{25}{2}\pi$

○ 25π

○ $25\sqrt{2}\pi$

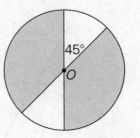

10. In the figure above, what fraction of the circle with center *O* is shaded?

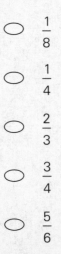

○ $\dfrac{1}{8}$

○ $\dfrac{1}{4}$

○ $\dfrac{2}{3}$

○ $\dfrac{3}{4}$

○ $\dfrac{5}{6}$

11. The hypotenuse of an isosceles right triangle has a length of h, and the triangle has an area of a. Which of the following must be true?

○ $a = 4h^2$
○ $a = 2h^2$
○ $a = h^2$
○ $4a = h^2$
○ $2a = h^2$

12. A cylinder has a volume of 180π cubic inches and the radius of its circular base is 6 inches. What is the length of the longest line segment that can be drawn from one point on the cylinder to another?

○ $\dfrac{30}{\pi}$

○ 12

○ 13

○ 5π

○ 6π

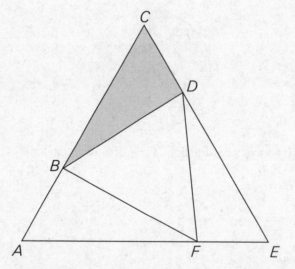

13. Equilateral triangle *BDF* is inscribed in equilateral triangle *ACE*, as shown in the figure above. The shaded region is what fraction of the area of triangle *ACE* ?

(1) $\angle DFE = 90°$
(2) The length of *AF* is $10\sqrt{3}$.

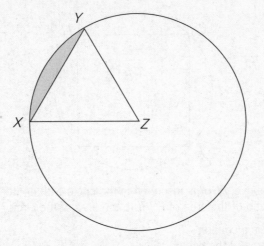

14. In the figure above, triangle *XYZ* is equilateral and has an area of $9\sqrt{3}$. Points *X* and *Y* are on the circle with center *Z*. What is the area of the shaded region?

○ $6\pi - 9\sqrt{3}$

○ $12\pi - 9\sqrt{3}$

○ $\left(9\sqrt{3} - 6\right)\pi$

○ $9\sqrt{3}\pi$

○ $36\pi - 9\sqrt{3}$

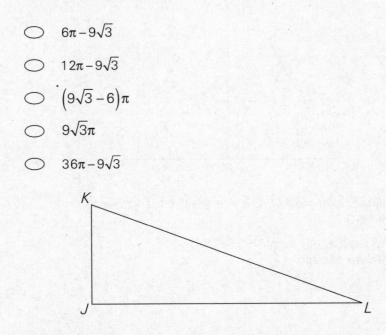

15. In the figure above, *JKL* is a right triangle. What is the area of triangle *JKL* ?

   (1) The length of *JK* is 3.
   (2) The length of *KL* is 6.

16. What is the slope of line *m* ?

   (1) The points (1,5) and (5,–7) lie on line *m*.
   (2) Line *m* is parallel to the line described by $3x + y = 17$.

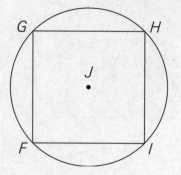

17. In the figure above, *FGHI* is inscribed in the circle with center *J*.
     What is the ratio of the area of *FGHI* to the area of the circle?

        (1) *FGHI* is a square.
        (2) The area of the circle is 8π.

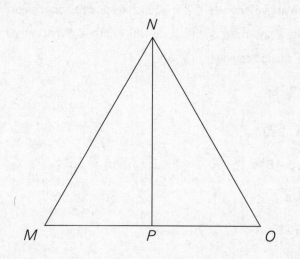

18. In the figure above, triangle *MNO* is equilateral. What is the area
     of triangle *MNO* ?

        (1) *NP* has a length of $5\sqrt{3}$.
        (2) *MN* has a length of 10.

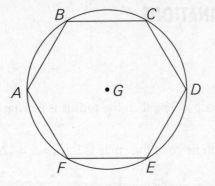

19. In the figure above, equilateral hexagon *ABCDEF* is inscribed in the circle with center *G*, which has a diameter of 16. What is the length of *AB* ?

   ○ 16
   ○ $8\sqrt{3}$
   ○ $6\sqrt{3}$
   ○ 8
   ○ $4\sqrt{3}$

20. If circle *O* is inscribed inside of equilateral triangle *T*, which of the following expresses the ratio of the radius of circle *O* to one of the sides of triangle *T* ?

   ○ 1 to 2
   ○ 1 to $\sqrt{2}$
   ○ 1 to $\sqrt{3}$
   ○ 1 to $2\sqrt{2}$
   ○ 1 to $2\sqrt{3}$

Challenge!
Take a crack at this high-level GMAT question.

ANSWERS AND EXPLANATIONS

Quiz 1

1. **E** If the area of the circle is 36π, then the radius is 6. That means $AO = 6$ and

   $CO = 6$. The circumference of the circle is $2 \times \pi \times 6 = 12\pi$. Because the slice is 90

   out of 360 degrees, it's a $\dfrac{90}{360} = \dfrac{1}{4}$ slice of the circle. So arc ABC is $\dfrac{1}{4}$ of the

   circumference, or $\dfrac{1}{4} \times 12\pi = 3\pi$. So the perimeter of the slice is

   $6 + 6 + 3\pi = 12 + 3\pi$. Choose E.

2. **C** When the side that's 12 inches is cut into three pieces, each piece will measure 4 inches. Therefore, each of the new rectangles will be a square measuring 4 inches by 4 inches. So the perimeter will be $4 + 4 + 4 + 4 = 16$ inches. The answer is C.

Quiz 2

1. **C** If $AB = BC$, then the triangle is isosceles and angle C equals angle A, measuring 30 degrees. Angles ADB and CDB form a straight line, so they must add up to 180 degrees. That means angle $CDB = 180 - 80 = 100$ degrees. You know that a triangle must add up to 180 degrees, so $n = 180 - 100 - 30 = 50$ degrees. The answer is C.

2. **B** If the square has an area of 100, then each side of the square has a length of

   $\sqrt{100} = 10$. WXZ is really a 45-45-90 right triangle, so you can apply the ratio. WX and WZ are each 10 units long, so $x = 10$. That means that XZ, the $x\sqrt{2}$

   side, is $10\sqrt{2}$ units long. Notice that you can get the same answer by just

   plugging $a = 10$ and $b = 10$ into the $a^2 + b^2 = c^2$ formula. However, you should

   also get familiar with the ratio method because there will be problems in which

   it may be the only thing you can use. Choose B.

Quiz 3

1. **A** Find the volume of the original cylinder. It's $\pi \times r^2 \times h = \pi \times 1^2 \times 20 = 20\pi$. The volume doesn't change when the shape does, so plug that volume into the formula for the new cylinder: $v = \pi \times r^2 \times h$ becomes $20\pi = \pi \times 2^2 \times h$, so $h = 5$. Choose A.

2. **C** You can start with (2,5) and work your way down the line by adding –2 to the y coordinate and 3 to the x coordinate. This leads to points (5,3), (8,1), and (11,–1). You can also start at (2,5) and work the other way by adding 2 to y and –3 to x. This leads to (–1,7). You can eliminate all those answers, leaving C as the only point not on the line. Choose C.

Alternatively, you can use the given point, (2,5), and the given slope, $m = -\dfrac{2}{3}$, to determine the line equation. Just plug those numbers into the format to get $5 = -\dfrac{2}{3}(2) + b$. You can solve that for $b = \dfrac{19}{3}$. Then you plug each point into the new line equation to see whether it fits. That way is more tedious, but it will work.

PRACTICE SET

1. **D** *OD* is the radius of the larger circle, so its area is 100π. If the shaded region is 36π, that leaves $100\pi - 36\pi = 64\pi$ for the area of the smaller circle. Choose D.

2. **B** This is not only a geometry question, but also a Plugging In question. Suppose the original length is 100 and the original width is 50. The original area is 5,000. The length is reduced by 10% to 90 and the width is reduced by 20% to 40. The new area is 3,600. That's a decrease of $5,000 - 3,600 = 1,400$. To make that a percent change, divide by the original amount: $\dfrac{1,400}{5,000} = 28\%$. Choose B.

3. **D** This is a good problem for Plugging In The Answers. Because the question asks for the *greatest* area, start with the largest answer and work your way down until you find one that works. E is too large. That rectangle would need a length and width of 2 and 20 or 5 and 8. Those are too big for a perimeter of 20. Next, try D. A rectangle with an area of 25 could have a length and width of 5 and 5, which gives a perimeter of 20. Choose D.

4. **B** Use the coordinates to determine the lengths of the necessary parts. The area of a triangle $= \dfrac{1}{2} \times$ Base $\times$ Height. Since the base must be perpendicular to the height, you can't just use two sides of the triangle. Instead use the vertical side *AC* as the base of the triangle and draw a horizontal line from the (5,9) point to the left, as in the figure below. The base *AC* has a length of 8 because it runs from $y = 2$ to $y = 10$. The height (the horizontal line you just drew) has a length of 3 because it goes from $x = 2$ to $x = 5$. So the area is $\dfrac{1}{2} \times 8 \times 3 = 12$. Choose B.

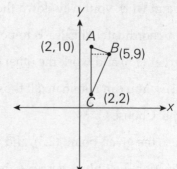

5. **B** Draw a line from B straight down to DC to split the quadrilateral into a rectangle and a triangle. See diagram below. The rectangle has a length and width of 10 and 4, for a total area of 40. The triangle has two sides of 3 and 4. They are perpendicular, so they can serve as the base and height. That gives an area of $\frac{1}{2} \times 3 \times 4 = 6$. So the total area of the quadrilateral is $40 + 6 = 46$. Choose B.

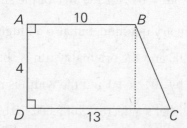

6. **C** Triangle MOP is a 30-60-90 right triangle, so use the $x : x\sqrt{3} : 2x$ ratio. MP has a length of 2 and it is the x side (the side opposite the 30-degree angle), so $x = 2$. MO is the hypotenuse, the $2x$ side, so it has a length of $2(2) = 4$. Choose C.

7. **D** The key to overlapping figures is to find the piece that bridges the two figures.

In this case, OX and OY are the legs of right triangle XOY, and they are also radii of the circle, so they are equal, which makes OXY a 45-45-90 right triangle.

Use the $x : x : x\sqrt{2}$ pattern. The hypotenuse is 5, so $x\sqrt{2} = 5$, and $x = \dfrac{5}{\sqrt{2}}$.

That means the radius of the circle is $r = \dfrac{5}{\sqrt{2}}$, and the area of the circle is $A = \pi r^2 = \pi \left(\dfrac{5}{\sqrt{2}} \right)^2 = \dfrac{25}{2} \pi$. Choose D.

8. **B** With a parallel line intersected by another line, only two sizes of angle are created. All of the big angles are equal to $3n$ and all of the small angles are equal to n. So $3n$ and n form a straight line and $3n + n = 180$. That means that $4n = 180$, so $n = 45$. Choose B.

9. **C** If the area of the square is 25, then each side of the square is 5. ABC is a 45-45-90 right triangle, so use the $x : x : x\sqrt{2}$ ratio. AB is one of the x sides, so $x = 5$. Since AC is the $x\sqrt{2}$ side, it has a length of $5\sqrt{2}$. The radius of the circle is half of AC, or $\dfrac{5\sqrt{2}}{2}$. The area of the circle is $\pi r^2 = \pi \times \left(\dfrac{5\sqrt{2}}{2}\right)^2 = \dfrac{25}{2}\pi$. Choose C.

10. **D** The two unshaded regions are vertical angles, so they are equal, at 45 degrees each. Two 45-degree slices are like one 90-degree slice, which is $\dfrac{90}{360} = \dfrac{1}{4}$ of the circle, because it covers 90 of the 360 degrees in the circle. That leaves $1 - \dfrac{1}{4} = \dfrac{3}{4}$ in the shaded region. Choose D.

11. **D** Draw your own diagram and plug in for the variables. Suppose the legs of the triangle are 3 each. The ratio for a 45-45-90 triangle is $x : x : x\sqrt{2}$. Since $x = 3$ (each leg), the hypotenuse is $h = 3\sqrt{2}$. The area of the triangle is $a = \dfrac{1}{2}$ (base)(height) $= \dfrac{1}{2} \times 3 \times 3 = \dfrac{9}{2}$, so $a = \dfrac{9}{2}$. Plug $h = 3\sqrt{2}$ and $a = \dfrac{9}{2}$ into the answers to see which one is true. In answer D, $4 \times \dfrac{9}{2} = 18$ and $\left(3\sqrt{2}\right)^2 = 18$, so choose D.

12. **C** This problem is similar to the Super Pythagorean situation. The longest line segment that can be drawn in the cylinder is one that goes from the edge of the top circle to the opposite edge of the bottom circle. That line is the hypotenuse of a right triangle formed by the height of the cylinder and the diameter of the bottom circle. The diameter of the circle is twice the radius, or $2 \times 6 = 12$ inches. Given the volume and radius of the cylinder, you can find its height. Plug in 180π for the volume and 6 for the radius into the volume formula: $v = \pi r^2 h$. The result is $180\pi = \pi \times 6^2 \times h$, which becomes $h = 5$. The legs of the right triangle are 5 and 12. That's the $5 : 12 : 13$ ratio, so the hypotenuse is 13. Choose C.

13. **A** Statement (1) tells you that $\angle DFE = 90°$, so add that to your diagram. (You did draw one on your scratch paper, didn't you?) Fill in 60° for each of the six angles forming corners of the two equilateral triangles. Because each triangle has 180°, $\angle FDE = 30°$. That leads to $\angle CDB = 90°$ and $\angle CBD = 30°$. If you keep going, you'll realize that each of the three small triangles is a 30-60-90 triangle. The middle sides of those triangles are all the same, because they're sides of an equilateral triangle. Since the triangles all follow the same 30-60-90 ratio, they are all the same size. Suppose the sides of each 30-60-90 triangle are x, $x\sqrt{3}$, and $2x$. You could use those lengths to find the area of BCD in terms of x. (It's $\dfrac{x^2\sqrt{3}}{2}$, if you're curious.) Each side of triangle ACE has a length of $x + 2x = 3x$. If you drop a height from point C, that forms another 30-60-90 triangle with a hypotenuse of $3x$. From there you can find the length of the height, allowing you to find the area of ACE, in terms of x. (It's $\dfrac{3\sqrt{3}x^2}{8}$, if you're curious.) Although you don't know the actual values, you can find the ratio of the areas. Narrow the choices to A and D. With statement (2), you're told the length of AF, but that's not enough. *Remember:* You can't trust the diagram for data sufficiency, only what you're actually told about the shapes. You don't know whether the BDF is just a bit smaller than ACE, tilted at just a slight angle, or whether BDF is much smaller than ACE, tilted at a greater angle. That will affect the size of the shaded region, so statement (2) is insufficient. Choose A.

14. **A** The easiest way to solve this one is to use Ballparking. The area of the triangle is $9\sqrt{3}$, which is about 15. From the diagram, the shaded region is much smaller than that, maybe 2 or 3. If you convert each answer, only A is anywhere close. To really solve this one, draw the height for the equilateral triangle, splitting it into two 30-60-90 triangles. That means you need the $x : x\sqrt{3} : 2x$ ratio. Using $2x$ for the base of triangle XYZ and $x\sqrt{3}$ for its height, you can set up the area formula: $9\sqrt{3} = \frac{1}{2} \cdot 2x \cdot x\sqrt{3}$. Solving that, you find $x = 3$, so each side of XYZ is 6, and so is the radius of the circle. With a radius of 6, the area of the circle is 36π. To find the shaded region, subtract the area of the triangle from the area of the slice of the circle. Since the slice has a 60-degree angle, it is a $\frac{60}{360} = \frac{1}{6}$ slice of the circle. That means its area is $\frac{1}{6} \times 36\pi = 6\pi$. So the area of the shaded region is $6\pi - 9\sqrt{3}$. Wasn't Ballparking a much simpler approach? Choose A.

15. **E** With statement (1), you have only one side of the triangle. If that is the height, you still need the base to find the area. Statement (1) is insufficient, so narrow your choices to B, C, and E. Statement (2) presents a similar situation: You have only one side, and you need a base and a height to find the area. Eliminate B. With both sides, it may appear that you have enough information. It seems that you could plug 3 and 6 into the Pythagorean theorem to find the length of JL and then use the area formula. However, you don't know which angle in the triangle is 90 degrees. In the figure, it appears that KL is the hypotenuse, but you can't be sure. If it is the hypotenuse, you get one answer, and if it's not the hypotenuse, you get another. Therefore, eliminate C and choose E.

16. **D** With statement (1), you could calculate the slope by using the x- and y-coordinates of the two points in the rise-over-run formula. $m = \frac{-7-5}{5-1} = \frac{-12}{4} = -3$. That's sufficient, so narrow the choices to A and D. With statement (2), you can manipulate the equation of the second line to $y = -3x + 17$, so its slope is -3. Since the lines are parallel, the first line's slope is also -3. Statement (2) is also sufficient, so choose D.

17. **A** With statement (1), you know the square-looking shape is actually a square. That means the diameter of the circle is equal to the diagonal of the square. You could plug in numbers, such as $s = 2$ for the side of the square. Using the 45-45-90 ratio, the diagonal would be $2\sqrt{2}$, which gives the circle a radius of $\sqrt{2}$. Since you know the side of the square and the radius of the circle, you could find their areas and compare them in a ratio. Statement (1) is sufficient, so narrow the choices to A and D. With statement (2), you know the actual area of the circle, but you don't know anything about *FGHI*. It could be a square, as it appears, or it could be a very skinny rectangle with little area. Since its area is changeable, you cannot find the ratio of its area to that of the circle. Statement (2) is insufficient, so choose A.

18. **B** Statement (1) may appear to be sufficient. Since the triangle is equilateral, its height will divide it into two 30-60-90 triangles. If you know one of the sides, you can use the 30-60-90 ratio to find the other sides. However, you don't know that *NP* is the height of the triangle. It appears that way in the figure, but there's no concrete indication that it forms a right angle with *MO*. Statement (1) is insufficient, so narrow your choices to B, C, and E. With statement (2), you have the length of *MN*. Since the triangle is equilateral, you can draw the height and use the 30-60-90 ratio find its length (which turns out to be $5\sqrt{3}$) and, subsequently, the area of the triangle. Statement (2) is sufficient, so choose B.

19. **D** Start by drawing a line from the center of the circle to each corner of the hexagon, like spokes of a wheel. Since the hexagon is equilateral, each angle formed by the spokes is equal. There are six of them, so each one is $\frac{360}{6} = 60°$. Each spoke is a radius of the circle, so they are all equal, meaning that the outer angles of each triangle are equal. Since 60° is already accounted for by the inner angle, each outer angle must be $\frac{120}{2} = 60°$. So each triangle is an equilateral triangle with sides equal to the radius of the circle, which is 8. Therefore, *AB* has a length of 8. Choose D.

20. **E** First, draw the height of the equilateral triangle from the tip of the triangle to the base. Since the triangle is equilateral, the height will create a 30 degree angle at the topmost angle. Now, notice that the height passes through the center of the circle. Draw the radius of the circle from the center of the circle to the side on the right. Since the circle is inscribed within the triangle, the radius will create a 90 degree angle at the point it touches the side of the triangle. Now, notice that you have created a right triangle with angle measurements 30, 60, and 90. So, set the radius, which is across from the 30 degree angle, to 1. Since the ratio of the sides of a 30-60-90 right triangle are 1, $1\sqrt{3}$, 2, you can set the side across from the 60 degree angle, or half the side of the equilateral triangle, equal to $1\sqrt{3}$. So, the side of the triangle is $2\sqrt{3}$. The ratio is therefore 1 to $\sqrt{3}$. Choose E.

10
Data Sufficiency 2

In Chapter 3, you learned about the data sufficiency format and the "AD or BCE" method that you should use to tackle it. In this chapter, you will see some more sophisticated techniques that will help you with specific types of data sufficiency questions.

SIMULTANEOUS EQUATIONS

In Chapter 8, you learned how to solve simultaneous equations that involve two variables. Here's the general rule for solving simultaneous equations: You need as many distinct equations as you have variables. For example, to solve for two variables, you need two distinct equations. To solve for three variables, you need three distinct variables.

For data sufficiency questions, you don't actually need to solve the equations; you just need to realize when you have enough information to do so. The key is recognizing equations and variables. In some cases, such as the following example, it's relatively easy.

1. If $x + y = 7$, what is x ?

    (1) $x - y = 1$
    (2) $y + z = 11$

Statement (1) is sufficient because you now have two distinct equations. That's enough to solve for both variables and answer the question. Narrow it down to A and D. Statement (2) is not sufficient, because it introduces a *third* variable and you only have *two* equations. You can't solve it, so A is the correct answer.

In other cases, identifying the variables and the equations becomes more difficult. Look at this next example.

2. Angela goes shopping. If she buys a total of 7 hats and belts, how many hats did she buy?

    (1) Angela buys one more hat than she does belts.
    (2) Angela buys a total of 11 belts and skirts.

This question has two variables: the number of hats and the number of belts. It also has one equation, hats + belts = 7. Statement (1) has one equation, hats − 1 = belts. Statement (2) has one equation, belts + skirts = 11, and one more variable, the number of skirts. It's essentially the same as question 1, just disguised as a word problem. The correct answer is also A. If you can spot the variables and equations in word problems, data sufficiency questions will be come much easier.

As mentioned above, to solve for the variables in simultaneous equations, you must have *distinct equations*. In other words, the equations must not be multiples of each other. For example, the equation $2x + 2y = 4$ is a multiple of the equation $x + y = 2$. (If you multiply both sides of the equation $x + y = 2$ by 2, you end up with the first equation, $2x + 2y = 4$.)

Here's an example:

3. What is the value of x ?

   (1) $2x + 4y = 16$

   (2) $6x + 12y = 48$

Statement (1) is only one equation with two variables. Therefore, it's not sufficient to solve for x. So, narrow your answers to B, C, and E. Statement (2) gives you only one equation with two variables, so it is also not sufficient, and you can eliminate choice B. At first glance you may think the answer is C, but don't be so hasty. Although you have two equations, the second equation is simply the first equation multiplied by 3. Since it is therefore a multiple of the first equation, the two equations are not distinct. Therefore, the answer is E.

OVERLAPPING RANGES

For a statement to answer the question, it must provide a single value for the number asked. If a statement narrows down the possibilities to a few numbers, but not just one, it is not sufficient to answer the question. However, if each statement narrows the possibilities to a small set and there is only one value in common, then those statements together are sufficient. Look at the following example:

1. What is x ?

   (1) x is an odd integer between 0 and 10.
   (2) x is a multiple of 5.

Statement (1) tells you that x is 1, 3, 5, 7, or 9; however, that's not a single value, so you can't answer the question. Narrow the answers to B, C, and E. Statement (2) tells you that x is 5, 10, 15, 20, 25, or some other multiple of 5. However, that's not a single value. Eliminate B. Both statements together are sufficient. The only value they share is 5, so x must equal 5. Choose C.

Quiz 1

1. What is the value of even integer n ?

   (1) $\sqrt{n}$ is an integer.
   (2) $20 < n < 50$

2. If a student's total cost for a semester's tuition, fees, and books was $11,250, how much was his cost for books that semester?

   (1) The cost for fees was 15 percent of the cost for tuition.
   (2) The combined cost for books and fees was 25 percent of the cost for tuition.

Remember!
For Data Sufficiency problems in this book, we do not supply the answer choices. The five possible answer choices are the same every time.

PIECES OF THE PUZZLE

The answer to a data sufficiency problem revolves around which pieces of information are sufficient to answer the question posed. If you can determine which pieces of information are missing, you can more easily recognize which statement(s) contain(s) those pieces of information. Identify the value for which the question asks and determine which numbers you need to get there. It's like putting together a jigsaw puzzle.

Look at this next example:

1. If Steve owns red, blue, and green marbles in the ratio of
    2 : 3 : 5, respectively, how many blue marbles does he own?

    (1) Steve owns 20 red marbles.
    (2) Steve owns a total of 100 red, blue, and green marbles.

Before you even look at the statements, try to figure out what information you'll need to answer the question. You know that a ratio plus any of the actual values will allow you to find all the other actual values. So look for actual values as you check each statement.

Statement (1) contains an actual value, so it is sufficient. Narrow the choices to A and D. Statement (2) has an actual value, so it is sufficient. The answer must be D.

This approach works well with any data sufficiency problem involving a formula of some sort. For example, many geometry questions involve some sort of formula. Look at the following example:

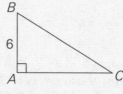

2. In triangle *ABC* above, the length of *AB* is 6. What is the area of triangle *ABC* ?

    (1) The length of *BC* is 10.
    (2) The length of *AC* is 8.

To calculate the area of a triangle, you need to know the base and the height. The question provides the height, so the missing piece is the base, *AC*. A statement that gives you the length of *AC* or allows you to calculate it is sufficient.

Statement (1) gives you the length of *BC*. Because *ABC* is a right triangle, you can use any two sides and the Pythagorean theorem to find the length of the third side. With (1) you have two sides so you can find *AC* and calculate the area. (*Note:* You may also have noticed that this triangle is a right triangle with its sides in the ratio 3 : 4 : 5. So you could calculate the length of *AC* without using the Pythagorean theorem, if you like.) Narrow the choices to A and D. Statement (2) tells you the length of *AC*. You can calculate the area, so choose D.

The pieces-of-the-puzzle approach is extremely useful for simplifying a tough data sufficiency question. By identifying the particular thing you need, you can focus on that while looking at the statements, rather than thinking through the whole process of solving the problem.

YES/NO QUESTIONS

Most of the data sufficiency questions you've seen so far ask for a specific value such as "What is x?" However, you will see some questions that ask not for a numerical value but for a *yes* or *no* answer. For example, look at the question below:

1. Is x an odd integer?

    (1) x is divisible by 3.
    (2) x is divisible by 2.

The question doesn't ask for the value of x. Instead it asks a yes/no question. A sufficient answer is either "Yes, x is odd," or "No, x is not odd." It's important to realize that "No" is an acceptable answer. The insufficient answer is "I can't tell from the information."

In the above question, look at statement (1). If x is divisible by 3, it could be odd (such as 3, 9, or 15) or even (such as 6, 12, or 18). From statement (1) you cannot tell for certain whether x is odd or not. You can't answer the question, so narrow the choices to B, C, and E. From statement (2), you know that x is even, so the answer to the question is "No, x is not odd." You have answered the question, so choose B. *Remember:* "No" is a sufficient answer.

Yes/No questions are among the most difficult on the Math section, mostly because they are very tricky. As you look at each statement, be sure to consider all of the possibilities that are consistent with the information in that statement. Considering only the obvious numbers will generally lead you directly to a trap answer.

2. If ABC and DEF are triangles, and the length of AB is greater than that of DE, is the area of ABC greater than that of DEF ?

    (1) The length of BC is greater than that of EF.
    (2) The length of AC is greater than that of DF.

Start by considering statement (1). You know that two sides of ABC are bigger than two sides of DEF. It makes sense that ABC could be greater in area than DEF. Just imagine stretching DEF in all directions and that could be ABC. But is ABC necessarily greater in area than DEF? A lot depends on that unknown third side for each triangle. Suppose that AC is tiny, so that ABC is a long, narrow wedge, as shown in ABC below. The area of DEF could be bigger than that of ABC in such a case, so you can't tell for certain whether or not ABC is bigger. "I can't tell" is insufficient, so write down B, C, and E.

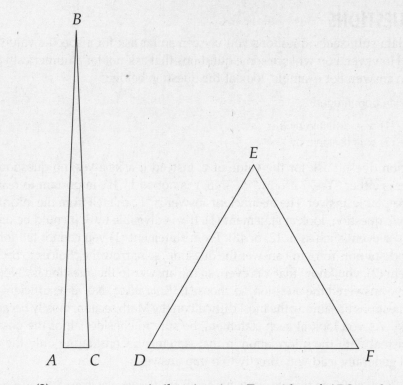

Statement (2) sets up a very similar situation. Two sides of *ABC* are bigger than two sides of *DEF*, but the third side of each is completely unknown. By the same reasoning you used with statement (1), statement (2) is insufficient. Cross off B.

Now put both statements together. Each side of *ABC* is bigger than the corresponding side of *DEF*. It seems natural to think that the area of *ABC* is bigger than that of *DEF*. That certainly *could* be true, but does it *have* to be true? No. Again, you need to imagine all of the possibilities. *ABC* could be very thin, even if all three sides are relatively long, as shown below.

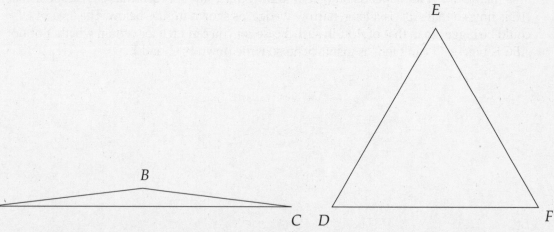

In the extreme case, the area of *ABC* is almost zero. Statements (1) and (2) together are still insufficient, even though your initial response says otherwise, so the answer is E. The key is to acknowledge the obvious possibility, but then to explore the counterintuitive possibilities.

PLUGGING IN FOR YES/NO DATA SUFFICIENCY

The Plugging In technique can be applied to Yes/No data sufficiency questions. It is very helpful in sorting out whether a particular statement leads always to "yes" or always to "no" or to "I can't tell." If a fact statement for a Yes/No question contains a variable, try plugging in various values for that variable to see whether you get "yes" or "no" in answer to the question. Be certain that you plug in only numbers that are consistent with the statement under consideration and with any information in the initial setup.

3. Is $xy < 0$?

    (1) $x < 0$
    (2) $y = x^2$

With statement (1), you know that x is negative. However, you don't know anything about y. If you plug in $x = -1$ and $y = -2$, then $xy = 2$, which is a "no" answer. On the other hand, you could plug in $x = -1$ and $y = 3$ to get $xy = -3$, which is a "yes" answer. Statement (1) is inconclusive, so write down B, C, and E.

With statement (2), you know that $y = x^2$. If $x = -2$, then $y = 4$ and $xy = -8$; that's a "yes." However, x could be positive. You need to forget statement (1) for the moment. If $x = 2$, then $y = 4$ and $xy = 8$, which is a "no" answer. Statement (2) overall leads to "I can't tell," so eliminate B.

With both statements, you know that x is negative and $y = x^2$. If $x = -2$, then $y = 4$ and $xy = -8$, which leads to "yes." No matter what negative number you plug in for x, y will be positive, making xy negative. Since you always get "yes," both statements together are sufficient, and the correct answer is C.

Plugging in numbers will be most effective when you select numbers carefully. Think about what types of numbers or combinations lead to "yes" answers versus those that lead to "no" answers. Then see whether both types of numbers are consistent with the statement you are considering. In the previous example, the issue was positive/negative, so you needed to see whether you could plug in both positive and negative numbers at each step.

QUIZ 2

1. Is it true that $x < y$?

    (1) $5x < 5y$
    (2) $xz < yz$

2. If p is a positive integer, is p even?

    (1) $4p$ is even.
    (2) $p + 2$ is odd.

PRACTICE SET

1. What is the value of n ?

    (1) $n^2 + 5n + 6 = 0$
    (2) $n^2 - n - 6 = 0$

2. If x and y are integers, does $x = y$?

    (1) $xy = y^2$
    (2) $x^2 = y^2$

3. Kevin buys beer in bottles and cans. He pays $1.00 for each can of beer and $1.50 for each bottle of beer. If he buys a total of 15 bottles and cans of beer, how many bottles of beer did he buy?

    (1) Kevin spent a total of $18.00 on beer.
    (2) Kevin bought 3 more cans of beer than bottles of beer.

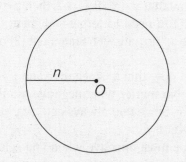

4. What is the area of the circle with center O above?

    (1) The circumference of the circle is 12π.
    (2) $n = 6$

5. Pete works at three part-time jobs to make extra money. What are his average earnings per hour?

    (1) Pete earned $500 for 20 hours at the first job, $150 for 10 hours at the second job, and $100 for 5 hours at the third job.
    (2) Pete earned an average of $25 per hour at the first job, $15 per hour at the second job, and $20 per hour at the third job.

6. If p is an integer, is p positive?

    (1) $pq > 0$ and $qr < 0$
    (2) $pr < 0$

7. If x is an integer, what is the value of x ?

    (1) x is the square of an integer.
    (2) $0 < x < 5$

8. If m and n are integers, is $mn \leq 6$?

    (1) $m + n = 5$
    (2) $1 \leq m \leq 3$ and $2 \leq n \leq 4$

9. If $2x + 3y = 11$, what is the value of x ?

    (1) $5x - 2y = 18$
    (2) $6y - 22 = -4x$

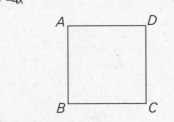

10. Is quadrilateral $ABCD$ above a square?

    (1) $AB = BC$
    (2) Angle ABC is a right angle.

11. At a certain baseball game, each of the spectators is either a Bullfrogs fan or a Chipmunks fan, and no one is both. What is the ratio of Bullfrogs fans to Chipmunks fans among spectators at the baseball game?

    (1) The number of Chipmunks fans among the spectators is 20% greater than the number of Bullfrogs fans.
    (2) The total number of spectators at the baseball game is 4,400.

12. What is the value of $x + y$?

    (1) $x - y = 70$
    (2) $x = 170 - y$

13. A pizzeria serves pizzas in three sizes: small, medium, and large. On Tuesday, the pizzeria served a total of 280 pizzas. How many large pizzas did the pizzeria serve on Tuesday?

    (1) On Tuesday, the pizzeria served 25% more small pizzas than medium pizzas.
    (2) On Tuesday, the number of medium pizzas served by the pizzeria was 80% of the number of large pizzas.

14. Is $\dfrac{1}{a} < \dfrac{1}{b+1}$?

 (1) $a = b$
 (2) $b > 0$

15. If x is a positive integer, is $x^2 - 1$ divisible by 3 ?

 (1) x is even.
 (2) x is divisible by 3.

16. If m and n are positive integers and $mn = 30$, what is the value of $m + n$?

 (1) $\dfrac{m}{5}$ is an integer.

 (2) $\dfrac{n}{2}$ is an integer.

17. What is the value of $\dfrac{a^2 b}{c}$?

 (1) $a = \dfrac{1}{b}$ and $c = \dfrac{1}{a}$.

 (2) $b = c$ and $a = 4c$.

18. Is 3^{p-2} greater than 1,000 ?

 (1) $3^{p+1} < 54{,}000$
 (2) $3^p < 3^{p-1} + 2{,}000$

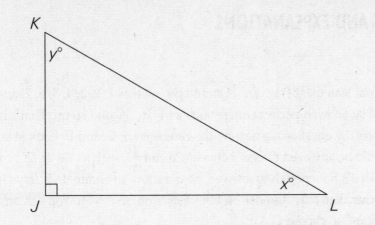

19. In right triangle *JKL*, shown above, what is the length of *KL* ?

    (1) The length of *JK* is 5.
    (2) $y = 2x$

20. If *f* is a positive integer, is $\sqrt{f+1}$ an integer?

    (1) *g* is an integer and $f = (g + 1)(g - 1)$.

    (2) *g* is an integer and $\dfrac{f+1}{g}$ is an integer.

Challenge!
Take a crack at this high-level GMAT question.

ANSWERS AND EXPLANATIONS

Quiz 1

1. **C** Look at statement (1). $\sqrt{n}$ is an integer such as 1, 2, 3, 4, 5, 6, 7, and so on. So n must be an even perfect square such as 4, 16, 36, and so on. That's not enough to answer the question, so narrow the choices to B, C, and E. Look at statement (2). n could be any even integer between 20 and 50, such as 22, 24, 26, and so on. That's not enough to answer the question, so eliminate B. Try (1) and (2) together. The only number on both lists is 36, so $n = 36$. You can answer the question, so choose C.

2. **C** The question itself provides one equation and contains three variables. Look at statement (1). This gives you a second equation. However, you need three equations to solve for three variables. You can't answer the question, so narrow the choices to B, C, and E. Look at statement (2). This provides another equation. However, you still have only two equations for three variables. You can't answer the question, so eliminate B. Try (1) and (2) together. Now you have three distinct equations and you can solve for all three variables. You can answer the question, so choose C.

Quiz 2

1. **A** Start with statement (1). If you divide both sides of the inequality by 5, you get $x < y$. So the answer to the question is "yes." Narrow the choices to A and D. Look at statement (2). The problem here is that you don't know what kind of number z is. If you plug in a positive number, such as $z = 4$, you get $x < y$ when you divide both sides by z. If you plug in a negative number, such as $z = -3$, then you get $x > y$ when you divide both sides by z. *Remember*: You have to flip the inequality sign when you multiply or divide by a negative number. You can't answer the question, so choose A.

2. **B** Look at statement (1). p could be either an odd number, such as $p = 3$, or an even number, such as $p = 2$. Both numbers fit the statement, so you can't answer the question. Narrow the choices to B, C, and E. Look at statement (2). You can plug in odd numbers such as $p = 3$. However, you can't plug in even numbers because they won't fit the statement. So p is odd and the answer is "no." You can answer the question, so choose B.

Practice Set

1. **C** Look at statement (1). If you factor it, you get $(n + 2)(n + 3) = 0$, which means that $n = -2$ or -3. That's not a single value, so you can't answer the question. Narrow the choices to B, C, and E. Try statement (2). This factors to $(n + 2)(n - 3) = 0$, so $n = -2$ or 3. This isn't a single value, so you can't answer the question. Eliminate B. Try (1) and (2) together. The only number that is on both lists is -2, so $n = -2$. You can answer the question, so choose C.

2. **C** Look at statement (1). If you plug in a positive number for y, such as $y = 2$, then $x = y$ and the answer is "yes." Same thing if you use a negative number, such as $y = -2$. However, if you plug in $y = 0$, then x could equal anything, so "no" is a possibility. You can't answer the question, so narrow the choices to B, C, and E. Try statement (2). If you plug in two positive numbers, such as $x = 2$ and $y = 2$, then $x = y$ and the answer is "yes." If you plug in a positive number and a negative number, such as $x = 2$ and $y = -2$, then the answer is "no." You can't answer the question, so eliminate B. Try (1) and (2) together. The only numbers that will fit both statements are those in which $x = y$. You can't use a positive and a negative because that won't fit statement (1). You can't use 0 for y and something else for x, because that won't fit statement (2). It must be true that $x = y$. The answer is "yes," so choose C.

3. **D** The question provides two variables, bottles and cans, and one equation, bottles + cans = 15. Look at statement (1). This provides another equation, $(1 \times \text{cans}) + (1.5 \times \text{bottles}) = 18$. You have two equations for two variables, so you can answer the question. Narrow the choices to A and D. Look at statement (2). This provides another equation, cans − 3 = bottles. You have two equations for two variables, so you can answer the question. Choose D.

4. **D** You know that the formula for the area of a circle is $A = \pi r^2$, so the missing piece is the radius. Look for that as you go through the statements. In statement (1), you're given the circumference, so you can solve for the radius by plugging $C = 12\pi$ into the equation $C = 2\pi r$. You can answer the question, so narrow the choices to A and D. Look at statement (2). This gives you the radius. You can answer the question, so choose D.

5. **A** To find an average, you need to know the total and the number of elements. So the missing pieces are the total money earned and the number of hours. Look for those in the statements. In statement (1) you can find both the total money earned and the number of hours worked. You can answer the question, so narrow the choices to A and D. Look at statement (2). You can find neither the total money earned nor the number of hours worked. *Remember:* Never average the averages. You can't answer the question, so choose A.

6. **E** Look at statement (1). You could plug in positive numbers for p and q and that would make r negative. The answer would be "yes." Or you could plug in negative numbers for p and q and that would make r positive. In that case, the answer would be "no." You can't answer the question, so narrow the choices to B, C, and E. Look at statement (2). You could plug in a positive number for p and a negative number for r and the answer would be "yes." Or you could plug in a negative number for p and a positive number for r and the answer would be "no." You can't answer the question, so eliminate B. Try (1) and (2) together. You could plug in $p = +$, $q = +$, and $r = -$. That would fit both statements and the answer would be "yes." Or you could plug in $p = -$, $q = -$, and $r = +$. That would fit both statements and the answer would be "no." You can't answer the question, so choose E.

7. **E** Look at statement (1). *x* must be a perfect square, such as 1, 4, 9, 16, and so on. However, you can't narrow it down to a single value. You can't answer the question, so narrow your choices to B, C, and E. Look at statement (2). *x* could be 1, 2, 3, or 4. You can't answer the question, so eliminate B. Try (1) and (2) together. Although the lists overlap, they share more than one value. *x* could be either 1 or 4. You can't answer the question, so choose E.

8. **A** Look at statement (1). If you plug in *m* = 1 and *n* = 4, then *mn* = 4 and the answer is "yes." If you plug in *m* = 2 and *n* = 3, then *mn* = 6 and the answer is "yes." If you plug in *m* = –5 and *n* = 10, then *mn* = –50 and the answer is "yes." Any numbers that will fit the statement will give you a "yes" answer. You can answer the question, so narrow the choices to A and D. Look at statement (2). If you plug in *m* = 1 and *n* = 2, then *mn* = 2 and the answer is "yes." If you plug in *m* = 3 and *n* = 4, then *mn* = 12 and the answer is "no." You can't answer the question, so choose A.

9. **A** The question provides one equation and two variables. Look at statement (1). This gives you another equation. With two equations for two variables, you can solve for *x*. You can answer the question, so narrow the choices to A and D. Look at statement (2). Although this seems to give you another equation, it really doesn't. The equation in (2) is the equation from the question rearranged and multiplied by 2. If you tried to set up the simultaneous equations and solve them, everything would cancel and you'd be stuck. *Remember:* You need a distinct equation for each variable. You can't answer the question, so choose A.

10. **E** Look at statement (1). It's possible that *ABCD* is a square. You could make all four sides equal and make all four angles right angles. However, it's also possible that it's not a square. Just because *AB* = *BC* doesn't mean that the other two sides are also the same. Don't let the diagram fool you. It's not necessarily drawn to scale. You can't answer the question, so narrow the choices to B, C, and E. Look at statement (2). By itself, this doesn't tell you much. It might be a square, but you don't know whether the sides are all the same or whether the other angles are also right angles. You can't answer the question, so eliminate B. Try (1) and (2) together. It might be a square, but it doesn't have to be. The other three angles don't have to be right angles and *CD* and *AD* might not equal *AB* and *BC*. See the diagram below. You can't answer the question, so choose E.

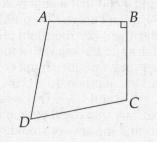

11. **A** Start by thinking about the pieces of the puzzle. You need the ratio of Bullfrogs fans to Chipmunks fans. Knowing both numbers would be enough, as it would be to know just the ratio itself. With statement (1), you can't find both numbers, because there are two variables but only one equation. However, you can find the ratio. Translate the statement to $c = 120\% \times b$, which becomes $\dfrac{c}{b} = \dfrac{120}{100}$. You can flip that upside down to get the ratio you want. Since (1) is sufficient, narrow the choices to A and D. With statement (2), you get the total number of spectators, but that doesn't help you with the number of either type of fan or the ratio of the two. Choose A.

12. **B** Start by thinking about the pieces of the puzzle that you need. You could answer the question either by knowing both numbers, x and y, or by knowing just their sum. With statement (1), you can't find both numbers; there are two variables and only one equation. You also can't manipulate the equation to get $x + y$ equal to some number. Since (1) is insufficient, narrow the choices to B, C, and E. With statement (2), you still can't solve for both variables, because there is only one equation. However, you can add y to both sides to get $x + y = 170$. That's sufficient to answer the question, so choose B.

13. **C** From the initial setup, you can derive the equation $s + m + l = 280$. With statement (1), you can get the equation $s = 125\% \times m$. However, you have only two equations, but three variables. You can't solve for l, so narrow the choices to B, C, and E. With statement (2), you can derive the equation $m = 80\% \times l$. However, that's still only two equations for three variables. Since (2) is insufficient, eliminate B. With both statements, you now have three variables for three equations. That's enough to solve for all three variables. Choose C.

14. **C** Tackle Yes/No questions by plugging in various numbers. With statement (1), both a and b could be 1, in which case the question becomes "Is $\dfrac{1}{1} < \dfrac{1}{2}$?" and the answer is "no." If both a and b are –1, then the question becomes "Is $-\dfrac{1}{1} < -\dfrac{1}{2}$?" and the answer is "yes." Statement (1) is insufficient, so narrow the choices to B, C, and E. With statement (2), knowing that b is positive doesn't tell you anything about a. If $a = 1$ and $b = 1$, the answer is "no." If $a = –1$ and $b = 1$, the answer is "yes." Since (2) is insufficient, eliminate B. With both statements, both a and b are equal and positive. If you plug in various numbers, such as $a = b = 1$ or $a = b = 5$, you'll always get "no." That answers the question, so choose C.

15. **B** With Yes/No questions, try Plugging In. For statement (1), if $x = 2$, then $x^2 - 1 = 3$, which is divisible by 3. If $x = 6$, then $x^2 - 1 = 35$, which is not divisible by 3. Since you can get both "yes" and "no," statement (1) is insufficient and you should narrow the choices to B, C, and E. For statement (2), if $x = 3$, then $x^2 - 1 = 8$, which is not divisible by 3. If $x = 6$, then $x^2 - 1 = 35$, which is not divisible by 3. For any x that is divisible by 3, the result is not divisible by 3, so the answer is "no." That's sufficient, so choose B.

16. **E** If $mn = 30$, then m and n could be any of the factors of 30: 1, 2, 3, 5, 6, 10, 15, or 30. With statement (1), m could be 5, making $n = 6$ and $m + n = 11$. If $m = 10$, then $n = 3$ and $m + n = 13$. m could also be 15 or 30. Since there is more than one answer, narrow the choices to B, C, and E. With statement (2), n could be 2, 6, 10, or 30. Each possibility leads to a different value for $m + n$, so (2) is insufficient; eliminate B. With both statements together, you could have $m = 15$ and $n = 2$, so $m + n = 17$. However, $m = 5$ and $n = 6$, with $m + n = 11$, also works. That's insufficient, so choose E.

17. **C** Try Plugging In. With statement (1), if $a = 1$, then $b = 1$ and $c = 1$, so $\dfrac{a^2 b}{c} = 1$.

However, if $a = 2$, then $b = \dfrac{1}{2}$ and $c = \dfrac{1}{2}$, so $\dfrac{a^2 b}{c} = \dfrac{2^2 \times \frac{1}{2}}{\frac{1}{2}} = 4$. Since more

than one answer is possible, (1) is insufficient. Narrow the choices to B, C, and

E. With statement (2), if $b = c = 1$, then $a = 4$, so $\dfrac{a^2 b}{c} = \dfrac{4^2 \times 1}{1} = 16$. However, if

$b = c = 2$, then $a = 8$, so $\dfrac{a^2 b}{c} = \dfrac{8^2 \times 2}{2} = 64$. More than one value is possible, so

eliminate B. With both statements together, Plugging In is much more difficult.

You could rely on the simultaneous equations rule of thumb. There are four

equations in three variables, so that should be enough to solve for all of the

variables. Algebraically, you can substitute $c = \dfrac{1}{a}$ into $a = 4c$ to get $a = 4 \times \dfrac{1}{a}$,

which becomes $a^2 = 4$. In $\dfrac{a^2 b}{c}$, the b and the c will cancel, so the question is

really "what is a^2?" Although a can be either 2 or –2, the answer is 4 in both

cases. Since there is one answer, choose C.

18. **B** With statement (1), if you divide both sides of the inequality by 3^3, or 27, you get $3^{p-2} < 2,000$. The answer could be either "yes" or "no," since values above and below 1,000 are possible. Narrow the choices to B, C, and E. With statement (2), subtract 3^{p-1} from both sides to get $3^p - 3^{p-1} < 2,000$. You can factor the left side to get $3^{p-1}(3 - 1) < 2,000$ or $3^{p-1}(2) < 2,000$, which becomes $3^{p-1} < 1,000$. If you divide both sides by 3, you get $3^{p-2} < 333\dfrac{1}{3}$, so the answer is "yes." Choose B.

19. **C** With right triangles, you need either two sides or one side and a special ratio (30-60-90 or 45-45-90) to find the other side(s). In statement (1), you have only one side of the triangle and you don't know whether the triangle fits one of the special angle patterns or not. Statement (1) is insufficient, so narrow the choices to B, C, and E. In statement (2), you know that the y angle is twice the size of the x angle, so the triangle is a 30-60-90 triangle. However, you don't know any of the sides. Statement (2) alone is not enough, so eliminate B. With both statements together, you have one of the sides and you know the triangle fits the 30-60-90 pattern, so you could solve for the missing side *KL*. Choose C.

20. **A** With Yes/No questions, try Plugging In. For statement (1), if $g = 2$, then $f = (2 + 1)(2 - 1) = 3$. $\sqrt{3+1} = 2$, so the answer is "yes." If $g = 5$, then $f = (5 + 1)(5 - 1) = 24$. $\sqrt{24+1} = 5$, so the answer is "yes" again. For any integer g (provided f is positive), you will get "yes." That answers the question, so narrow the choices to A and D. With statement (2), if $g = 1$, then f could be any positive integer. Some values for f will give "yes" for an answer and some will give "no." That's insufficient, so choose A.

Assorted Topics 2

PROBABILITY

The probability that a particular event will occur is expressed as a fraction (or a decimal or percent) between 0 and 1. For example, the probability that a flipped coin will come up heads is $\frac{1}{2}$, and the probability that it will rain on a certain day might be 30%. However, it wouldn't make sense to say that the probability of something was more than 1 (absolutely certain to occur) or less than 0 (no chance of occurring). For most GMAT problems involving probability, you should use the following formula:

$$\text{Probability of } x = \frac{\text{\# of outcomes that include } x}{\text{\# of all possible outcomes}}$$

To calculate the probability of an event, take the number of all potential outcomes and put it in the denominator of a fraction. Then take the number of favorable outcomes, those that match the event, and put it in the numerator of the fraction.

For example, suppose you have a box containing 20 chocolates, of which 10 are filled with fudge, 6 with creme, and 4 with caramel. If you choose a chocolate at random and bite into it, there are 20 potential outcomes, one for each chocolate. The probability of choosing one with fudge filling is $\frac{10}{20}$ or $\frac{1}{2}$. Suppose you like fudge and caramel but hate creme filling. (What is that stuff, anyway?) There are 10 + 4 = 14 chocolates that have fudge or caramel, so the probability of getting a chocolate you like is $\frac{14}{20}$ or $\frac{7}{10}$.

Note that this fraction method applies only when you have an equal chance of getting each of the possible outcomes. In other situations, such as with a lopsided coin, the question will provide you with the necessary probability.

INDEPENDENT EVENTS

Many problems involve the probability of several events occurring. To find the probability of a series of events, find the probability for each separate event and then multiply them together. Suppose a question asks for the probability of getting heads on three coin flips in a row. The chance of getting heads on each separate coin flip is $\frac{1}{2}$, so the probability of getting three in a row is $\frac{1}{2} \times \frac{1}{2} \times \frac{1}{2} = \frac{1}{8}$.

In the previous example, the events were independent, meaning that the result on one coin flip did not affect the probabilities for other coin flips. When events are independent, you can calculate the probability for each separate event without regard for what happens with other events. Try this next example.

1. Two dice, each with six sides numbered 1 through 6, are tossed. What is the probability that both dice will come up with either a 1 or a 2 ?

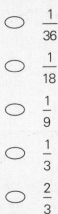

$\bigcirc$ $\dfrac{1}{36}$

$\bigcirc$ $\dfrac{1}{18}$

$\bigcirc$ $\dfrac{1}{9}$

$\bigcirc$ $\dfrac{1}{3}$

$\bigcirc$ $\dfrac{2}{3}$

The probability that the first die will result in a 1 or a 2 is 2 out of 6, or $\dfrac{2}{6} = \dfrac{1}{3}$. The probability is the same for the second die. To get the probability that both events will occur, just multiply the two probabilities: $\dfrac{1}{3} \times \dfrac{1}{3} = \dfrac{1}{9}$. So the answer is C.

DEPENDENT EVENTS

In some cases, a series of events are dependent. The result of one event affects the probabilities for later events. This often happens if things are used up during some process. For dependent events, always assume that earlier events had the desired result when you determine the probability for each later event.

Suppose there are 4 marbles in a jar, 3 blue and 1 red. What is the probability of drawing 2 blue marbles from the jar? Well, the probability that the first marble is blue is $\dfrac{3}{4}$. However, there are now only 3 marbles left, 2 blue and 1 red (assume that you successfully picked a blue marble the first time). The probability that the second marble is blue is $\dfrac{2}{3}$, so the probability of picking 2 blue marbles is $\dfrac{3}{4} \times \dfrac{2}{3} = \dfrac{1}{2}$. Now try the following example.

2. Frank has a box containing 6 doughnuts: 3 jellies and 3 cinnamon twists. If Frank eats 3 doughnuts, chosen randomly from the box, what is the probability that he eats 3 jelly doughnuts?

○ $\frac{1}{2}$

○ $\frac{1}{3}$

○ $\frac{1}{8}$

○ $\frac{1}{20}$

○ $\frac{1}{36}$

The probability that the first doughnut is a jelly is $\frac{1}{2}$. Assuming he gets a jelly, the probability that the second doughnut is a jelly is $\frac{2}{5}$, because there are 2 jellies left out of 5 doughnuts. Assuming he got 2 jellies already, the probability that the third is a jelly is $\frac{1}{4}$, because there is 1 jelly left out of 4 doughnuts. To find the probability that all three events happened, multiply the probabilities: $\frac{1}{2} \times \frac{2}{5} \times \frac{1}{4} = \frac{1}{20}$. The answer is D.

"NOT" PROBABILITY

Sometimes it's easier to calculate the probability that something will *not* happen than to calculate the probability that it *will* happen. If the probability that something *will happen* is x, then the probability that it *won't happen* is $1 - x$. For example, suppose there is a 40% chance that it will rain tomorrow. That means there is a $1 - 0.4 = 0.6$ or 60% chance that it will not rain tomorrow. Suppose you need to find the probability that you will get at least 1 head when you flip a coin 5 times. The hard way to do it would be to find the probabilities of getting exactly 1 head, exactly 2 heads, exactly 3 heads, exactly 4 heads, and exactly 5 heads, and then add them all up. The easy way is to find the probability that you do *not* get at least 1 head. That means you get 5 tails. The probability of that is simply $\frac{1}{2} \times \frac{1}{2} \times \frac{1}{2} \times \frac{1}{2} \times \frac{1}{2} = \frac{1}{32}$. So the probability that you will get at least 1 head is $1 - \frac{1}{32} = \frac{31}{32}$. Try the following example.

3. A six-sided die, with sides numbered 1 through 6, is rolled three times. What is the probability that the sum of the three rolls is at least 4 ?

○ $\dfrac{1}{216}$

○ $\dfrac{1}{54}$

○ $\dfrac{1}{2}$

○ $\dfrac{53}{54}$

○ $\dfrac{215}{216}$

This problem is easier if you start with the probability that the sum of the rolls is less than 4. The only way that can happen is to get a 1 on each of the three rolls. The probability of getting a 1 is $\dfrac{1}{6}$, so the probability of getting a 1 three times is $\dfrac{1}{6} \times \dfrac{1}{6} \times \dfrac{1}{6} = \dfrac{1}{216}$. The probability that you will get at least 4 is $1 - \dfrac{1}{216} = \dfrac{215}{216}$. The correct answer is E.

FUNCTIONS

Function problems usually contain some bizarre symbols or strange terms. A question might test a function such as $x \# y = x^2 + y^2 + 2xy$ or use an odd term such as *hyper-prime*. However, a function problem is really just an exercise in following directions. The question must define the function for you, either as a formula or as a description of how to manipulate the numbers. Just plug the numbers you're given into that definition. Here's an example.

1. If $a @ b = 3a^2 + 2b - 1$, then $2 @ 3 =$

○ 12
○ 17
○ 30
○ 37
○ 41

Just plug in $a = 2$ and $b = 3$ into the formula the question provides. You get $2 @ 3 = 3(2)^2 + 2(3) - 1 = 12 + 6 - 1 = 17$. The answer must be B.

Sometimes the GMAT indicates a function by using strange terms rather than a symbol. You may even see something that has a real-life use, such as the net present value of an annuity or some other financial function. Don't worry. The question will provide the directions, either as a formula or a step-by-step description. All you have to do is plug in the numbers and do the calculation.

RATES

A number of GMAT questions deal with how fast someone can complete a task (e.g., paint a wall or build widgets) or how fast someone travels. These problems revolve around that person's rate. The formula for rate can be expressed a couple of ways.

$$\text{Amount} = \text{Rate} \times \text{Time}$$

$$\text{Rate} = \frac{\text{Amount}}{\text{Time}}$$

Just fill in the numbers the question provides and solve for the other one. Look at this example.

1. If Albert can travel 200 miles in 4 hours, how many hours will it take Albert, traveling at the same constant rate, to travel 350 miles?

   ○ 5
   ○ 6
   ○ 7
   ○ 8
   ○ 10

The key number is usually the rate. Find it if the question doesn't state it. Albert's rate (or speed) is $\frac{200}{4} = 50$ per hour. He needs to travel 350 miles. Plug those numbers into the formula to get $350 = 50 \times \text{Time}$, which is solved as $\text{Time} = \frac{350}{50} = 7$ hours. The answer is C.

If several people are working together, just add their individual rates to find their combined rate. For example, if Joe can paint 10 square feet per hour and Jack can paint 8 square feet per hour, then they paint 18 square feet per hour when they work together. This principle also applies if two people are traveling toward each other. Add their rates to find how quickly they close the gap. Suppose Alice and Brenda are 300 miles apart and begin driving toward each other. If Alice drives at a speed of 40 miles per hour and Brenda drives at a speed of 60 miles per hour, they get closer at a rate of $40 + 60 = 100$ miles per hour. So they will meet in $\frac{300}{100} = 3$ hours. Try the following example:

2. Mark can process 30 insurance claims per hour. Bruce can process 15 claims per hour. Mark starts working on a batch of 555 insurance claims. Two hours later, Bruce begins working with Mark until the batch is finished. How many hours did Mark spend working on the batch?

   ○ 2
   ○ 11
   ○ 13
   ○ 22
   ○ 26

If Mark works alone for 2 hours, he processes 2 × 30 = 60 claims, leaving 555 − 60 = 495 claims to go. When Bruce joins Mark, they work at the combined rate of 30 + 15 = 45 claims per hour, so they need $\dfrac{495}{45} = 11$ hours to finish the batch. So Mark spends a total of 2 (alone) + 11 (with Bruce) = 13 hours working on the batch. The correct answer is C.

If the task or the distance is undefined, you may want to use the Plugging In technique. Make up a number for the amount of work or the distance and solve the problem from there. Try the following example:

3. Working alone, Bud can complete a particular task in 6 hours. Lou, working alone, can complete the same task in 8 hours. If Bud and Lou work together, how many hours will it take them to complete the task?

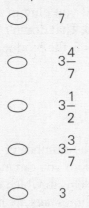

○   7

○ $3\dfrac{4}{7}$

○ $3\dfrac{1}{2}$

○ $3\dfrac{3}{7}$

○   3

The task is undefined, so make up a number for it. Suppose the task is 48 units (because it works well with 6 and 8). Bud can complete the task in 6 hours, so his individual rate is $\dfrac{48}{6} = 8$ units per hour. Lou's rate is $\dfrac{48}{6} = 6$ units per hour. Combined, they work at a rate of 8 + 6 = 14 units per hour. To complete 48 units, they will need $\dfrac{48}{14} = \dfrac{24}{7} = 3\dfrac{3}{7}$ hours.

The correct answer is D. Note that the answer is not $\dfrac{6+8}{2} = 7$ hours or $\dfrac{1}{2} \times 7 = 3\dfrac{1}{2}$ hours.

Don't fall for those Joe Bloggs traps. Use the formula and work it out.

DIGIT PROBLEMS

In digit problems, one digit of a number is replaced by a symbol or letter. For example, the problem may contain a number such as 11,8#3, where # represents the missing digit. Usually, you need to find the value or the range of possible values for the missing digit. Remember that there are only 10 possible values for a single digit: 0 through 9.

You can usually solve a digit problem by applying the Plugging In The Answer technique. Try the numbers from the answer choices until you find one that fits. Look at the following example:

$$
\begin{array}{r}
510 \\
\times \quad \# \\
\hline
2,\#\#0
\end{array}
$$

1. In the multiplication above, # represents a single digit. What digit does # represent?

   - ○ 2
   - ○ 3
   - ○ 4
   - ○ 5
   - ○ 6

Just try out the different answers until you find one that fits. If you plug in # = 2, the product is 1,020, which doesn't fit. With # = 3, the product is 1,530. That doesn't fit either. Plug in # = 4 and the product is 2,040. That doesn't work. With # = 5, the product is 2,550. That works, so the answer is D.

COMBINATIONS AND PERMUTATIONS

Problems involving combinations and permutations deal with the number of different ways to arrange a group of things or the number of different selections you can make from a group of things. One critical distinction to make is between problems in which the order of the things *does* matter and problems in which the order of the things *does not* matter.

Suppose you're scheduling speakers for a seminar. You have three people—A, B, and C—available but you need only two different people, one for the morning and one for the afternoon. Your choices are A then B, A then C, B then A, B then C, C then A, and C then B. That's a total of six different pairs. Notice that order does matter. You want to count "A then B" and "B then A" as two different pairs.

Now suppose that you're choosing fruits to make a health shake. You need two different fruits and you have three from which to choose—A, B, and C. You could choose A and B, A and C, or B and C. That's only three different pairs (not pears). You don't count "A and B" and "B and A" as two different pairs because they're just going into the blender together anyway.

When order matters, the different arrangements are called permutations. When order doesn't matter, the different arrangements are called combinations. The names aren't that important, but you do need to understand the difference and be able to identify which one the question wants.

There are three basic patterns you will see on the GMAT. You may also see questions that mix these three patterns together, but the key is to understand how to handle each of the three basic models: combination from different sources, permutation from the same source, and combination from the same source.

COMBINATION (DIFFERENT SOURCES)

When you have a single decision to make, the number of possible outcomes is easy to determine: It's simply the number of options for that one decision. For example, if you need to choose a shirt to wear and you have 12 different shirts, then there are 12 possible outcomes.

When you have more than one decision to make, you find the number of possible outcomes by multiplying the numbers of options for the decisions together. Suppose you need to choose a shirt and a pair of pants, and you have 12 different shirts and 5 different pairs of pants. Multiply the number of options for shirts and the number of options for pants to get $12 \times 5 = 60$ possible outcomes. Try this example.

1. Nick is enrolling in classes for next quarter. He must choose a math class, a language class, a science class, and a humanities class. If there are 3 math classes, 2 language classes, 1 science class, and 5 humanities classes available, how many different groups of classes could Nick choose?

   ○ 4
   ○ 5
   ○ 11
   ○ 24
   ○ 30

Nick has to make four decisions—one for each type of class—so multiply those four numbers together: $3 \times 2 \times 1 \times 5 = 30$. The correct answer is E.

The previous example involves choosing items from different sources. The math class Nick chooses must come from the math list, not the language list or one of the others. With these different source questions, just multiply the number of options for each decision. The result is the number of possible combinations. Nick didn't have to decide the order of the classes, just which ones would be included in the group.

PERMUTATION (SAME SOURCE)

In some problems, you will need to choose several items from the same list. For example, you may need to choose 3 books to read from a list of 6 books and determine in what order to read them. For each book that you must select, you are making a decision. However, the number of options changes with each decision because you have already used up some of the possible selections. When selecting the first book, you have 6 options. However, when you select the second book, you've already crossed one off the list, so there are only 5 options left. Then there are 4 options for the third book. So, the number of possible outcomes is $6 \times 5 \times 4 = 120$ possible reading lists.

Note that this process results in the number of permutations, not combinations. If the six books are A, B, C, D, E, and F, you are counting ABC as separate from CAB. That's what you want if you must determine the order in which you will read the books.

Try this next example.

2. Mandy is judging a talent contest involving 5 dogs. She must select the top 3 dogs and award a blue ribbon to the most talented
dog, a red ribbon to the second-most talented, and a white ribbon
to the third-most talented. How many different arrangements of
ribbon-winners are possible?

○ 3
○ 5
○ 12
○ 15
○ 60

This is a permutation problem because the order of the dogs matters. Awarding A
the blue ribbon, B the red, and C the white is different from awarding B the blue, A the
red, and C the white. Mandy makes three selections: the first dog, the second dog, and
the third dog. In selecting the first dog, Mandy can choose any of the 5 dogs. In selecting the second, she has only 4 dogs left, and 3 dogs for the third choice. Thus, she has
$5 \times 4 \times 3 = 60$ possible permutations of ribbon-winners. The correct answer is choice E.

So far, the method for the calculation of combinations from different sources and the
method for the calculation of permutations from the same source are very similar—just
multiply the number of options for the choices together. When you learn to find combinations from the same source, it gets a bit trickier. It's important to correctly identify which
type of problem you're dealing with, so you can use the proper method for calculating the
answer.

COMBINATION (SAME SOURCE)

Suppose Mandy didn't need to determine the ranking among the top 3 dogs, but rather
merely had to choose the best 3 to receive doggie treats. She is still selecting 3 from a list
of 5, but now the order of the 3 doesn't matter. This is a combination chosen from the same
source.

The number of combinations will always be smaller than the number of permutations
in selecting a certain number of items from some list. Think of the process of selecting a
permutation as first choosing one of many possible groups and then putting that particular
group in order. With a combination, you would stop after selecting the group. The number of permutations is the number of combinations multiplied by the number of ways to
arrange a particular group.

Suppose you must choose a group of songs from a list and then choose the order in
which to play those songs. Say there are 10 possible groups of songs that you could choose.
If there are 6 ways to arrange a given group of songs, you will end up with $10 \times 6 = 60$
possible arrangements, or permutations.

To find the number of combinations, you will work backward through the above process. First, pretend you are finding the number of permutations. Then, divide that number
by the number of ways to arrange a particular group. This process of "factoring out the
order" will leave you with the number of possible groups, or combinations. See how this
method works on the following problem.

3. Eric is ordering a pizza. He wants three different toppings on his pizza, and the available toppings are pepperoni, sausage, black olives, green peppers, and mushrooms. How many different combinations of toppings are available?

- ○ 5
- ○ 10
- ○ 15
- ○ 30
- ○ 60

This is a combination problem, because Eric doesn't care about the order in which the toppings are selected, just which ones are in the group selected. To find a combination, start by finding the permutation. If he were selecting them in order, he would have 5 choices for the first topping, 4 for the second, and 3 for the third. That gives you $5 \times 4 \times 3 = 60$ possible permutations. Of course, that's not the number you want, because it treats pepperoni-sausage-mushrooms as different from mushrooms-sausage-pepperoni.

Next, determine how many ways a group of three toppings can be arranged. This is equivalent to choosing 3 from a list of 3. There are 3 options for the first choice, 2 for the second, and only 1 for the third, so 3 toppings can be arranged in $3 \times 2 \times 1 = 6$ different ways.

Finding the combination is the same as taking the permutation number, 60, and factoring out the number of ways to order a given group, 6. So the number of combinations is $\dfrac{5 \times 4 \times 3}{3 \times 2 \times 1} = \dfrac{60}{6} = 10$. The correct answer is choice B.

MEDIAN, MODE, AND RANGE

In Chapter 6, you learned how to find the average of a group of numbers. The GMAT also tests some close cousins of the average, namely the median, mode, and range of a set of numbers.

To calculate the median of a group of numbers, first arrange the numbers in order, either ascending or descending. The median is simply the middle number. If there is an even number of things in the group, there won't be a single middle number. In that case, the median is the average of the two middlemost numbers.

The mode of a group of numbers is the number that appears the most times. If every number is different, there is no mode.

The range of a set of numbers is the difference between the greatest number in the set and the least number in the set. Just subtract.

Suppose you have this set of numbers: 1, 5, –5, 3, 1, 2, and 8. To find the median, arrange them in order: –5, 1, 1, 2, 3, 5, and 8. The number in the middle is 2, so the median is 2. The mode in this set is 1 because it shows up twice while each of the other numbers shows up once. The range of the set is $8 - (-5) = 13$.

PRACTICE SET

1. Alex drives to and from work each day along the same route. If he drives at a speed of 80 miles per hour on the way to work and he drives at a speed of 100 miles per hour on the way from work, which of the following most closely approximates his average speed in miles per hour for the round trip?

    ○   80.0
    ○   88.9
    ○   90.0
    ○   91.1
    ○   100.0

2. When a certain coin is flipped, the probability that it will land on heads is $\frac{1}{2}$ and the probability that it will land on tails is $\frac{1}{2}$. If the coin is flipped three times, what is the probability that all three results are the same?

    ○ $\frac{1}{8}$

    ○ $\frac{1}{4}$

    ○ $\frac{3}{8}$

    ○ $\frac{1}{2}$

    ○ $\frac{7}{8}$

3. Joe is choosing books at the bookstore. He has a list of 7 books that he would like to buy, but he can afford to buy only 3 books. How many different groups of books could Joe buy?

    ○   210
    ○   155
    ○   70
    ○   35
    ○   21

$$\frac{\begin{array}{r} \# \\ + @ \end{array}}{\&}$$

4. In the addition above, #, @, and & each represent a distinct, positive digit. If & is even, what is the value of # ?

    (1) # and @ are even and & = 6
    (2) # < @

5. If Max can complete a job in 4 hours and Nick can complete the same job in 6 hours, how many fewer hours do Max and Nick working together need to complete the job than Max alone needs to complete the job?

    ○   1.6
    ○   2.4
    ○   3.2
    ○   3.4
    ○   5.0

6. If a set of numbers consists of 10, 15, 0 , 3, and x, and the range of the set is 30, what are the possible values for the median of the set?

    ○   −15 and 30
    ○   15 and 10
    ○   0 and 3
    ○   3 and 15
    ○   3 and 10

7. If the area of a number is defined as the difference between that number's greatest and least prime factors, what is the area of 100 ?

    ○   0
    ○   2
    ○   3
    ○   5
    ○   9

Remember!
For Data Sufficiency problems in this book, we do not supply the answer choices. The five possible answer choices are the same every time.

8. Carol is having friends over to watch home movies. She has 6 reels of home movies, but she and her friends have time to watch only 3 of them. Carol must decide which reels to watch and in what order. How many different orderings does Carol have from which to choose?

○ 120
○ 96
○ 60
○ 36
○ 20

9. A jar contains 5 marbles: 3 red and 2 blue. If two marbles are drawn randomly from the jar, what is the probability that they will be different colors?

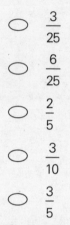

○ $\dfrac{3}{25}$

○ $\dfrac{6}{25}$

○ $\dfrac{2}{5}$

○ $\dfrac{3}{10}$

○ $\dfrac{3}{5}$

10. Oscar is running in a straight line away from Nancy at the rate of 20 feet per second. Nancy is chasing Oscar at the rate of 25 feet per second. If Oscar has a 100-foot head start, how long, in seconds, will it take Nancy to catch Oscar?

○ 4
○ 5
○ 10
○ 20
○ 100

11. A cupboard holds 10 cans, of which 3 contain pumpkin puree. If a group of 4 cans is randomly selected from the cupboard, what is the probability that the group includes the 3 cans containing pumpkin puree?

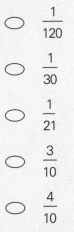

○ $\dfrac{1}{120}$

○ $\dfrac{1}{30}$

○ $\dfrac{1}{21}$

○ $\dfrac{3}{10}$

○ $\dfrac{4}{10}$

12. Mo is planning a dinner party and must create a menu consisting of 1 soup, 1 entree, 3 different side dishes, and 2 different desserts. If Mo has 3 possible choices for the soup, 2 for the entree, 5 for the side dishes, and 3 for the desserts, how many different menus can Mo create?

○ 2,160
○ 180
○ 120
○ 90
○ 7

13. From a group of 10 students, 7 girls and 3 boys, a teacher must choose 2 girls and 2 boys to present book reports. How many different arrangements of students, in order, are possible?

○ 252
○ 504
○ 1,008
○ 1,512
○ 5,040

14. Each candle in a particular box is either round or square and either scented or unscented. If 60% of the candles are round, what is the probability that a candle selected randomly from the box will be unscented?

    (1) If a candle is scented, it has an 80% chance of being round.
    (2) If a candle is square, it has a 25% chance of being scented.

15. The greatest number in a set of 4 numbers is 70. What is the average (arithmetic mean) of the set?

    (1) The median of the set is 25.
    (2) The range of the set is 70.

16. Anthony, Brad, and Cris are inviting 2 friends each to a party. If Anthony has 4 friends from which to choose, Brad has 2, and Cris has 5, how many different groups of 6 invitees are possible?

    ○ 40
    ○ 60
    ○ 66
    ○ 462
    ○ 720

17. Ric begins walking up a mountain trail, ascending at a constant rate of 200 feet per hour. Sixty minutes later, Josie begins walking down the same trail, starting at a point 1,700 feet higher than Ric's starting point. If Josie descends at a constant rate of 300 feet per hour, how many feet will Ric have ascended when the two meet?

    ○ 600
    ○ 680
    ○ 800
    ○ 850
    ○ 900

18. If $x \& y = x^2 - 2y$, what is the value of $a \& 2$?

    (1) $3 \& a = 13$
    (2) The value of a is either 2 or –2.

19. Jack is making a list of his 5 favorite cities. He will choose 3 cities in the United States from a list of 5 candidates. He will choose 2 cities in Europe from a list of 3 candidates. How many different lists of cities, ranked from first to fifth, can Jack make?

○   30
○   360
○   1,800
○   3,600
○   6,720

20. If $f(n) = xa^n$, what is the value of $f(5)$?

(1) $f(0) = 3$

(2) $f(4) = 48$

Challenge!
Take a crack at this high-level GMAT question.

ANSWERS AND EXPLANATIONS

Practice Set

1. **B** The distance is undefined, so make one up. Suppose his trip is 400 miles each way. On the way to work, he travels at 80 miles per hour and completes the trip in $\frac{400}{80} = 5$ hours. On the way from work, he travels 100 miles per hour and completes the trip in $\frac{400}{100} = 4$ hours. For the round trip, he travels $400 + 400 = 800$ miles in $5 + 4$ hours. That's an average speed of $\frac{800}{9} = 88.89$ miles per hour. B is the correct answer.

2. **B** It doesn't really matter which way the first flip ends up, so don't count that probability. The probability that the second flip is the same as the first is $\frac{1}{2}$. The probability that the third flip matches is also $\frac{1}{2}$. So the probability that the last two flips match the first is $\frac{1}{2} \times \frac{1}{2} = \frac{1}{4}$. Choose B.

3. **D** This is a single-source combination problem. For the first of his 3 chosen books, Joe can pick from 7 titles; he has 6 choices for the second book, and 5 choices for the third book. So multiply: $7 \times 6 \times 5 = 210$. But wait, you're not done yet! Don't forget to divide 210 by the number of ways you can arrange the group of 3 books he selected: 3 ways for his first choice, 2 ways for his second choice, and 1 way for his third choice, or $3 \times 2 \times 1 = 6$. The correct answer is 35, so choose D.

4. **C** Look at statement (1). If both # and @ are even, positive digits that add up to 6, then one of them is 2 and one of them is 4. However, you can't tell which one is which. You can't answer the question, so narrow the choices to B, C, and E. Look at statement (2). This isn't much help by itself. There are several possible values for #, @, and &. You can't answer the question, so eliminate B. Try (1) and (2) together. From (1), you know that # and @ are 2 and 4. From (2), you know that # is the smaller of the two. So # = 2 and @ = 4. You can answer the question, so choose C.

5. **A** The task is undefined, so make up a value, say 48 units. Max can complete 48 units in 4 hours, so his rate is $\dfrac{48}{4} = 12$ units per hour. Nick can complete 48 units in 6 hours, so his rate is $\dfrac{48}{6} = 8$ units per hour. Combined, Max and Nick work at the rate of $12 + 8 = 20$ units per hour and can complete the job in $\dfrac{48}{20} = 2.4$ hours. That's $4 - 2.4 = 1.6$ fewer hours than Max alone needs.

Choose A.

6. **E** For the range to be 30, either x is the highest number and $x = 30$ or x is the lowest number and $x = -15$. If $x = 30$, the set is 0, 3, 10, 15, and 30, so the median would be 10. If $x = -15$, the set is −15, 0, 3, 10, 15, so the median would be 3. So the possible values for the median are 3 and 10. Choose E.

7. **C** The prime factorization of 100 is $2 \times 2 \times 5 \times 5$. So the greatest prime factor is 5 and the least is 2. That's a difference of $5 - 2 = 3$. Choose C.

8. **A** Order is important, so set up a permutation (same source). Carol must choose 3 reels. She has 6 options for the first reel, then 5 options for the second, and 4 options for the third. That gives you $6 \times 5 \times 4 = 120$ possible arrangements (or permutations).

9. **E** The probability that the first marble will be red is $\dfrac{3}{5}$. Assuming the first one is red, the probability that the second marble will be blue is $\dfrac{1}{2}$ because there are 4 marbles left, 2 of which are blue. So the probability of getting red then blue is $\dfrac{3}{5} \times \dfrac{1}{2} = \dfrac{3}{10}$. However, getting blue then red would also be acceptable. The probability that the first marble is blue is $\dfrac{2}{5}$. Assuming that the first marble is blue, the probability that the second marble is red is $\dfrac{3}{4}$, because 3 of the remaining 4 marbles are red. So the probability of getting blue then red is $\dfrac{2}{5} \times \dfrac{3}{4} = \dfrac{3}{10}$. Because either of these patterns is acceptable, add the probabilities to find the probability that the two marbles are different colors: $\dfrac{3}{10} + \dfrac{3}{10} = \dfrac{6}{10} = \dfrac{3}{5}$. Choose E.

10. **D** If Oscar is traveling 20 feet per second and Nancy is traveling 25 feet per second, then Nancy is gaining on Oscar at the rate of $25 - 20 = 5$ feet per second. So it will take her $\dfrac{100}{5} = 20$ seconds to close the 100-foot gap. Choose D.

11. **B** There are 4 ways to select 3 pumpkins and 1 other: PPPO, PPOP, POPP, and OPPP. For PPPO, the probability is $\frac{3}{10} \times \frac{2}{9} \times \frac{1}{8} \times \frac{7}{7} = \frac{6}{720} = \frac{1}{120}$. For PPOP, the probability is $\frac{3}{10} \times \frac{2}{9} \times \frac{7}{8} \times \frac{1}{7} = \frac{1}{120}$. For POPP, the probability is $\frac{3}{10} \times \frac{7}{9} \times \frac{2}{8} \times \frac{1}{7} = \frac{1}{120}$. For OPPP, the probability is $\frac{7}{10} \times \frac{3}{9} \times \frac{2}{8} \times \frac{1}{7} = \frac{1}{120}$.

Since any of the four ways is acceptable, the overall probability is

$\frac{1}{120} + \frac{1}{120} + \frac{1}{120} + \frac{1}{120} = \frac{4}{120} = \frac{1}{30}$. Choose B.

12. **B** Break this complex problem into several sub-problems. Mo has 3 possibilities for the soup. She has 2 possibilities for the entree. She needs to choose a group of 3 side dishes from a list of 5. That's a combination, so she has $\frac{5 \times 4 \times 3}{3 \times 2 \times 1} = 10$ possible groups of side dishes. She will choose 2 of 3 possible desserts. That's another combination, so she has $\frac{3 \times 2}{2 \times 1} = 3$ possible groups of desserts. Soups, entrees, side dishes, and desserts are a different source problem, so multiply her options together: $3 \times 2 \times 10 \times 3 = 180$ possible menus. Choose B.

13. **D** Break this complex problem into several sub-problems. Choosing 2 boys from a list of 3 is a combination. The teacher has $\frac{3 \times 2}{2 \times 1} = 3$ possible pairs of boys. Choosing 2 girls from a list of 7 is another combination. The teacher has $\frac{7 \times 6}{2 \times 1} = 21$ possible pairs of girls. Choosing a pair of boys and a pair of girls is a different source problem. The teacher has $3 \times 21 = 63$ possible combinations. However, the question asks for an arrangement, so you must figure out how many ways each group could be arranged. Arranging 4 students from a list of 4 gives you $4 \times 3 \times 2 \times 1 = 24$ ways to arrange each possible group, or $24 \times 63 = 1,512$ possible arrangements. Choose D.

14. **C** You know that 60% of the candles are round, so 40% are square. With statement (1), you know that 80% of the scented candles are round, so 20% are square. However, you can't determine the split between scented and unscented, so you can't answer the question. Narrow the choices to B, C, and E. With statement (2), you learn that 25% of square candles are scented, so 75% are unscented. That means 40% × 75% = 30% of all candles are square and unscented and 40% × 25% = 10% of all candles are square and scented. However, you don't know how the round candles are split between scented and unscented. Eliminate B. With both statements together, you know that 10% of all candles are square and scented. Those represent 20% of scented candles, so solve the equation 20% × s% = 10% to get s = 50% of all candles are scented, so 50% are unscented. That tells you the probability, so choose C.

15. **C** Start by seeing which pieces of the puzzle you need. You know there are four numbers, so you need the total in order to find the average. With statement (1), you can determine that the middle two numbers add up to 50, because the median of an even set is the average of the two middle numbers. You also know that the biggest number is 70; however, you're missing information about the smallest number. Statement (1) is insufficient, so narrow the choices to B, C, and E. With statement (2), you can tell that the smallest number must be 0, since the range is equal to the largest number minus the smallest number. With (2) alone, however, you don't know anything about the middle numbers. Eliminate B. With both statements, you know that the largest number is 70, the smallest is 0, and the two in the middle sum to 50. Although you don't know the middle numbers individually, you know the total of all four numbers is 0 + 50 + 70 = 120, so the average must be 30. Choose C.

16. **B** Break this problem into pieces. Anthony must choose a group of 2 friends from a list of 4. That's a combination, so he has $\frac{4 \times 3}{2 \times 1} = 6$ possible groups. Brad has $\frac{2 \times 1}{2 \times 1} = 1$ possible group of invitees. Cris has $\frac{5 \times 4}{2 \times 1} = 10$ possible groups. Combining their lists is a different source problem, so there are 6 × 1 × 10 = 60 possible groups of invitees. Choose B.

17. **C** Break this problem into two phases: the first when Ric is the only walker and the second when both are walking. The first phase is 1 hour, so Ric travels 200 × 1 = 200 feet up. Thus, he is now 1,700 − 200 = 1,500 feet below Josie. When they are walking together, they travel at a combined rate of 200 + 300 = 500 feet per hour, because after each hour they are 500 feet closer together. At this rate, it takes them $\frac{1,500}{500} = 3$ hours to meet. Ric has walked a total of 4 hours, so he has traveled 200 × 4 = 800 feet. Choose C.

18. **D** The missing piece of the puzzle is the value of a to plug into the formula for the function. With statement (1), you can set up the equation $3^2 - 2a = 13$, which you can solve for $a = -2$. That's sufficient, because you could plug that into the formula to find $a \& 2$. Narrow the choices to A and D. With statement (2), you have two possible values for a. However, since the formula tells you to square a, it doesn't matter whether it is positive or negative. Thus both values of a lead to the same value for $a \& 2 = 2^2 - 2(2) = 0$. You can answer the question, so choose D.

19. **D** Break this problem into sub-problems. Jack must choose a group of 3 U.S. cities and a group of 2 European cities, and then place them in order. Choosing 3 U.S. cities from a list of 5 is a combination; he has $\dfrac{5 \times 4 \times 3}{3 \times 2 \times 1} = 10$ possible groups of U.S. cities. Choosing 2 European cities from a list of 3 is also a combination; he has $\dfrac{3 \times 2}{2 \times 1} = 3$ possible groups of European cities. Combining the U.S. and European lists is a different source problem; he has $10 \times 3 = 30$ possible groups of 5 cities. For each group, there are $5 \times 4 \times 3 \times 2 \times 1 = 120$ possible ways to rank them. So there are $30 \times 120 = 3{,}600$ possible arrangements. Choose D.

20. **E** First evaluate statement (1). If you plug 0 into the function, you get $f(0) = xa^0$, or $f(0) = x$. Since you also know from the statement that $f(0) = 3$, you now know that $x = 3$. However, without knowledge of a, you cannot solve. So, narrow your answers to B, C, and E. Statement (2) by itself does not allow you to solve for anything since plugging it into the function yields $f(4) = xa^4 = 48$. You do not know the x or a values. Eliminate choice B. Now, try the statements together. From statement (1), $x = 3$, so statement (2) can now be read as $f(4) = 3a^4 = 48$. At first glance, this looks sufficient to solve for a, but you must consider that a could be either negative or positive. Therefore, the combination is not sufficient. Choose E.

12

Quantitative
Practice Section

INSTRUCTIONS

This practice section contains 37 questions covering a range of math topics similar to those you will see on the real GMAT. It recreates (as much as is possible on paper) the experience you will have in taking the Quantitative section of the GMAT. Set a timer for 75 minutes and try to answer every question in that amount of time.

A few reminders:

- Start slowly; then gradually pick up speed to finish the section.

- Do the questions in order. You must choose an answer before you move on to the next question, and you cannot go back to a previous question.

- Set up your scratch paper and use it to do all of your work.

- *Important:* Answer every question, so you may have to guess on some of the tougher questions.

- Use the methods and concepts you have learned, especially elimination methods and the various versions of Plugging In.

- *Remember:* In the data sufficiency questions that you've worked on throughout this book, we removed the five answer choices since those are always the same. Here in the practice section, we've added them back in, since you will see them on the real GMAT.

The section is designed to simulate the performance of someone who gets about 75% of the questions right and receives a score of about 40 (on the 0–60 scale).

Good luck!

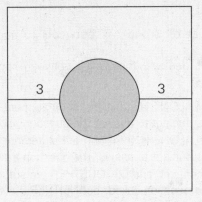

1. In the figure above, a circular hole is cut in the center of a square sheet of metal. If the area of the sheet was 100 square centimeters before the hole was cut, what is the approximate area of the remainder of the sheet, in square centimeters, after the hole is cut?

   ⟨⟩ 12.57
   ⟨⟩ 49.73
   ⟨⟩ 50.27
   ⟨⟩ 71.73
   ⟨⟩ 87.43

2. If $a > b$, how much greater than b is a ?

   (1) b is one-fourth the value of a.
   (2) The sum of a and b is 100.

   ⟨⟩ Statement (1) ALONE is sufficient, but statement (2) alone is not sufficient to answer the question asked.
   ⟨⟩ Statement (2) ALONE is sufficient, but statement (1) alone is not sufficient to answer the question asked.
   ⟨⟩ BOTH statements (1) and (2) TOGETHER are sufficient to answer the question asked; but NEITHER statement ALONE is sufficient.
   ⟨⟩ EACH statement ALONE is sufficient to answer the question asked.
   ⟨⟩ Statements (1) and (2) TOGETHER are NOT sufficient to answer the question asked, and additional data specific to the problem are needed.

3. If $\dfrac{z^2 + 6z + 9}{z^2 - 9} = 2$, what is the value of z ?

   ⟨⟩ 9
   ⟨⟩ 6
   ⟨⟩ 3
   ⟨⟩ –3
   ⟨⟩ –9

4. What is the value of j ?

    (1) The product of 2 and j is between 10 and 32, exclusive.

    (2) When j is divided by 2, the result is between 4 and 10, inclusive.

○ Statement (1) ALONE is sufficient, but statement (2) alone is not sufficient to answer the question asked.

○ Statement (2) ALONE is sufficient, but statement (1) alone is not sufficient to answer the question asked.

○ BOTH statements (1) and (2) TOGETHER are sufficient to answer the question asked; but NEITHER statement ALONE is sufficient.

○ EACH statement ALONE is sufficient to answer the question asked.

○ Statements (1) and (2) TOGETHER are NOT sufficient to answer the question asked, and additional data specific to the problem are needed.

5. The monthly fee for a certain cellular telephone plan is $0.25 per minute for the first 200 minutes of calling time, plus $0.50 for each minute above 200 minutes. Was the fee for June less than $60 ?

    (1) Calling time for June was 180 minutes.

    (2) For 460 minutes of calling time, the fee would be four times as great as that for June.

○ Statement (1) ALONE is sufficient, but statement (2) alone is not sufficient to answer the question asked.

○ Statement (2) ALONE is sufficient, but statement (1) alone is not sufficient to answer the question asked.

○ BOTH statements (1) and (2) TOGETHER are sufficient to answer the question asked; but NEITHER statement ALONE is sufficient.

○ EACH statement ALONE is sufficient to answer the question asked.

○ Statements (1) and (2) TOGETHER are NOT sufficient to answer the question asked, and additional data specific to the problem are needed.

6. Of the pages produced by a printing press, 15% are unusable. How many pages must be produced per minute by the printing press to yield 1,020 usable pages in an hour?

○ 17
○ 20
○ 23
○ 24
○ 25.5

7. In the equation $2x - cy = 18$, c is a constant. If the value of y is 2 when x is 6, what is the value of x when y is 3 ?

    ○ $-\dfrac{9}{2}$

    ○ -4

    ○ -3

    ○ 4

    ○ $\dfrac{9}{2}$

8. If p is a price in whole cents, which of the following could NOT be the result of increasing p by 20%?

    ○ $1.20
    ○ $1.25
    ○ $1.38
    ○ $1.80
    ○ $2.52

9. If the total price for n copies of a book is $31.50, what is the price per copy of the book?

    (1) If twice as many copies were bought for the same total price, the price per copy would be $1.75.
    (2) If 4 fewer copies were bought for the same total price, the price per copy would be $2.80 greater.

    ○ Statement (1) ALONE is sufficient, but statement (2) alone is not sufficient to answer the question asked.
    ○ Statement (2) ALONE is sufficient, but statement (1) alone is not sufficient to answer the question asked.
    ○ BOTH statements (1) and (2) TOGETHER are sufficient to answer the question asked; but NEITHER statement ALONE is sufficient.
    ○ EACH statement ALONE is sufficient to answer the question asked.
    ○ Statements (1) and (2) TOGETHER are NOT sufficient to answer the question asked, and additional data specific to the problem are needed.

10. Torry has submitted $\frac{2}{5}$ of his homework assignments, and he received an average grade of 75 for those assignments. If he wishes to receive an average grade of 90 for all of his homework assignments, the average grade for Torry's remaining homework assignments must be what percent greater than the average grade for the assignments he has already submitted?

   ○   15%
   ○   20%
   ○   25%
   ○ $33\frac{1}{3}\%$
   ○   40%

11. For all numbers m and n, m @ $n = (2m - n)(m + n)$. If $m = 3$ and $n = 4$, then n @ $m =$

   ○   35
   ○   14
   ○   7
   ○   –7
   ○   –14

12. A certain school teaches fourth, fifth, and sixth grades only, with 150 students in each grade. During one day of a blizzard, 10% of the fourth-grade students, $\frac{1}{6}$ of the fifth-grade students, and 60 of the sixth-grade students do not attend school. The student attendance on that day is approximately what percent less than full attendance?

   ○   11%
   ○   16%
   ○   22%
   ○   31%
   ○   33%

13. Before adding to her collection, Laura had 207 antique figurines stored in 9 boxes. After adding to her collection, she had 386 figurines in 12 boxes. What was the approximate percent increase in the average number of figurines per box?

   ○   9%
   ○   33%
   ○   40%
   ○   50%
   ○   86%

14. The product of the sum of 3 consecutive prime numbers and the greatest integer less than the least of the prime numbers is 30. What is the largest of the 3 prime numbers?

   ○   2
   ○   3
   ○   5
   ○   7
   ○   11

15. A rectangular box, with dimensions of 12 inches by 18 inches by 10 inches, contains soup cans. If each can is a cylinder with a radius of 3 inches and a height of 5 inches, what is the maximum number of soup cans that the box can contain?

   ○   6
   ○   12
   ○   15
   ○   30
   ○   48

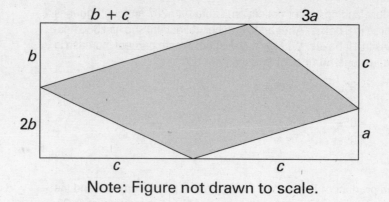

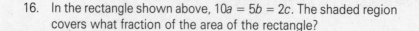

Note: Figure not drawn to scale.

16. In the rectangle shown above, $10a = 5b = 2c$. The shaded region covers what fraction of the area of the rectangle?

- ○ $\dfrac{3}{5}$
- ○ $\dfrac{11}{20}$
- ○ $\dfrac{1}{2}$
- ○ $\dfrac{9}{20}$
- ○ $\dfrac{2}{5}$

17. A jar contains only green pencils and red pencils. If the jar contains a total of 225 pencils, what percentage of the pencils are green?

    (1) The jar contains 75 red pencils.
    (2) The jar contains twice as many green pencils as red pencils.

- ○ Statement (1) ALONE is sufficient, but statement (2) alone is not sufficient to answer the question asked.
- ○ Statement (2) ALONE is sufficient, but statement (1) alone is not sufficient to answer the question asked.
- ○ BOTH statements (1) and (2) TOGETHER are sufficient to answer the question asked; but NEITHER statement ALONE is sufficient.
- ○ EACH statement ALONE is sufficient to answer the question asked.
- ○ Statements (1) and (2) TOGETHER are NOT sufficient to answer the question asked, and additional data specific to the problem are needed.

18. If x and y are integers such that $x^2 = y$ and $xy = 125$, then $x - y =$

○ −30
○ −20
○ −5
○ 5
○ 20

19. A circular hoop with a radius of 12.5 inches is rolled in a straight line on a flat surface. If each revolution of the hoop requires 10 seconds to complete, approximately how many minutes are necessary to roll the hoop 75 feet across the surface?

○ 1
○ 2
○ 3
○ 4
○ 5

20. In the most recent mayoral election for City Y, 63% of all votes were cast for the winning candidate. How many votes were cast for the winning candidate?

(1) 500,000 people were eligible to vote in the election.
(2) 55,500 votes were cast for candidates other than the winning candidate.

○ Statement (1) ALONE is sufficient, but statement (2) alone is not sufficient to answer the question asked.
○ Statement (2) ALONE is sufficient, but statement (1) alone is not sufficient to answer the question asked.
○ BOTH statements (1) and (2) TOGETHER are sufficient to answer the question asked; but NEITHER statement ALONE is sufficient.
○ EACH statement ALONE is sufficient to answer the question asked.
○ Statements (1) and (2) TOGETHER are NOT sufficient to answer the question asked, and additional data specific to the problem are needed.

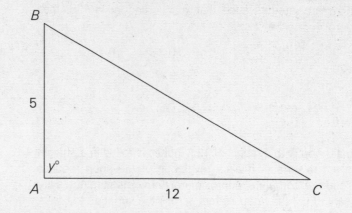

21. In the figure above, what is the area of triangle *ABC* ?

    (1) The length of *BC* is 13.
    (2) *y* = 90

    ○ Statement (1) ALONE is sufficient, but statement (2) alone is not sufficient to answer the question asked.

    ○ Statement (2) ALONE is sufficient, but statement (1) alone is not sufficient to answer the question asked.

    ○ BOTH statements (1) and (2) TOGETHER are sufficient to answer the question asked; but NEITHER statement ALONE is sufficient.

    ○ EACH statement ALONE is sufficient to answer the question asked.

    ○ Statements (1) and (2) TOGETHER are NOT sufficient to answer the question asked, and additional data specific to the problem are needed.

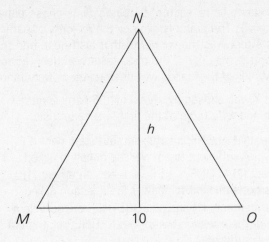

22. In the figure above, if the length of *MO* is 10, is *MNO* an equilateral triangle?

      (1) The length of *MN* is 10.

      (2) $h = 5\sqrt{3}$

    ○   Statement (1) ALONE is sufficient, but statement (2) alone is not sufficient to answer the question asked.

    ○   Statement (2) ALONE is sufficient, but statement (1) alone is not sufficient to answer the question asked.

    ○   BOTH statements (1) and (2) TOGETHER are sufficient to answer the question asked; but NEITHER statement ALONE is sufficient.

    ○   EACH statement ALONE is sufficient to answer the question asked.

    ○   Statements (1) and (2) TOGETHER are NOT sufficient to answer the question asked, and additional data specific to the problem are needed.

23. In each of five taste tests, each of 51 participants chose either Brand *X* or Brand *Y*. The brand chosen by the majority of participants in a taste test was the winner of that taste test, and the brand that won the majority of the taste tests was deemed the better brand. Which of the brands was deemed the better brand?

   (1) Brand *X* was chosen by a total of 155 participants.
   (2) One brand won three of the first four taste tests.

   ○ Statement (1) ALONE is sufficient, but statement (2) alone is not sufficient to answer the question asked.
   ○ Statement (2) ALONE is sufficient, but statement (1) alone is not sufficient to answer the question asked.
   ○ BOTH statements (1) and (2) TOGETHER are sufficient to answer the question asked; but NEITHER statement ALONE is sufficient.
   ○ EACH statement ALONE is sufficient to answer the question asked.
   ○ Statements (1) and (2) TOGETHER are NOT sufficient to answer the question asked, and additional data specific to the problem are needed.

24. How many prime numbers are less than integer *k*?

   (1) $18 < k < 27$
   (2) $23 < k < 30$

   ○ Statement (1) ALONE is sufficient, but statement (2) alone is not sufficient to answer the question asked.
   ○ Statement (2) ALONE is sufficient, but statement (1) alone is not sufficient to answer the question asked.
   ○ BOTH statements (1) and (2) TOGETHER are sufficient to answer the question asked; but NEITHER statement ALONE is sufficient.
   ○ EACH statement ALONE is sufficient to answer the question asked.
   ○ Statements (1) and (2) TOGETHER are NOT sufficient to answer the question asked, and additional data specific to the problem are needed.

25. How many baseball cards do Keith, Pat, and Steve own in total?

  (1) Keith and Pat together own half as many baseball cards as Steve does.
  (2) Keith and Steve together own 109 baseball cards, and Pat and Steve together own 126 baseball cards.

  ◯ Statement (1) ALONE is sufficient, but statement (2) alone is not sufficient to answer the question asked.
  ◯ Statement (2) ALONE is sufficient, but statement (1) alone is not sufficient to answer the question asked.
  ◯ BOTH statements (1) and (2) TOGETHER are sufficient to answer the question asked; but NEITHER statement ALONE is sufficient.
  ◯ EACH statement ALONE is sufficient to answer the question asked.
  ◯ Statements (1) and (2) TOGETHER are NOT sufficient to answer the question asked, and additional data specific to the problem are needed.

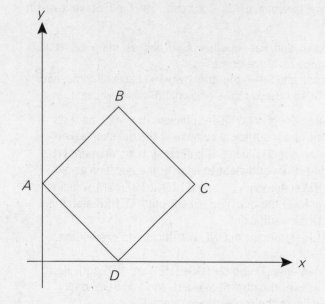

26. What is the area of square *ABCD*, as shown in the coordinate plane above?

> (1) Point *A* has coordinates (0,4).

> (2) Points *B* and *D* have coordinates (4,8) and (4,0), respectively.

○ Statement (1) ALONE is sufficient, but statement (2) alone is not sufficient to answer the question asked.

○ Statement (2) ALONE is sufficient, but statement (1) alone is not sufficient to answer the question asked.

○ BOTH statements (1) and (2) TOGETHER are sufficient to answer the question asked; but NEITHER statement ALONE is sufficient.

○ EACH statement ALONE is sufficient to answer the question asked.

○ Statements (1) and (2) TOGETHER are NOT sufficient to answer the question asked, and additional data specific to the problem are needed.

27. If x, y, and z are distinct integers, which integer is the median of the set $\{x, y, z\}$?

    (1) $x + y < z$
    (2) $x > y$

   ◯ Statement (1) ALONE is sufficient, but statement (2) alone is not sufficient to answer the question asked.
   ◯ Statement (2) ALONE is sufficient, but statement (1) alone is not sufficient to answer the question asked.
   ◯ BOTH statements (1) and (2) TOGETHER are sufficient to answer the question asked; but NEITHER statement ALONE is sufficient.
   ◯ EACH statement ALONE is sufficient to answer the question asked.
   ◯ Statements (1) and (2) TOGETHER are NOT sufficient to answer the question asked, and additional data specific to the problem are needed.

28. If both m and n are negative integers, which of the following must be positive?

   ◯ $\dfrac{m}{n} - 1$

   ◯ $m(n + 1)$

   ◯ $mn - 5$

   ◯ $m^2 + n^2 - 1$

   ◯ $mn + 3n$

29. Two bottles are partially filled with water. The larger bottle currently holds $\frac{1}{3}$ of its capacity. The smaller bottle, which has $\frac{2}{3}$ of the capacity of the larger bottle, currently holds $\frac{3}{4}$ of its capacity. If the contents of the smaller bottle are poured into the larger bottle, the larger bottle will be filled to what fraction of its capacity?

○ $\frac{5}{6}$

○ $\frac{3}{4}$

○ $\frac{2}{3}$

○ $\frac{7}{12}$

○ $\frac{1}{2}$

30. In a certain office, the ratio of men to women is $\frac{3}{4}$. If 10 men were added to the office, the ratio of men to women would be $\frac{7}{6}$. How many men and women total are currently in the office?

○ 18
○ 24
○ 28
○ 42
○ 52

31. If the radius of a cylinder is half the length of the edge of a cube, and the height of the cylinder is equal to the length of the edge of the cube, what is the ratio of the volume of the cube to the volume of the cylinder?

○ $\dfrac{2}{\pi}$

○ $\dfrac{\pi}{4}$

○ $\dfrac{4}{\pi}$

○ $\dfrac{\pi}{2}$

○ 4

32. If x and y are distinct prime numbers, which of the following could be true?

○ $\dfrac{x^y}{y}$ is an odd integer.

○ $x^2y^3 = x^2$

○ $\dfrac{y^x}{4}$ is an even integer.

○ $\dfrac{xy}{2}$ is an even integer.

○ $x^y = y^x$

33. Three men and 2 women will present 5 consecutive speeches, 1 by each person, at a conference. If the order of the speakers is determined randomly, what is the probability that at least 2 of the men's speeches will be consecutive?

○ $\dfrac{3,124}{3,125}$

○ $\dfrac{9}{10}$

○ $\dfrac{4}{5}$

○ $\dfrac{16}{25}$

○ $\dfrac{1}{2}$

34. Three children, John, Paul, and Ringo, are playing a game. Each child will choose either the number 1 or the number 2. When one child chooses a number different from those of the other two children, he is declared the winner. If all of the children choose the same number, the process repeats until one child is declared the winner. If Ringo always chooses 2 and the other children select numbers randomly, what is the probability that Ringo is declared the winner?

○ $\dfrac{1}{6}$

○ $\dfrac{1}{4}$

○ $\dfrac{1}{3}$

○ $\dfrac{1}{2}$

○ $\dfrac{2}{3}$

35. Is q an integer?

    (1) $3q$ is an integer.
    (2) $5q$ is an integer.

    ◯ Statement (1) ALONE is sufficient, but statement (2) alone is not sufficient to answer the question asked.

    ◯ Statement (2) ALONE is sufficient, but statement (1) alone is not sufficient to answer the question asked.

    ◯ BOTH statements (1) and (2) TOGETHER are sufficient to answer the question asked; but NEITHER statement ALONE is sufficient.

    ◯ EACH statement ALONE is sufficient to answer the question asked.

    ◯ Statements (1) and (2) TOGETHER are NOT sufficient to answer the question asked, and additional data specific to the problem are needed.

36. Line k passes through the points (6,2) and P and has a slope of $-\dfrac{3}{5}$. If the line that passes through the origin and point P has a slope of -2, which of the following are the xy-coordinates for point P ?

    ◯ $\left(-\dfrac{40}{7}, \dfrac{80}{7}\right)$

    ◯ $(-4,8)$

    ◯ $(-3,6)$

    ◯ $\left(\dfrac{11}{5}, -\dfrac{22}{5}\right)$

    ◯ $\left(\dfrac{28}{13}, -\dfrac{56}{13}\right)$

37. Will must choose a 3-character computer password, consisting of 1 letter from the alphabet and 2 distinct digits, in any order. From how many different passwords can Will choose?

    ◯ 390
    ◯ 2,340
    ◯ 4,680
    ◯ 7,020
    ◯ 14,040

ANSWERS AND EXPLANATIONS

1. **E** If the area of the uncut square was 100, then each side of the square is 10. Given that the line on each side of the circle is 3, the diameter of the circle is $10 - 3 - 3 = 4$, so the radius is 2. That means the area of the circle is $\pi r^2 = 2^2\pi = 4\pi$, or approximately 12.4 (using 3.1 as an approximation for π). Thus, the area of the cut sheet is about $100 - 12.4 = 87.6$. Choose E.

2. **C** You can translate statement (1) into $b = \frac{1}{4}a$. However, that's only 1 equation in 2 variables; you can't solve that. For example, you could have $a = 8$ and $b = 2$, in which case $a - b = 6$, or you could have $a = 16$ and $b = 4$, in which case $a - b = 12$. Narrow your choices to B, C, and E. You can translate statement (2) into $a + b = 100$. Once again, that's only 1 equation in 2 variables; there are many possible solutions. Eliminate B. With both statements together, you have 2 equations in 2 variables. You can solve that system to find a and b and then calculate $a - b$. Choose C.

3. **A** Try Plugging In The Answers. With C, $z = 3$, so $\dfrac{z^2 + 6z + 9}{z^2 - 9} = \dfrac{9 + 18 + 9}{9 - 9} = \dfrac{36}{0}$, which is undefined, so eliminate C. With A, $z = 9$, so

   $\dfrac{z^2 + 6z + 9}{z^2 - 9} = \dfrac{81 + 54 + 9}{81 - 9} = \dfrac{144}{72} = 2$. That matches what the question stated, so

   A is the right answer. Alternatively, you could factor the quadratic terms to get

   $\dfrac{z^2 + 6z + 9}{z^2 - 9} = \dfrac{(z+3)(z+3)}{(z+3)(z-3)} = \dfrac{z+3}{z-3}$. Solve $\dfrac{z+3}{z-3} = 2$ to get $z = 9$. Choose A.

4. **E** Translate statement (1) into $10 < 2j < 32$. Divide by 2 to get $5 < j < 16$. More than one value is possible, so narrow the choices to B, C, and E. Translate statement (2) into $4 < \dfrac{j}{2} < 10$. Multiply by 2 to get $8 < j < 20$. Since more than one value is possible, eliminate B. Combining both statements, you still have more than one possible value for j, such as $j = 9$ or $j = 10$. Choose E.

5. **D** With statement (1), you can find the fee for June; it is $180 \times 0.25 = \$45$. You can answer the question, so narrow the choices to A and D. With statement (2), you can find the fee for 460 minutes by using the two rates ($.25 for the first 200 minutes and $.50 for 260 minutes over 200) and then dividing the result by 4 to get the fee for June. Since you can answer the question, choose D.

6. **B** Try Plugging In The Answers. With C, the press produces 23 pages per minute or $23 \times 60 = 1{,}380$ pages in an hour. Of those, $15\% \times 1{,}380 = 207$ are unusable, so there are $1{,}380 - 207 = 1{,}173$ usable pages. That's too many, so eliminate C and try B. At 20 pages per minute, the press produces $20 \times 60 = 1{,}200$ pages in an hour. Of those, $15\% \times 1{,}200 = 180$ are unusable, leaving $1{,}200 - 180 = 1{,}020$ usable pages. That's what the question stated, so choose B.

7. **E** Plug $x = 6$ and $y = 2$ into the equation to get $2(6) - 2c = 18$. Solve that to get

$c = -3$. That means the equation is $2x + 3y = 18$. (Be careful with the negative

signs!) Plug $y = 3$ into that to get $2x + 3(3) = 18$, which you can solve to get

$x = \dfrac{9}{2}$. Choose E.

8. **B** This question is essentially about divisibility. If you increase p by 20%, you get

$1.2p$. Since p must be in whole cents, change each answer into cents by moving

the decimal point 2 places to the right, and then divide each answer by 1.2.

You're looking for the one that isn't an integer after the division. B becomes

$\dfrac{125}{1.2} = 104.1\overline{6}$. Choose B.

9. **D** Let p = price per copy. From the given information, you can set up the equation $n \times p = \$31.50$. To find p, you need the value of n. You can translate statement (1) into $2n \times \$1.75 = \$31.50$. There is only one variable, so you can solve that for n, and then plug that into the original equation to find the price. Statement (1) is sufficient, so narrow the choices to A and D. You can translate statement (2) into $(n - 4) \times (p + \$2.80) = \$31.50$. Although there are two variables in this equation, you also have the equation from the initial setup. With two equations for two variables, you can solve for p. Statement (2) is sufficient, so choose D.

10. **D** Since the number of homework assignments is never defined, you can plug in your own number, such as 10 assignments. To work with averages, you should set up average circles, as shown below. For the homework already submitted, Torry has $\frac{2}{5} \times 10 = 4$ assignments, with an average grade of 75. So, he has a total of $4 \times 75 = 300$ points on these assignments. Since he has 10 assignments total, to get an average grade of 90, Torry needs $10 \times 90 = 900$ points. That means he needs to get $900 - 300 = 600$ total points on his remaining assignments. Since there are 6 assignments remaining, that works out to an average grade of $\frac{600}{6} = 100$ per assignment. The formula for percent change is $\frac{\text{difference}}{\text{starting \#}}$. In this case, that is $\frac{100 - 75}{75} = \frac{1}{3} = 33\frac{1}{3}\%$. Choose D.

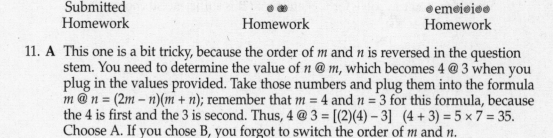

Submitted Homework   Homework   Homework

11. **A** This one is a bit tricky, because the order of m and n is reversed in the question stem. You need to determine the value of $n @ m$, which becomes 4 @ 3 when you plug in the values provided. Take those numbers and plug them into the formula $m @ n = (2m - n)(m + n)$; remember that $m = 4$ and $n = 3$ for this formula, because the 4 is first and the 3 is second. Thus, 4 @ 3 = $[(2)(4) - 3]\ (4 + 3) = 5 \times 7 = 35$. Choose A. If you chose B, you forgot to switch the order of m and n.

12. **C** With 150 students in each of 3 grades, there are 3   150 = 450 students altogether. During the blizzard, 10% × 150 = 15 fourth-graders, $\frac{1}{6} \times 150 = 25$ fifth-graders, and 60 sixth-graders miss school. That is 15 + 25 + 60 = 100 students absent. To find percent change, divide the difference by the starting number. In this case, $\frac{100}{450} = \frac{2}{9} = 22.\overline{2}\%$. Choose C.

13. **C** Set up an average circle, as shown below, to find Laura's average figurines per box before the addition. 207 figurines in 9 boxes is $\frac{207}{9} = 23$ figurines per box. After the addition, she has $\frac{386}{12} =$ approximately 32 figurines per box. Feel free to round off numbers, because the question says "approximate." The percent change is $\frac{32 - 23}{23} = \frac{9}{23} \approx 39\%$. The closest answer is 40%, so choose C.

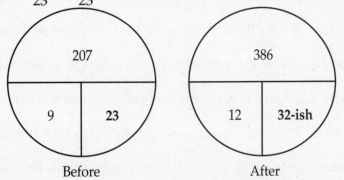

Before   After

14. **D** Try Plugging In The Answers. You can eliminate A and B right away, because 2 and 3 can't be the largest of 3 consecutive primes. With D, the three consecutive primes are 3, 5, and 7. Their sum is 3 + 5 + 7 = 15. The largest integer smaller than 3 is 2. The product is 15 × 2 = 30, which matches what the question says. Choose D.

15. **B** An obvious thing to do would be to calculate the volume of the box,

$12 \times 18 \times 10 = 2{,}160$ cubic inches, and the volume of the cylinder,

$\pi r^2 h = 3^2 \times 5 \times \pi = 45\pi$ cubic inches. If you divide the volumes, you get

$\dfrac{2{,}160}{45\pi} = \dfrac{48}{\pi} \approx 15.3$, which seems to imply that 15 cans would fit. However, that

trap answer ignores the dead space that comes from putting round objects in a

rectangular box. If you stack the cans side by side in rows, each one takes up

6 inches (the diameter) in each horizontal direction. So you can fit $\dfrac{12 \times 18}{6 \times 6} = 6$

cans in each horizontal layer. Since the box is 10 inches tall and the cans are

5 inches tall, you can fit 2 layers, or $2 \times 6 = 12$ cans. Choose B.

16. **B** Plug in some numbers for a, b, and c that match the equations. Suppose $a = 2$,

$b = 4$, and $c = 10$. Take those values and fill in the lengths on the perimeter of the

rectangle. That makes the rectangle a 12×20 rectangle, so the area is 240. Since

each corner is a right angle, you can find the area of each of the four triangles

at the corners. The area of the upper-left triangle is $\dfrac{1}{2} \times 4 \times 14 = 28$. The area of

the upper-right triangle is $\dfrac{1}{2} \times 6 \times 10 = 30$. The area of the lower-left triangle is

$\dfrac{1}{2} \times 8 \times 10 = 40$. The area of the lower-right triangle is $\dfrac{1}{2} \times 2 \times 10 = 10$. The total

area of the triangles is $28 + 30 + 40 + 10 = 108$, so the shaded region is

$240 - 108 = 132$. As a fraction of the whole rectangle, the shaded region is

$\dfrac{132}{240} = \dfrac{11}{20}$. Choose B.

17. **D** From the initial setup, you can write the equation $g + r = 225$. With statement (1), you can substitute $r = 75$ to find the number of green pencils. Statement (1) is sufficient, so narrow your choices to A and D. With statement (2), you can write the equation $g = 2r$. With two equations and two variables, you can solve for the number of green pencils. Statement (2) works, so choose D.

18. **B** Substitute x^2 for y in the equation $xy = 125$. That gives you $x^3 = 125$, so $x = 5$. Now plug that into the equation $x^2 = y$ to get $y = 5^2 = 25$. So $x - y = 5 - 25 = -20$. Choose B.

19. **B** The circumference of the hoop will tell you how far the hoop travels in one revolution. The formula for circumference is $C = 2\pi r$. In this case, the circumference of the hoop is $(2)(\pi)(12.5) = 25\pi$ = approximately 75 inches. Convert this measurement to feet (because the problem wants to know how many minutes it takes the hoop to roll 75 feet). To make this conversion, divide 75 inches by 12 (the number of inches in a foot): $75 \div 12 = 6.25$. Now you can set up the following ratio:

$$\frac{10 \text{ seconds}}{6.25 \text{ feet}} = \frac{x \text{ seconds}}{75 \text{ feet}}$$

Cross multiply to obtain the following equation:

$6.25x = 750$

$x = 120$ seconds

Divide 120 seconds by 60 (the number of seconds in a minute). The result is $120 \div 60 = 2$ minutes. Choose B.

20. **B** You know that 63% of all votes cast were for the winner. To find the actual number of votes for the winner, you need to know the total number of votes cast. Statement (1) tells you the number of eligible voters, but the actual number of votes cast might be smaller. That's insufficient, so narrow the choices to B, C, and E. With statement (2), you know that 37% of votes cast equals 55,500, since 63% for the winner implies 37% for the others. You can use that equation, $0.37x = 55,500$, to find the total number of votes, which allows you to answer the question. Statement (2) is sufficient, so choose B.

21. **D** You know that $AB = 5$ and $AC = 12$. What you don't know is whether they are the base and height of the triangle. Base and height must be perpendicular, so you need to know whether y is a right angle. With statement (1), you know that BC is 13. That means the triangle is a right triangle, and you can plug 12 and 5 in for the base and height to find the area of the triangle. Narrow the choices to A and D. With statement (2), y is a right angle, so you can use 12 and 5 as the base and height. Statement (2) also works, so choose D.

22. **E** With statement (1), you know that two of the sides are equal. The triangle could be equilateral, if all three are equal, but that's not necessarily the case. Imagine that NO is very small, while the other sides are equal. Narrow the choices to B, C, and E. With statement (2), knowing that $h = 5\sqrt{3}$ may make you think that the triangle is equilateral. However, that's true only if the middle line is perpendicular to MO, so that it becomes the height of the triangle. Imagine that the line leans to the right instead of pointing straight up. Eliminate B. With both statements together, you still can't conclude that the middle line is the height of the triangle. See the following diagram for a counterexample. Choose E.

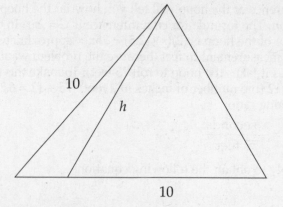

10

h

10

23. **E** With statement (1), you know that Brand X was chosen by an overall majority of participants, but you don't know whether that translates into a majority in three of the contests. It's possible that Brand X had received 51 votes in two of the taste tests, winning those, but only 17 or 18 votes in each of the others, losing those, so that Brand Y was the overall winner. Narrow the choices to B, C, and E. With statement (2), you know that the winner won three of the first four contests, so that the last one was moot, but you don't know which brand that was. Eliminate B. With both statements, Brand X still could be the overall winner or the loser, and knowing the order of the wins and losses wouldn't change them. Choose E.

24. **B** With statement (1), primes 2, 3, 5, 7, 11, 13, and 17 are definitely less than k, but you don't know whether 19 and 23 are less than k. Narrow the choices to B, C, and E. With statement (2), primes 2 through 23 are less than k. You don't know whether 29 is greater than k or equal, but in either case, it's not less than k. That's enough to answer the question, so choose B.

25. **C** You're looking for the value of $k + p + s$. With statement (1), you can write the equation $k + p = \dfrac{s}{2}$. But that's only one equation for three variables, which is insufficient to solve the system and answer the question. Narrow the choices to B, C, and E. With statement (2), you can write the equations $k + s = 109$ and $p + s = 126$. However, two equations are not enough to solve for all three variables. Eliminate B. With both statements together, you have three variables for three equations, which is enough to find all three variables and answer the question. Choose C.

26. **B** With statement (1), you don't know whether the distance from the origin to A is the same as the distance from the origin to D. If it were the same, you could apply the Pythagorean theorem to find the length of the side of the square and then its area. Since you don't know if it's the same, then you can't find the side of the square. That's not sufficient, so narrow the choices to B, C, and E. With statement (2), you know that the distance between B and D is 8. That's the diagonal of the square. You could use the 45-45-90 triangle ratio to find the sides of the square and then its area. Choose B.

27. **E** Try Plugging In. With statement (1), suppose $x = 5$, $y = 3$, and $z = 10$; the median would be x. However, if $x = 5$, $y = -20$, and $z = 0$, the median would be z. That's two possible answers, so narrow the choices to B, C, and E. With statement (2) alone, you don't know anything about z and whether it's bigger or smaller than x or y. Eliminate B. With both statements together, you could still use the two sets of numbers plugged in above. With two possible answers, that's still insufficient. Choose E.

28. **D** Plug In. If $m = -2$ and $n = -3$, then you can eliminate A and E. Try weird numbers such as 1, or –1 in this case. If $m = n = -1$, then you can eliminate B and C. Choose D.

29. **A** Plug In for the amount of water. Suppose the large bottle has a capacity of 36 gallons. (The number 36 works nicely with the 3s and the 4 in the fractions.) It currently contains $\frac{1}{3} \times 36 = 12$ gallons of water. The small bottle has a capacity of $\frac{2}{3} \times 36 = 24$ gallons and currently holds $\frac{3}{4} \times 24 = 18$ gallons of water. If you combine the water, you get $12 + 18 = 30$ gallons of water, which is $\frac{30}{36} = \frac{5}{6}$ of the capacity of the larger bottle. Choose A.

30. **D** Try Plugging In The Answers and the ratio box. The ratio of men to women is 3 to 4 at the start, so the ratio total is 7 people. With C, you have an actual total of 28, so the multiplier is $\frac{28}{7} = 4$, giving you $3 \times 4 = 12$ men and $4 \times 4 = 16$ women to start. Adding 10 men gives you 22 men and 16 women, or a $\frac{22}{16} = \frac{11}{8}$ ratio. That's not correct. Eliminate C and try another answer. With D, you have an actual total of 42, so the multiplier is $\frac{42}{7} = 6$, giving you $3 \times 6 = 18$ men and $4 \times 6 = 24$ women to start. Adding 10 men gives you 28 men and 24 women, or a $\frac{28}{24} = \frac{7}{6}$ ratio. That matches the information in the question, so choose D.

31. **C** Try Plugging In. Suppose the cube has an edge of 4 units. That means the height of the cylinder is 4 and its radius is 2. The cube has a volume of $4^3 = 64$. The volume of the cylinder is $\pi r^2 h = 2^2 \times 4 \times \pi = 16\pi$. The ratio of the cube to the cylinder is $\frac{64}{16\pi} = \frac{4}{\pi}$. Choose C.

32. **C** Try Plugging In. You'll probably need to try several sets of numbers, and you need one of the answers to be true at least once. The key is to try $y = 2$. If $x = 3$ and $y = 2$, then C becomes $\frac{8}{4} = 2$, which is an even integer. None of the other answers are ever true if x and y are different from each other and primes. (*Remember:* 1 is not prime.) Choose C.

33. **B** The best way to solve this problem is first to find the probability that there are *not* at least 2 consecutive men's speeches and then subtract that probability from 1. The only way to avoid having consecutive men's speeches is to alternate man-woman-man-woman-man. For the first spot, there are 3 men out of 5 people. For the second spot, there are 2 women out of 4 people; and so on. That probability is $\frac{3}{5} \times \frac{2}{4} \times \frac{2}{3} \times \frac{1}{2} \times \frac{1}{1} = \frac{12}{120} = \frac{1}{10}$. That's the probability of what you *don't* want to occur, so the probability of what you *do* want is $1 - \frac{1}{10} = \frac{9}{10}$. Choose B.

34. **C** The best way to think about this question is to focus on the final round, the one in which two children choose one number and one child chooses the other, so that there is a winner. It doesn't really matter whether this is the first round or the hundredth, the probabilities will come out the same. In this final round, there are three possibilities: Ringo chooses 2 while both John and Paul choose 1; Ringo and John choose 2 while Paul chooses 1; and Ringo and Paul choose 2 while John chooses 1. Each of the three possibilities is equally likely, and Ringo wins in only one of them, so the probability that he wins is $\frac{1}{3}$. Choose C.

35. **C** With Yes/No questions, try Plugging In. For statement (1), you can plug in both an integer, such as $q = 2$, and a non-integer, such as $q = \frac{1}{3}$. Since you can get both "yes" and "no" answers, narrow the choices to B, C, and E. For statement (2), you can plug in both an integer, such as $q = 2$, and a non-integer, such as $q = \frac{1}{5}$. That's insufficient, so eliminate B. With both statements together, you can plug in an integer such as $q = 2$, but there are no non-integers that fit both statements. Since you can get only the "yes" answer, that is sufficient. Choose C.

36. **B** The easiest way to solve this problem is Plugging In The Answers. The correct answer must have the right slope for both line k and the line through the origin. Using the formula for slope, you need both $\dfrac{y-2}{x-6} = -\dfrac{3}{5}$ and $\dfrac{y-0}{x-0} = -2$. All of the answers work for the line through the origin, but only answer B also works for line k. With B, $\dfrac{8-2}{-4-6} = \dfrac{6}{-10} = -\dfrac{3}{5}$ and $\dfrac{8-0}{-4-0} = \dfrac{8}{-4} = -2$. Choose B.

37. **D** There are three orders in which Will can set up his password: letter-digit-digit, digit-letter-digit, and digit-digit-letter. The number of permutations for letter-digit-digit is $26 \times 10 \times 9 = 2{,}340$. Since the digits must be distinct, there are only nine options left for the second digit after the first is chosen. Digit-letter-digit and digit-digit-letter each have 2,340 permutations as well, so Will has $2{,}340 + 2{,}340 + 2{,}340 = 7{,}020$ possibilities from which to choose. Choose D.

13

Integrated Reasoning Basics

For 2012, the GMAT gains a new section called the Integrated Reasoning section. If you are taking your GMAT on or after June 5, 2012, you'll need to prepare for the Integrated Reasoning section because it will be part of your test! We've prepared some resources to help you get ready. This chapter reviews the basics of the new section, including a rundown on all four new question types. We've also included a chapter that explains some strategies that will help you handle these new questions. Finally, this book includes two complete Integrated Reasoning sections with explanations so that you can practice.

There's one caveat, however, before we get started. At the time this chapter was written, GMAC had released many—but not all—of the details about the new section. So, you should also check our website www.PrincetonReview.com for the most up-to-date information about the new Integrated Reasoning section. As we learn more, we'll post what we find out to help you better prepare.

No More Issue Essay
GMAC has not only decided that there will only be one essay on the GMAT, they've also decided that there will only be one type of essay. The Argument essay stays and the Issue essay is history when the new test launches.

MEET THE INTEGRATED REASONING SECTION

The Integrated Reasoning section, which takes the place of one of the GMAT essays, is 30 minutes long. You'll see it as the second section of your test. Officially, there are only 12 questions, which sounds pretty great. However, most of those questions have multiple parts. So, for example, a Table Analysis question—one of the new question types we'll discuss—usually has four statements that you need to evaluate. Your answer to the question really consists of four separate responses. For the entire section, you'll actually need to select approximately 30 different responses.

INTEGRATED REASONING IS NOT ADAPTIVE

Unlike the Quantitative and Verbal sections, the Integrated Reasoning section is not adaptive. So, you won't see harder questions if you keep answering questions correctly. That's good news because it means that you'll more easily be able to focus your attention on the current question rather than worrying whether you correctly answered the previous question!

Test writers refer to non-adaptive sections as linear. Pacing for a linear section is different from the pacing that we reviewed for the adaptive Quantitative and Verbal sections. As of this writing, GMAC has not released any information about how the Integerated Reasoning section is scored. As soon as we know that, we'll have specific pacing advice posted on our website. So, be sure to check out www.PrincetonReview.com and the online tools that come with this book.

Even without knowing the specifics of how the Integrated Reasoning section is scored, we can still offer two general pacing guidelines.

> ## Pacing Guidelines
>
> 1. Work the easier questions first. As you'll see, many Integrated Reasoning questions call for more than one response per question. Work the easier questions first.
>
> 2. Don't get stubborn. With so many questions to answer in only 30 minutes, the Integrated Reasoning section can seem very fast paced. Spending too much time on one question means that you may not get to see all of the questions. Sometimes it's best to guess and move on.

THERE'S A CALCULATOR

There's an onscreen calculator available for use during the Integrated Reasoning section. The calculator is not available, however, for the Quantitative section. For the Quantitative section, you still need to perform any necessary calculations by hand.

The calculator for the Integrated Reasoning section is relatively basic. It provides buttons to perform the four standard operations: addition, subtraction, multiplication, and division. In addition, buttons to take a square root, find a percent, and take a reciprocal round out the available functions. Other buttons allow you to store and recall a value in the calculator's memory.

To use the calculator, open it by clicking on the "calculator" button in the upper left corner of your screen. The calculator will generally open in the middle of your screen, but you can move it around so that you can see the text of the problem or the numbers on any charts or graphs that are part of the question. The calculator is available for all Integrated Reasoning questions. You can enter a number into the calculator either by clicking on the onscreen number buttons or by typing the number on the keyboard.

Here's what the calculator looks like:

Calculator ✕

M	Backspace	CE	C
MC	7 8 9	/ sqrt	
MR	4 5 6	* %	
MS	1 2 3	– 1/x	
M+	0 +/- . + =		

Click on buttons, or click in answer window to use keyboard

For the most part, the keys on the onscreen calculator work as you might expect. However, a few keys may not work as expected. Oddly enough, that's particularly true if you are used to a more sophisticated calculator. So, here are a few tips about using some of the calculator keys:

MC is the memory clear key. Use this key to wipe out any values that you have stored in the calculator's memory.

MR is the memory recall key. Use this key to return any value that you have stored in the memory to the calculation area. For example, if you want to divide the number currently on your screen by the number in the memory, you would enter the key sequence / MR =.

MS is the memory store key. Use this key to store the number currently on the screen in the calculator's memory.

M+ is the memory addition key. Use this key to add the current onscreen number to the number in the calculator's memory. For example, if 2 is stored in the calculator's memory and 3 is on the screen, then clicking M+ will result in 5 being stored in the calculator's memory.

Backspace clears the last digit entered. Use this key to correct mistakes when entering numbers without clearing the entire number. For example, if you entered 23 but meant to enter 25, click backspace and then enter 5.

CE CE is the clear entry button. Use this button to correct a mistake when entering a longer calculation without starting over. For example, suppose you entered 2*3+5, but you meant to enter 2*3+9. If you click on CE right after you enter 5, your screen will show 6, the result of 2*3, and you can now enter +9= to finish your intended calculation.

C C is the clear key. Use this key when you want to start a new calculation. In our previous example, if you click C after you enter 5, the intermediate result, 6, is not retained.

sqrt sqrt is the square root key. Click this key after you enter the number for which you want to take the square root. For example, if you enter 4 sqrt, the result 2 will be displayed on your screen.

% % is the key used to take a percentage without entering a decimal. For example, if you want to take 20% of 400, enter 400*20%. The result 80 will now show on your screen. Note that you do not need to enter = after you click %.

1/x 1/x is used to take a reciprocal. Click this key after you enter the number for which you want to take the reciprocal. For example, the keystroke 2 followed by 1/x produces the result 0.5 on your screen. Again, note that you do not need to enter = after you click 1/x.

Be sure that you thoroughly understand the way the keys for the onscreen calculator work so you avoid errors and wasted time when you take your GMAT.

Calculator Practice Tip
When you practice for the Integrated Reasoning section, use a calculator similar to the calculator provided by GMAC. If you are doing online practice, use the onscreen calculator. If you are working problems from this book, use a basic calculator rather than that fancy calculator that you might still have from your high school or college math classes.

THE QUESTION TYPES

There are four question types in the Integrated Reasoning section. These question types are used mostly to test the same type of content that is tested in the Quantitative section. So, expect to calculate percents and averages. You'll also be asked to make a lot of inferences based on the data presented in the various charts, graphs, and tables that accompany the questions. So, the format of these questions may take some getting used to, but the content will probably seem familiar.

Let's take a more detailed look at each of the new question types.

TABLE ANALYSIS

Table Analysis questions present data in a table. If you've ever seen a spreadsheet, you'll feel right at home. Most tables have 5 to 10 columns and anywhere from 6 to 25 rows. You'll be able to sort the data in the table by each column heading. The sort function, however, is fairly basic. For example, when you interact with data in tables currently, you're used to how you can sort first by a column (such as state) and then another column (such as city) to produce an alphabetical list of cities by state. The tables in the Table Analysis questions don't allow you to do that. You can sort only one column at a time.

Here's what a Table Analysis question looks like:

Sort By Select... ▼ **1**

National Park		Visitors			Area	
Name	State	Number	% change	Rank	Acres	Rank
Grand Canyon	AZ	4,388,386	0.9	2	1,217,403	11
Yosemite	CA	3,901,408	4.4	3	791,266	16
Yellowstone	WY	3,640,185	10.5	4	2,219,791	8
Rocky Mtn.	CO	2,955,821	4.7	5	265,828	26
Zion	UT	2,665,972	-2.5	8	145,598	35
Acadia	ME	2,504,208	12.4	9	47,390	47
Bryce	UT	1,285,492	5.7	15	35,835	50
Arches	UT	1,014,405	1.8	19	76,519	42
Badlands	SD	977,778	4.7	22	242,756	28
Mesa Verde	CO	559,712	1.7	30	52,122	46
Canyonlands	UT	435,908	-0.1	36	337,598	23

The table above gives information for 2010 on total visitors and total acreage for 11 U.S. National Parks. In addition to the numbers of total visitors and total acreage for each National Park, the table also provides the percent increase or decrease over the total visitors for 2009 and the rank of the National Park for total visitors and total acreage in 2010.

Each column of the table can be **2** sorted in ascending order by clicking on the Select button above the table and choosing, from the drop-down menu, the heading of the column on which you want the table to be sorted.

Consider each of the following **3** statements about these National Parks. For each statement, indicate whether the statement is true or false, based on the information provided in the table.

True False **5**

○ ○ The park that experienced the greatest percent increase in visitors from 2009 to 2010 also had the least total acreage.

○ ○ The park with the median rank by the number of visitors is larger than only one other park by acreage.

○ ○ Exactly 20% of the parks with ranks less than 40 by acreage and showing positive growth in visitors were in Utah (UT).

○ ○ The total number of visitors at Arches in 2009 was less than 1,000,000.

The circled numbers won't be on your screen when you take the Integrated Reasoning section. We've added those so we can explain the different parts of a Table Analysis question. Here's what each circled number represents:

1 The Select button is a drop-down box that allows you to sort a column in ascending order. When opened, the box will display all of the different ways that you can sort the data in the table. For this table, for example, the possibilities are National Park Name, National Park State, Visitors Number, Visitors % change, Visitors Rank, Area Acreage, and Area Rank. You can always sort by every column.

2 These are the standard directions for a Table Analysis question, which are the same for every Table Analysis question. So, when you've read these directions once, you don't really need to bother reading them again.

3 These lines are additional directions, which are slightly tailored to the question at hand. However, they'll always tell you to base your answers on the information in the table. These directions will also always tell you which type of choice you are making for each statement: true/false, yes/no, agree/disagree, and so on. Again, you can probably get by without reading these most of the time.

4 These lines explain the table. Mostly, this information recaps the column headings from the table. Occasionally, you can learn some additional information by reading this explanatory text. For example, the explanatory text for this table states that the Visitors Number column is for 2010 and that the % change column shows the change from 2009 to 2010.

5 These statements are the questions. Typically, there are four statements. You must evaluate and select an answer for each. If you try to move to the next question without selecting a response for one or more statements, a pop-up window will open to inform you that you have not selected an answer for all statements. You cannot leave any part of the question blank.

Take a few moments to read through the statements in the example. Notice that the questions ask you to do things such as calculate a percentage or find a median. That's typical for Table Analysis questions. By now, you can probably see just how helpful the sorting function can be in answering some questions.

GRAPHICS INTERPRETATION

Now, let's take a look at Graphics Interpretation questions. For this question type, you are given one chart, graph, or image and asked to answer three questions based on that information. The questions are statements that include one drop-down box. You select your answer from the drop-down box to complete the statement.

Here's an example of a Graphics Interpretation question:

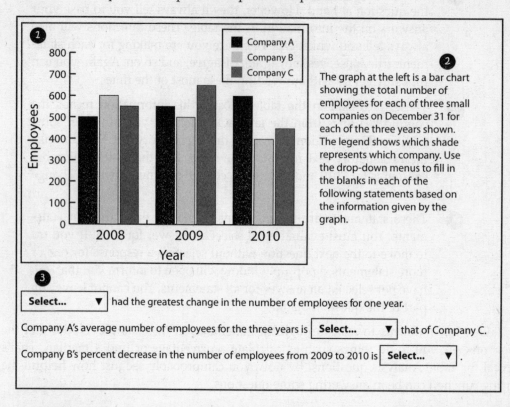

The graph at the left is a bar chart showing the total number of employees for each of three small companies on December 31 for each of the three years shown. The legend shows which shade represents which company. Use the drop-down menus to fill in the blanks in each of the following statements based on the information given by the graph.

3

[Select... ▼] had the greatest change in the number of employees for one year.

Company A's average number of employees for the three years is [Select... ▼] that of Company C.

Company B's percent decrease in the number of employees from 2009 to 2010 is [Select... ▼].

As with the Table Analysis questions, we've added the circled numbers so we can point out the different things that you'll see on your screen for a Graphics Interpretation question. Here's what each circled number represents:

1 The chart, graph, or image is always in the upper left of the screen. As shown here, the chart takes up a good deal of the screen. It will certainly be large enough that you can clearly extract information from it. You can expect to see a variety of different types of charts or graphs, including scatterplots, bar charts, line graphs, and circle (or pie) charts. For the most part, you'll see fairly standard types of graphs, however. Be sure to check any labels on the axes as well as any sort of included legend.

2 These lines are an explanation of the graph or chart. Mostly, you'll be told what the chart represents as well as what individual lines, bars, or sectors may represent. Sometimes, you'll be given some additional information, such as when measurements were made. For example, in this example, you are told that the bars show the numbers of employees for each firm on December 31 of the year in question. This information is typically extraneous to answering the questions. The explanatory information always ends with the same line about selecting your answers from the drop-down menu.

③ These are the questions. Graphics Interpretation questions typically include three statements. Each statement is generally a single sentence with one drop-down menu. Each drop-down menu usually includes three to five answer choices. Choose the answer choice that makes the statement true.

For the most part, Graphics Analysis questions ask you to find relationships and trends for the data. You can also be asked to calculate percentage increases or decreases, averages, and medians.

TWO-PART ANALYSIS

In many ways, the Two-Part Analysis questions are most similar to standard math questions. You'll typically be presented with a word problem that essentially has two variables in it. You'll need to pick an answer for each variable that makes some condition in the problem true.

Here's an example of a Two-Part Analysis question:

Two families buy new refrigerators using installment plans. Family A makes an initial payment of $750. Family B makes an initial payment of $1,200. Both families make five additional payments to pay off the balance. Both families pay the same amount for their refrigerators, including all taxes, fees, and finance charges. ①

In the table below, identify a monthly payment, in dollars, for Family A and a monthly payment, in dollars, for Family B that are consistent with the installment plan described above. Make only one selection in each column. ②

Family A	Family B	Monthly payment (in dollars)
○	○	50
○	○	80
○	○	120 ③
○	○	160
○	○	250
○	○	300

As you might have surmised, we have once again added the circled numbers so we can describe the different parts of the question. Here's what each circled number represents:

① This first block of text is the actual problem. In this case, it contains the description of the two variables in the problem. It also includes the condition that needs to be made true. As with any word problem, make sure that you read the information carefully. For these problems, also make sure that you are clear about which information goes with the first variable and which information goes with the second.

2 This part of the problem tells you how to pick your answers. Mostly it tells you to pick a value for column A and a value for column B, based on the conditions of the problem. This part is mostly boilerplate text that is slightly varied from problem to problem.

3 These are the answer choices. Two-Part Analysis questions generally have six answer choices. Choose only one answer choice for each column. It is possible that the same number is the answer for both columns. So, if that's what your calculations indicate, go ahead and choose the same number for both columns.

Most Two-Part Analysis questions can be solved with math that is no more sophisticated than simple arithmetic. There is one exception to that, however. While most Two-Part Analysis questions are math problems, you may see one that looks like a Critical Reasoning question. For these, you'll be given an argument and must do something like pick one answer that strengthens and one answer that weakens the argument.

MULTI-SOURCE REASONING

Multi-Source Reasoning questions present information on tabs. The information can be text, charts, graphs, or a combination. In other words, GMAC can put almost anything on the tabs! The layout looks a little bit like Reading Comprehension because the tabbed information is on the left side of your screen while the right side shows the questions.

Here's an example of a Multi-Source Reasoning question:

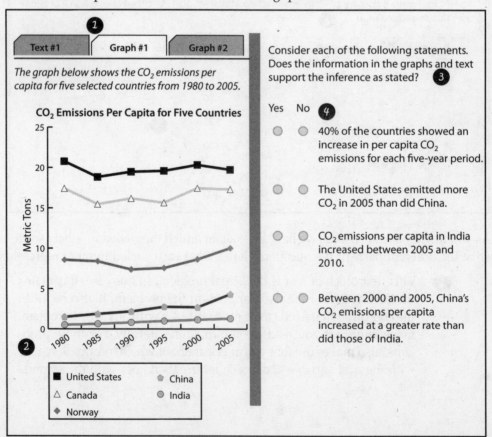

As we've done for the other three new question types, we've added circled numbers to indicate the different parts of the question. Here's what each circled number represents:

1 The tabs appear across the top left of the screen. Some questions have two tabs and some, as in this example, have three. The tabs typically give you some sort of indication about what's on the tab. The currently selected tab is white, while the unselected tabs are grey. GMAC can put almost anything on each tab, including graphs, tables, charts, text, or some combination. It's a good idea to take a few seconds to get your bearings before attempting the questions. Make sure you know what is on each tab and how the information on one tab relates to information on the other tab or tabs.

2 The information for each tab appears on the left of the screen. In this case, the information is a graph. When you see a chart or a graph, be sure to check out the axes. Also look for a legend or other information to help explain the information shown by the graph or chart. For tables, check the column headings so you better understand the table. Finally, don't neglect to read any supplied headings for the chart, graph, or table. Sometimes, that's all you need for the chart to make sense.

3 These are the basic instructions for responding to the statements. These instructions help to explain how you need to evaluate each statement. Here, for example, you need to determine whether the statements are valid inferences. In other cases, you may be asked to evaluate the statements for a different choice, such as true or false.

4 These are the actual questions. You need to pick a response for each statement. If you fail to respond to one or more statements, you won't be able to advance to the next question in the section. In other words, these statements work just like the statements for the Table Analysis questions.

Multi-Source Reasoning questions usually come in sets. Each set typically consists of three separate questions. Two of those questions are generally in the statement style shown in the preceding example. It's also possible to get a standard multiple-choice question as part of the set. A standard multiple-choice question has five answer choices and you select one response.

You may need information from more than one tab to respond to a statement or multiple-choice question. Don't forget to think about the information on the other tabs while evaluating the statements. That's why it's important to take a few moments to get familiar with what's on each tab before you start work on the questions.

ABOUT THE AUTHOR

Jack Schieffer has worked at The Princeton Review since 1989. He has taught courses for almost .every type of test, and he was the Director of Research & Development for the GMAT course from 1996 to 1998. In his spare time, he is pursuing a Ph.D. in economics.

NOTES

NOTES

NOTES

NOTES

NOTES

NOTES

NOTES

NOTES